Justice as Improvisation

Justice as Improvisation: The Law of the Extempore theorises the relationship between justice and improvisation through the case of the New York City cabaret laws. Discourses around improvisation often imprison it in a quasi-ethical relationship with the authentic, singular 'other'. The same can be said of justice. This book interrogates this relationship by highlighting the parallels between the aporetic conception of justice advanced by the late French philosopher Jacques Derrida and the nuanced approach to improvisation pursued by musicians and theorists alike in the new and emerging interdisciplinary field of Critical Studies in Improvisation (CSI). *Justice as Improvisation* re-imagines justice as a species of improvisation through the formal structure of the most basic of legal mechanisms, judicial decision-making, offering law and legal theory a richer, more concrete understanding of justice: not further mystery or mystique, but a negotiation between abstract notions of justice and the everyday practice of judging. Improvisation in judgment calls for ongoing, practical decision-making as the constant negotiation between the freedom of the judge to take account of the otherness or singularity of the case *and* the existing laws or rules that both allow for and constrain that freedom. Yes, it is necessary to judge, yes, it is necessary to decide, but to judge *well*, to decide *justly*, that is a music lesson perhaps best taught by critical improvisation scholars.

Sara Ramshaw is a Lecturer in Law at Queen's University Belfast. She holds a LLB and LLM from the University of British Columbia, a PhD from Birkbeck School of Law, and is a former Postdoctoral Fellow with the Improvisation, Community and Social Practice project in Canada.

Justice as Improvisation

The law of the extempore

Sara Ramshaw

Routledge
Taylor & Francis Group
a GlassHouse Book

First published 2013
by Routledge
2 Park Square, Milton Park, Abingdon, Oxon OX14 4RN

A GlassHouse Book
Simultaneously published in the USA and Canada
by Routledge
711 Third Avenue, New York, NY 10017

Routledge is an imprint of the Taylor & Francis Group, an informa business

British Library Cataloguing in Publication Data
A catalogue record for this book is available from the British Library

Library of Congress Cataloging in Publication Data
A catalog record for this book has been requested

ISBN: 978-0-415-51017-2 (hbk)
ISBN: 978-0-203-07328-5 (ebk)

Typeset in Garamond
by Taylor & Francis Books

For my parents, Eleanor and Chris

Contents

Acknowledgements

This book has been many years in the making.

My first encounter with the New York City cabaret laws took place in 1996 as a LLM student at the University of British Columbia Law School where Paul Chevigny's book *Gigs: Jazz and the Cabaret Laws in New York City* was required reading in Wes Pue's Legal History module. Since that time, Wes has encouraged and supported my interest in this subject. For that, I thank him.

To Peter Fitzpatrick, my PhD supervisor, who guided this work at the beginning and continues to inspire. Thanks also to Shelby Fitzpatrick, for much-welcomed escapes to The Old Vicarage during my PhD days.

To the singular community of scholars – fellow postgraduate students and academic staff alike – at Birkbeck School of Law, for ideas shared and friendships made: (in alphabetical order) Maria Aristodemou, Jose-Manuel Barreto, Jose Bellido, Elisabetta Bertolino, Brenna Bhandar, Anna Chronopoulou, Barry Collins, Costas Douzinas, Michelle Everson, Adam Gearey, Pablo Ghetti, Ben Golder, Piyel Haldar, Patrick Hanafin, Richard Joyce, Myrsini Koromantzou, Gil Leung, Elena Loizidou, Fiona Macmillan, Nathan Moore, Les Moran, Stewart Motha, Linda Mulcahy, Sundhya Pahuja, James Ressel, Victoria Ridler, Anton Schütz, Matt Stone, Patricia Tuitt, Illan Wall, Thanos Zartaloudis, and many others who I have undoubtedly failed to mention.

To all those involved in the Social Science and Humanities Research Council of Canada (SSHRC) Major Collaborative Research Initiative (MCRI) project 'Improvisation, Community and Social Practice' (ICASP), who taught me about improvisation and community, especially Ajay Heble, Ellen Waterman, Daniel Weinstock, Desmond Manderson, Tina Piper, David Lametti, Eric Lewis, Daniel Fischlin, Frédérique Arroyas, Ben Authers, Rob Wallace, Rebecca Caines, Tracy Nicholls, Melvin Backstrom, Michelle Peek, Kim Thorne, and others met along the way at various ICASP conferences and colloquiums, reading groups and less formal gatherings.

To my PhD examiners, Professors Des Manderson and Roger Cotterrell, for their generous and invaluable advice.

To the Institute for Jazz Studies at Rutgers University, for its hospitality and openness with its collection.

To all those who engaged with my research and offered valuable feedback on papers and presentations, especially Tina Mai Chen, David Churchill and Greg Smith at the Department of History, University of Manitoba; Diana Brydon at the Center for Globalization and Cultural Studies, University of Manitoba, where I was a Visiting Associate in Spring 2009; my colleagues at the School of Law at Queen's University Belfast (QUB); Paul Stapleton and all those at the QUB's Sonic Arts Research Centre (SARC), whose interest in my research defied disciplinary boundaries. The same applies to Marcel Cobussen, whose work on deconstruction and music sparked my own interest in Derrida and improvisation.

To my family and friends, in Canada and elsewhere, especially my grandmother Jean, my sisters Heather and Christine, as well as Geoff, Vicki, Koriena, Tamara, Marie-Hélène, Annie and Ann.

This research would not have been possible without the generous financial backing from the following agencies and funding schemes: ICASP Postdoctoral Fellowship, in partnership with Centre de recherche en éthique de l'Université de Montréal (CRÉUM); Goodenough College, Bilbrough Bursary; SSHRC Doctoral Fellowship; Edward Boyle/Alberta Research Scholarship; University of London Central Research Fund Grant; Universities U.K., Overseas Research Students Tuition Scholarship; Birkbeck College, Ronnie Warrington Doctoral Fellowship; and the British Columbia Law Foundation Graduate Fellowship.

Portions of this book have been revised and rewritten from essays published elsewhere, specifically Ramshaw, S. (2003) 'Nearing the Wild Heart: The Cixousian "Feminine" and the Quest for Law's Origins', *Australian Feminist Law Journal*, 19: 11–27 (Special Issue: Divining the Source: Law's Foundation and the Question of Authority); Ramshaw, S. (2006) 'Deconstructin(g) Jazz Improvisation: Derrida and the Law of the Singular Event', *Critical Studies in Improvisation*, 2(1). Online. Available HTTP: www.criticalimprov.com/article/view/81/188 (accessed 2 September 2012); Ramshaw, S. (2010a) 'The Creative Life of Law: Improvisation, Between Tradition and Suspicion', *Critical Studies in Improvisation*, 6(1) (Special Issue: *Lex Non Scripta, Ars Non Scripta*: Law, Justice, and Improvisation). Online. Available HTTP: www.criticalimprov.com/article/view/1084/1700 (accessed 2 September 2012); and Ramshaw, S. (2010b) 'Jamming the Law: Improvised Theatre and the "Spontaneity" of Judgment', *Law Text Culture*, 14: 133–59 (Special Issue: Law's Theatrical Presence). I thank the publishers for permission to use these texts.

Finally, to Eugene.

Chapter 1

Introduction

The law of the extempore

Eric Lewis, jazz musician and philosophy professor at McGill University in Montréal, tells of a group of US Navy SEALs tasked with putting out a large number of offshore oil fires. The job was extremely dangerous, and they studied a detailed training manual to prepare themselves for all possible eventualities. Despite this meticulous preparation, the work resulted in numerous casualties and had a very low success rate. The fires, it seemed, refused to follow prescribed plans.[1] The naval academy, looking for a solution to this dilemma, adopted principles of improvisation in their training, inculcating some basic principles and a sense that the SEALs should trust themselves to react appropriately to the situation on the ground. This resulted in far fewer casualties and far more fires being successfully extinguished.[2]

Justice as Improvisation applies the wisdom of this story to the law with the understanding that it is indeed necessary to improvise; this is not surprising. Improvisation hums 'in the background of all life' (Toop 2008: 139); everyone improvises (Snow 2004: 49). It is indeed necessary to improvise, but to improvise *well*, well, that's another story (Derrida 2004a: 332).

Discourses around improvisation often imprison it in a quasi-ethical relationship with the authentic, singular 'other',[3] either denying, or making extremely difficult, any definitional structure (Fischlin and Heble 2004: 31; Cobussen 2008a: 6).[4] 'Improvisation', writes Bailey (1992), 'is always changing and adjusting, never fixed, too elusive for analysis and precise description' (ix). Any attempt to define or describe improvisation is thus said to constitute 'a misrepresentation, for there is something central to the spirit of voluntary improvisation which is opposed to the aims and contradicts the idea of documentation' (ix; see also Nachmanovitch 1990: 12).[5]

The same can be said of justice. The only agreement as to the meaning of justice is that there is no agreement (Manderson 2000: 192). Nevertheless, as with improvisation, we cannot escape it. Justice, argues Manderson, 'is hard to explain exactly because it is felt to be bedrock and self-evident' (192). Might then the bon mot of Paul Simon, that 'improvisation is too good to leave to chance' (quoted in Fischlin and Heble 2004: 31), likewise concern justice? Applied to improvisation, it suggests that 'the rhetoric of chance (and therefore spontaneity) is best set aside when it comes to improvisation' (31). As Fischlin and Heble powerfully articulate, '[t]he paradox (and anxiety) of a chance that can't be left to chance neatly encapsulates how improvisation voids definitional modes of knowing in its polymorphous ability to be both chance and nonchance simultaneously' (31).

One response to this anxiety, at least as it pertains to improvisation, is to recognize and interrogate further its inherently contradictory nature, as that which flouts form (Soules 2004: 274) even as it is most defined by it, by its ability to 'reinvent or comment on already established forms' (Fischlin and Heble 2004: 31). The task of working through these paradoxes and separating improvisation from its mythic image falls on critical improvisation scholars. Offering some limited designation, one definition of improvisation adopted in Critical Studies in Improvisation (CSI)[6] is that of a 'musical practice … [that] embodies real-time creative decision making, risk-taking, and collaboration'[7] (Heble[8] and Siemerling 2010: 4). Despite the *musical* focus of this definition, CSI research is currently pursued in 'a range of overlapping fields of inquiry' (4), such as postcolonial studies, cultural studies, literary studies, African American studies, black performance, history, psychology, theatre studies and gender studies (4).

Justice as Improvisation adds to the above list the discipline of law.[9] The wide-ranging appeal of improvisation as a model or subject of study demonstrates 'the need to consider improvisation not simply as a musical form, but, perhaps more urgently, as a complex social phenomenon that mediates transcultural inter-artistic exchanges that produce new conceptions of identity, community, history, and the body' (4). In the words of Heble and Siemerling: 'musical practices in which improvisation figures prominently *are* social practices' (5, emphasis in original):

> Particularly for music-makers whose explorations question settled habits of response and judgment, improvisation becomes an important locus of resistance to orthodoxies of the imagination (knowing), of relations with others (community) and of relations to the materials of the world around us (instruments). Improvised music has the potential for reshaping possible relations among these materials of existence – knowing, community, instruments – in ways that can fundamentally inform and transform contemporary cultural debate.
>
> (Heble and Siemerling 2010: 5; see also Fischlin and Heble 2004: 11)

Musical improvisation is herein explored as a model for social change with a view to shaping political, cultural, and ethical dialogue and action.[10] *Justice as Improvisation* re-imagines justice as a species of improvisation through the formal structure of the most basic of legal mechanisms, judicial decision-making, offering law and legal theory a richer, more concrete, understanding of justice. Not further mystery or mystique, but a negotiation between abstract notions of justice and the everyday practice of judging. Improvisation in judgment calls for ongoing, practical decision-making as the constant negotiation between the freedom of the judge to take account of the otherness or singularity of the case *and* the existing laws or rules that both allow for and constrain that freedom. Yes, it is necessary to judge, yes, it is necessary to decide, but to judge *well*, to decide *justly*, that is a music lesson perhaps best taught by critical improvisation scholars.

Justice as Improvisation thereby builds on the insights offered by CSI and calls for the study of law and improvisation within its 'broader, theoretical context' (Landgraf 2011: 94), insisting that *all law is improvisation.*[11] To provide some 'minimal structures',[12] which allow for a fuller discussion of the fundamentally improvisational nature of law, this interrogation 'takes place'[13] (Finn 2008: 203) through the case study of the New York City (NYC) cabaret laws, or, more specifically, on the NYC Cabaret Employee's Identification Card system of regulation. Originally applying solely to chefs, waiters, dishwashers and the like, the regulations governing cabaret employees underwent reform in 1943 to include musicians and entertainers, who until the late 1960s would be required to hold an ID card in order to work in a licensed cabaret club. The introduction of these 'police cards', as they were otherwise known, occurred roughly contemporaneously to the emergence in after-hours night clubs in Harlem of a new and supposedly 'wild', improvisatory brand of jazz – bebop. While the temporal connection between the ID cards and the birth of bebop in Harlem is of enormous legal historical significance, and deserves careful and considered treatment elsewhere, it is, for me, less theoretically interesting than the oppositional relation simultaneously created and troubled by the NYC 'police cards', as between law and improvisation. Through the 'police cards', law was positioned as determinate and general against a wildly singular improvisation. These laws, though, were not beyond dispute or challenge, indicating that the opposition between law and improvisation can never be purely settled or determined.

This is not the first book to engage with the NYC cabaret laws. Two notable examples of other research done in this area include *The Police Card Discord* (1993) by Maxwell Cohen and *Gigs: Jazz and the Cabaret Laws in New York City* (1991) by Paul Chevigny. Both authors are lawyers who, along with their musician clients, challenged the cabaret laws in their variant guises over the years: Cohen in the late 1950s, Chevigny in the mid-1980s and then again in the mid-2000s. They both approach the subject from a civil libertarian stance, focusing on the rights of the musicians involved and the denigrating power of the cabaret system of regulation. *Justice as Improvisation* is not really about the NYC cabaret laws, though, and offers little novelty in this regard. What this account offers, which is missing in Cohen and Chevigny's books, is an analysis of the creative life of law, which brings law in line with jazz, not in opposition to it, *through* improvisation.

From this case study, certain inevitabilities follow, such as a concentration on the improvised music of the bebop era. While other possible entries into the study of law, justice and improvisation convincingly present themselves – the most obvious being the 'free jazz' or 'free improvisation' movement of the 1960s (Gioia 1997: 338)[14] – compelling grounds exist, I believe, for an almost exclusive focus on bebop. Adding to the obvious temporal connection mentioned above, is the broader *social*, as opposed to the purely musical, significance assigned to improvisation following the 'bebop revolution' (Kofsky 1998a: 112; Kofsky 1998b: 80; Spellman 1985: vii), which led to the generalized characterization of improvisation as 'wild' and other, individualistic and revolutionary, in society. As George Lewis (2004b) explains: 'Bebop's challenge to the dominant culture was not limited to musical concerns; in fact, bebop musicians challenged traditional notions of intra- and extramusicality' (135). Bebop musicians, in other words, not only radically redefined 'African-American improvisative musicality' (135); they directly challenged, by extension, 'the entire social order' (135). Accordingly, the broader social significance of improvisation, brought to the fore with the advent of bebop, is as important to this study of law and justice as the music itself.[15]

Following on from the above, the conception of law proffered in this book – as that which is fundamentally improvisational in nature – rests on four basic premises. First, improvisation and law share the same 'structural tension' (Landgraf 2011: 25) in that their meaning rests on the aporetic[16] relation between singularity and generality, repetition and alteration:[17] 'singularity, originality, or immediacy are already tied to repetition' (4), just as generality, stability and predictability involve constant alteration. Outside this relation, 'these notions cannot be communicated, understood, or even recognized' (4). This shared tension, this 'law of the singular event' (Derrida 2004b: 8), is what I am calling here 'the law of the extempore'.

To aid comprehension in this regard, the spectral guidance of Jacques Derrida is required. Attempts to summarize deconstructive[18] 'theory' or the Derridean 'method'[19] inevitably run the risk of 'simplifying the complexity of Derrida's thought' (Beardsworth 1996: xv). Nonetheless, they are essential to understanding deconstruction's critique of traditional metaphysics as that which privileges presence over absence in its 'desire for fully constituted meaning and grounds' (McNeill and Feldman 1998: 354). My intention here is not to detail fully, if such were possible, Derrida's project. Instead, I will focus solely on a few concepts that are particularly relevant to a deconstructive reading of the singular and the general.

First, communication begins, as Derrida does (Bennington 1993: 24), with the 'sign', as that which must not only represent a thing in its singularity ('signifier') – *this* book, for example – but also the 'concept' of a book in general ('signified'). Without this 'unity' between the 'word' and the 'thing', 'the whole of language would be reduced to a list of proper names of things, and would not in fact be a language' (25). Every sign, in other words, be it written or spoken, 'must be repeatable' (58): 'a "sign" which was essentially singular and which could be used only once would not be a sign' (58). While singularity does in a sense exist – 'what is said is said once, here and now, in such and such a place, at such and such a date' (59) – these '"once only" events of speech' (59) are only made possible through '*iterability*' or repetition and alteration, as Derrida reveals:

> … as soon as there is a mark, that is, the possibility of repetition, as soon as there is language, generality has entered the scene and the idiom compromises with something that is not idiomatic: with a common language, concepts, laws, general norms.
>
> (Derrida 1995b: 200)

Deconstruction thus highlights the 'problematic relation between the singular and the general' (Attridge 1992a: 181) and casts doubt on the possibility of pure distinction.

Derrida takes a certain 'revenge' (Bennington 1993: 71) on speech through his 'invention' of the 'witticism' *différance* (70–1), which inserts an 'a' in place of the 'e' in the French word *différence*, in order to capture the 'dual movement' (Smith 2005: 44) of difference and deferral that the latter signifies (Attridge and Baldwin 2004). Vengeance is unleashed by the fact that the difference between the two words is 'only marked in writing' (both *différance* and *différence* are pronounced the same way in French), obliging speech 'to take its own written trace as its reference' if it wants to 'say this difference' (Bennington 1993: 70–1).

The difference and deferral of *différance* means that 'every element of the system only gets its identity in its difference from the other elements' (74); and every element is marked by all that it is not (74–5). Of note, the absent other element is not absent in the sense of being 'present elsewhere' (75); it is instead a *trace*: 'Every trace is a trace of a trace' (75); and '*différance* is subject to *différance*' (74). Thus, all that is 'present' in an 'element' is 'the other, "absent" element, which must, for language to be possible, present this alterity *as* alterity' (75; emphasis in original). To present absence 'as such', though, does not make it present and this presents a challenge to the presence/absence dichotomy (75). This is not to say that Derrida is a 'thinker of absence, emptiness, nothing' (76). In Bennington's words: '"Trace" attempts to name this entwinement of the other-in-the-same which is the condition of the same itself' (76). It is therefore the notion of the trace, which 'permits the possibility of thinking beyond the binary opposition of presence and absence' (Smith 2005: 76) and, by analogy, it challenges all oppositional constructions, including that between the singular and the general, improvisation and law. Chapter 3 offers a more comprehensive examination of Derrida's thought in this regard.

The second basic premise of this book in relation to law's fundamentally improvisational qualities is that conventional definitions of law render invisible or ignore its singular or unpredictable elements. In keeping with the 'orthodox jurisprudence of modernity'[20] (Douzinas et al. 1991: ix), law persists as a unified subject, '"out there", perfectly formed, complete and coherent, waiting to be discovered' (Douzinas et al. 1991: x). In these accounts, it endures, at least in its generic or conventional sense, as 'a body of rules of action or conduct prescribed by controlling authority, and having legal binding force' (Black 1990: 884). The ideal of the rule of law means that 'everyone is bound by the law' (Pue 2000: 17, emphasis omitted). Moreover, it is 'presume[d] that before citizens' liberties and freedoms are restricted, the full protection of constitutional rights and the political protections provided by our parliamentary system of government will be brought into play' (17, emphasis omitted). Determinations of what is and what is not lawful remain under the control of the democratically elected legislature; police are employed to enforce these laws and courts adjudicate any alleged infractions or disputes over meaning (17).

As Piper (2010) observes, '[l]aw rarely exists in its stereotyped, positivist form' (1). That said, less conventional interpretations of law are also found wanting in their refusal to recognize law's singular elements. Gerald Postema's 'Melody and Law's Mindfulness of Time' (2004) is but one example of this. In this essay, melody[21] is offered as a 'metaphor and model' (205) in which to 'understand the role of time in law's characteristic normativity' (205). Postema conceives law as a 'distinctive kind of normative order' (206), one which

> ... seeks to guide the practical reasoning and the actions of self-directing, intelligent agents, and ... provides these agents with a framework within which they can publicly justify their actions and demand justification from others, especially from those who exercise political power over them.
>
> (Postema 2004: 206)

For Postema, in law's normative features lie 'the deep truth about law wherever it is found' (206). His application of the metaphor of melody to law thereby becomes a model through which to discover the *form* law's characteristic normativity takes (206).[22]

To the existing dominant models of law's normativity in jurisprudence, namely those of *nomos* (reasons) and *thesmos* (commands), Postema adds melody or *melos* (207). This third model is of particular value to jurisprudence and law for it 'highlights the temporal dimensions of law's normativity that the other models leave in the shadows' (207). Melody, argues

Postema, orders time through the constituent elements of '*attention, memory, and anticipation*' (208, emphasis added). Admittedly, this is 'true of experience generally' (208), but Postema makes a special case for melody:

> Musical thinking is a kind of rule-following: To grasp a melody *in media res* [in the middle of a sequence of events] is to project the direction of musical movement on the basis of what is sounding and what has already sounded. Melody-thinking is holistic thinking, that is, thinking in temporal sound patterns and melodic lines as notes are sounding, keeping in mind the path already marked out and anticipating where it will go next.
>
> In music, the past, present, and future are related internally by the emerging melodic pattern. Grasping a melody, especially hearing it for the first few times, can be flexible or revisable on both ends of the melodic line. In the middle of its unfolding, the hearer projects the line on the basis of her memory of the partial sequence already fading into the past. If the projection matches the direction, her grasp of the meaning of the past is confirmed. If it goes in a surprising direction, not only is she forced to rethink its anticipated future, but equally she must give altered significance to the sequence already heard. She now hears a different melody from what she thought she was hearing – the pattern is different, hence the musical significance of the melodic moments already sounded is different. The present and anticipated future of the melody alters its past.
>
> (Postema 2004: 208)

For Postema then 'melody, or rather the kind of mindfulness involved in grasping a melody, offers a model that promises to illuminate law's characteristic normativity' (208).

Postema's conception of law, while attractive, is inherently flawed. He looks to 'precedent-sensitive judicial reasoning' (214) in order to understand law's mindfulness of time. His description of melody as 'attention, memory, and anticipation' (208) is applied to the following effect:

> Deciding cases governed by precedent is like grasping a melody as it is being played ... It involves *attention* to present circumstances, *memory* of past decisions, and *anticipation* of the direction in which the rule or *ratio* is moving. The past is essential to precedent-sensitive reasoning, but it is not simply backward-looking ... Law's memory is always bent to the present in anticipation of the future. Equally, its focus on the future is from the threshold of past and present. At any point in the arc traced by the *ratio* decision-makers interact with decision-makers going before them and coming after them.
>
> (Postema 2004: 214, emphasis added)

What is missing from Postema's melodic formulation of law's mindfulness of time is any mention of the *unanticipated* or *unprecedented*, which, as this book will detail, is equally essential to law as those of attention, memory and anticipation. Throughout his essay, Postema's focus is the 'general' nature of law's essence:

> The bulk of legal norms … must be *general*. This is not just because this is a cheaper and more efficient mode of social control than case-by-case micro-management of behavior, but also because law's task is to guide people engaged in complex patterns of social interaction over time.
>
> (Postema 2004: 219, emphasis in original)

Thus, the 'meaningful ordering of time' (207) of which Postema's law is mindful is actually that of generality and linearity, even if the past, present and future interact in a complex fashion (214). No attention is paid by Postema to the time of the singular, to that of the unanticipated, unprecedented, or the 'to come', which is not a coming at all, but a promise; 'the time of the promise', says Derrida (1997a: 306), always outside time, extempore.[23]

Improvisation's mindfulness of time is worth noting here. Most discussions of improvisation stress '*performative immediacy*' (Landgraf 2011: 4, 19, emphasis added). In its 'ad hoc delivery' (19), or 'real-time creative decision making, risk-taking, and collaboration' (Heble and Siemerling 2010: 4), 'improvisation highlights the uniqueness of the "event" that is its performance' (Landgraf 2011: 19). Both Derrida and CSI, however, force us to rethink the notion of improvisation as pure singularity and immediacy. Instead, improvisation, as CSI theorists continually underscore, retrospectively develops and builds on its own history (17). Moreover, for Derrida, the distinction between a planned or prescribed act and an 'improvised doing',[24] as Landgraf calls it, is always already unsettled (21). The law of the extempore must thereby engage certain *constraints*, be them 'temporal, material, technical, genre-specific, linguistic, cultural, or societal' (18), which may broadly be termed as 'law'. Yet, this 'law', which can never be fully planned or determined in advance, must be somewhat unpredictable or extempore.

The third premise, or underlying aim, of *Justice as Improvisation* is the desire to reclaim the singular in and for law. While some limited work has been undertaken, as Chapter 5 details, on highlighting form and structure in improvisation (broadly conceived as the 'laws' of improvisation), there has been less success at unmasking the essential extempore in law. A detailed accounting of the history of improvisation in relation to the NYC jazz scene in Chapter 4 hints at possible reasons behind this concealment. At its origin, jazz and, more specifically, bebop jazz improvisation, was positioned as wild and revolutionary, not only musically speaking, but also socially. While numerous explanations exist for the suppression of jazz in the past other than its improvised nature and various types of music *not* associated with improvisation in the same way have met with legal restriction, such as rock and rap music,[25] law's relationship to singularity and otherness is clear. Law must eschew all spontaneous or unpredictable elements. This can be starkly contrasted to the prevailing perception of jazz as that which is founded solely upon pure spontaneous improvisation. Both conceptions are, when deconstructed, ultimately found wanting. Derrida thus reclaims the wildly singular as necessary for justice. The openly responsive dimension of both law and improvisation, although never complete or absolute, glances towards the singular other and keeps alive the possibility of creativity, ethics, democracy and justice, to which Chapter 7 will return.

The fourth and final principle focused upon in this book is the creative potential of justice *as* improvisation. Although not without controversy, improvisation is frequently, almost instinctively, associated with creativity and innovation (Postema 1987: 303). In light of this inherent pairing of improvisation and innovation, improvisational scholars in particular attack Derrida for his supposedly negative conception of improvisation, as that which is 'decidedly lacking in … a positive concept of creation' (Gallope 2011: 14). Repeatedly cited in support of this claim are Derrida's remarks in an unpublished interview, which are repeated in Kirby Dick and Amy Ziering Kofman's film *Derrida* (2002):

> It's not easy to improvise, it's the most difficult thing to do. Even when one improvises in front of a camera or microphone, one ventriloquizes or leaves another to speak in one's place the schemas and languages that are already there. There are already a great number of prescriptions that are prescribed in our memory and in our culture. All the names are already preprogrammed. It's already the names that inhibit our ability to ever really improvise. One can't say what ever one wants, one is obliged more or less to reproduce the stereotypical discourse. And so I believe in improvisation and I fight for improvisation. But always with the belief that it's impossible. And there where there is improvisation I am not able to see myself. I am blind to myself. And it's what I will see, no, I won't see it. It's for others to see. The one who is improvised here, no I won't ever see him.
>
> (Derrida 2004c; Dick and Kofman 2005: 93)

Based on these, and similar, statements,[26] theorists such as Gallope (2011) assert that, instead of embracing the creative potential of improvisation,[27] Derrida 'instinctively resorts to gestures of disorientation, insecurity, and incompetence' (17). Gary Peters, in his otherwise absorbing *The Philosophy of Improvisation* (2009), similarly describes Derrida's 'model' of improvisation as 'rather limited' (96). Even Edgar Landgraf (2011), who best seems to understand Derrida's conceptualization of improvisation, looks to Luhmann's systems theory to redress the 'dead end marked by Derrida's thought' (38).

Accusations of negativity and nihilism are not new to Derrida, or to scholars who embrace his ideas.[28] Yet, reading improvisation's 'impossibility' through the Derridean concept of *différance*, we find that Derrida is not biased against the singular or improvisation. Instead, for Derrida, improvisation exists as the paradoxical mediation between the singular and the generalized recognition of said singularity, which is necessary for improvisation to be recognized as such. Deconstruction here is another name for creativity and inventiveness (Derrida 1989: 42). Gallope (2011) argues that 'without an orientation in lived time, there is no philosophical basis to argue for a better or virtuous form of improvisation' (16) and thus no possibility of advancing a more just unpredictability or improvised justice. Taking its cue from Derrida himself, *Justice as Improvisation* challenges Gallope's claims and instead envisages great creative potential in deconstruction (and thus in any deconstruction of law and improvisation). As only Derrida can convey: ' … it's that music, that which happens where it wasn't expected, well, it must create, well, it must create, it must create, it must be created where it is expected without expecting' (Derrida 2004a: 334).

On that note, *Justice as Improvisation* proceeds as follows. Subsequent to this initial introductory chapter, Chapter 2 introduces the case study around which the book is structured. Its purpose is threefold. First, it establishes the positioning of law as general against a wildly singular improvisation through the NYC cabaret laws. In late 1926, the Board of Aldermen of NYC determined that there was 'altogether too much running "wild"' in NYC cabaret clubs, and that action needed to be taken. Action came in the form of the cabaret licensing laws. In June 1940, the Police Commissioner created the New York Police Department (NYPD) Cabaret Rules and Regulations to place further control on the employees of these clubs by way of the Cabaret Employees' Identification Cards, or 'police cards' as they were informally called. This system of regulation enabled police to fingerprint and photograph people who worked in licensed places, and to issue identification cards, denying cards to those considered not of good character. Having initially escaped regulation, musicians and performers were added to the employees covered under the regulations in 1943. Upon their inclusion, jazz musicians became its 'most vulnerable victims' (Cohen 1993: ix). It became unlawful for a club to hire a person who did not have a so-called 'police card' and denied were cards to anyone with a criminal record, regardless of how petty or distant the crime.

The NYC cabaret laws were never beyond dispute or challenge, though, offering a second justification for the case study. The controversy in which the 'police cards' were from their inception embroiled indicates that the opposition between the general (law) and the singular (other) is never purely settled or determined. To begin with, NYC Mayor James 'Jimmy' Walker, NYC's most famed regular nightclub customer, led the passing of the cabaret laws. Then, with control over these laws being transferred to the NYPD in 1931, further paradoxes arose. For instance, as Chapter 2 describes, the Seabury Commission disclosed that many members of the police force were either active or silent partners in thousands of these clubs. Although Judge Seabury's investigations eventually led to the resignation of Walker in 1933, the NYC cabaret licensing laws continued, but not without contest. Throughout the years, the legitimacy of the identity card requirement was challenged several times in the New York County Supreme Court and its administration was charged with 'petty graft, corruption and personal influence' (Nicholson 1995: 167). The Governor of New York State, Nelson Rockefeller, was eventually petitioned in 1960 with a request to investigate the illegal activity surrounding the 'police cards' (Gelb 1960b: 1).

This leads me to the third basis for the case-study approach. Of interest is how the law relating to the NYC 'police cards' adapted to changing social attitudes regarding singularity and otherness, jazz (and race), over the years, leading ultimately to their repeal in 1967. Reform required the introduction of improvisation into law for change to occur. The necessary but paradoxical relationship between singularity and generality thereby coalesced by way of this 'unusual regulatory scheme' (*Chiasson v NYC* 1986: 641). Although a concentrated focus on the case study fades with the closing of Chapter 2 (although it does re-appear for brief consideration in Chapter 6), its spectral presence haunts[29] the remainder of the analysis.

Chapter 3 will move from the particular to the general through a Derridean reading of the aporetic relation between singularity and generality. Many reject the application of Derrida's work to the discipline of law,[30] regarding him as a 'philosophical aesthete who tirelessly sought if not to avoid the law at least to waive or suspend it' (Goodrich 2008: 229). 'Derrida made no contribution to law. He had nothing to say about positive law' (230). Or so Goodrich begins his epitaph to the philosopher. And later: 'So Derrida had nothing direct to say to lawyers. He said nothing explicit about the law that lawyers practice' (230). And yet 'Derrida's encounter with law' was 'both pivotal and emblematic' (231), as Goodrich explains:

> The paradox of his work, its central tenet and key, was a literary resistance to law, a refusal of the anti-intellectualism of lawyers, and yet his most famous conceptual innovation, the neologism and practice of deconstruction, eventually comes to be defined as justice. Deconstruction is justice. Which entails of necessity that deconstruction is dependent upon law, defined by legality, and of course by endless deferral of the moment of passage from justice to law, from thought to decision. He was indeed rigorous. He never got to talk about law, he never seemed to want to, he held off. What he did do, however, was take lawyers to task,

> directly or more often indirectly, by reintroducing what law has historically separated itself from: amity, community, femininity, felicity.
>
> (Goodrich 2008: 233)

So, too, Derrida had nothing to say directly to musicians, especially jazz musicians, about music or improvisation, as Chapter 3 notes. And yet, in an interview he conducted with Ornette Coleman before joining him on stage at the 1997 Paris La Villette Jazz Festival for an improvised jazz–text collaboration,[31] the 'substantial connections' between his and Coleman's work were made glaringly obvious (Brody 2011). What Derrida, and only he, thus offers this study is a 'relationship of inevitable interaction' between law and improvisation, which Manderson (2000) finds vital to any exploration of the aesthetic dimensions of law and justice (31).

Chapter 4, together with Chapter 5, interrogates the tripartite relationship between improvisation, singularity and alterity through one of the most 'visible and easy to grasp' (Hatch and Weick 1998: 604) instantiations of improvisation, namely that of jazz music.[32] To the question 'What is jazz?' Louis Armstrong purportedly replied, 'Man, if you have to ask, you'll never know' (quoted in Hyman 2004: 3).[33] This celebrated response, 'parried with mystification' (DeVeaux 1997: 6), has become authority for the position that jazz is defined solely by its un-define-ability, by its inability to be tied down, contained or fixed in content. A music 'create[d] … ex nihilo' (Jarrett 2004: 319), or the 'sound of surprise' (Cotterrell 1976: 6).

To equate jazz so fully and inevitably with improvisation is not without its problems – not the least of which is the impoverished view, dominating the West, regarding the techniques of improvisation, which Chapter 5 details extensively. To the uninitiated, improvising jazz musicians 'seem to be making all of it up as they go along' (Gabbard 2004: 315; see also Demsey 2000: 788; Stewart 2003: 96). This perception is not only decidedly incorrect it has 'racist' (Derrida 2004b: 332) undertones. Improvisation, in accordance with this understanding, is envisaged as 'ultraprimitive' (Gilroy 2000b: 294; Gabbard 2004: 300), 'instinctive' (Townsend 2000: 8), 'unconscious' (Finkelstein 1948: 17; Gabbard 2004: 301); 'compensation for a deficiency (the inability to read written music), or [.] a freakish kind of gift (the jazz musician as the spontaneous, innocent, "natural" player)' (Townsend 2000: 8). Despite the enormous 'skill and devotion, preparation, training and commitment' (Bailey 1992: xii), which goes into jazz improvisation, listeners continue to place all their belief 'in the mystical "improvisational genius"' (Finkelstein 1948: 73), that 'ego-driven mystic who is unable to describe his or her own creative process' (Lewis 2004a: 170).

While attentive to this dilemma,[34] it is the case that certain types of jazz have, in the past, focused quite extensively on improvisation, thereby contributing to this vision of jazz as 'largely improvisational in nature' (Hall 1999: 1599; Lewis 2004b: 134). Take bebop,[35] for example. Developed between 1939 and 1941 in after-hours jam sessions at Monroe's Uptown House and Minton's Playhouse in Harlem, NYC[36] (Ward and Burns 2001: 291), bebop adopted the improvisational focus of the jam session – 'where the paramount concern was unbroken momentum' (DeVeaux 1997: 377). In so doing, the improvised solo moved to the fore of the performance (Belgrad 1998: 180) and 'radically revised the prevailing definition of jazz'[37] (DeVeaux 1997: 202).

Through a detailed history of the NYC jazz scene, particularly as it relates to the bebop era, Chapter 4 outlines the inter relationship of jazz and improvisation, focusing on jazz's role in shaping the image of improvisation as wild and/or wildly inventive, which, in turn, profoundly influenced, both musically and conceptually, jazz. Early representations of jazz as wild can be traced to the music's racialized conceptualisation and its lineage to African tribal music and ritual. The continued association of jazz with wildness in the bebop era, the same era that saw the emergence of the NYC 'police cards', was based not only in racialized conceptions of primitivism and savagery, but also the 'culture of spontaneity' (Belgrad 1998) and the supposed inventiveness of improvisation as extemporary and unpredictable. That solo and ensemble improvisation was central to bebop contributed to its wild formlessness. Reinforcing the image of improvisation as extemporary in the bebop era was the music's connection to the jam session, that seemingly lawless space, which both spawned bebop jazz and gave it its improvisational focus. That these jam sessions originally took place in out-of-the-way, after-hours Harlem nightspots and involved a great deal of racial mixing, simply contributed to bebop's wild reputation and solidified the close association between improvisation, singularity and alterity.

Not wishing to underestimate the importance of definitional openness, especially when writing about improvisation (Fischlin and Heble 2004: 31), Chapter 5 reveals how descriptions which focus almost entirely on 'spontaneity and the ex nihilo act are "astonishingly incomplete"' (Stanyek 2004: 95). This chapter thereby complicates the tripartite relation outlined in Chapter 4, while, at the same time, demystifying improvisation, moving beyond the 'remarkably tenacious, yet quite erroneous, view of the improviser as an inspired individual guided only by intuition' (Martin 2002: 134). As Gary Peters (2005) writes, '[b]y placing an emphasis on "self-expression" and "collective interaction", the musical account of improvisation, while important, has proved less engaged with the particular *structures* of improvisation' (300, emphasis in original). Intended here is the broadening of this perspective through the work of critical improvisation theorists. CSI debunks key myths surrounding improvisation, such as its formlessness and individualistic nature, via extended discussions of the 'jazz form', the importance of tradition and the communal aspects of improvisation. Ultimately, it is the relationship between the singular and general delectations, which provide meaning and content to improvisation.

Chapters 6 transposes the structure–freedom paradox of improvisation, outlined in Chapters 4 and 5, to the legal realm, revealing how and why law must, mirroring improvisation, be both structured and free, general and singular. Judicial precedent and discretion provide focus here. Notwithstanding the determinacy offered to law by the doctrine of *stare decisis*, freedom is imbued into its very essence. So too is the seeming illimitable freedom of legal discretion curtailed by the unpredictable. This paradox of freedom and structure at the heart of the common law is interrogated further through judicial decision-making pertaining to case law on the NYC 'police cards'. Illustrated is that every judicial act comprises a complex and paradoxical array of structured and free elements, of singularity *and* generality.

The recognition of law's paradoxes by legal theorists, however, only takes us so far. As Derrida (2005c) best expresses, without undecidability or irresolution, society 'would be a machine functioning without us, without responsibility, without decision, ultimately without ethics, or law, or politics' (128). Thus, Chapter 7 returns to Derrida in pursuit of the creative potential of deconstructive legal improvisation. Here, 'the "post-Force of Law" Derrida' (Thurschwell 2008: 154), as a philosopher concerned with 'ethical and political responsibility' (154; de Ville 2011: 8), is read alongside the Derrida who performed with Ornette Coleman at La Villette Jazz Festival, while beckoning CSI scholars back on stage. The anticipated outcome of this synthesis is a recognition of the openly responsive dimension of improvisation, which, although never complete or absolute, glances towards the singular other and keeps alive the possibility of democracy, ethics, resistance and justice in society. Deconstruction as justice as improvisation, we might even say.

Thinking about law in terms of improvisation has the potential, writes Piper (2010), to 'excite the legal imagination and suggest something instructive about the dynamic nature of the law' (4). With these aims in mind, the closing section of the book applies the principles of improvisation to precedent-sensitive judicial decision-making to offer some practical suggestions for making more visible the singular elements of law. Improvisation teaches us that the question of 'how to go on' in law 'involves neither merely acquiring a repertoire of routine reactions to routine situations, nor grasping a general proposition (let alone a systemic theory) logically independent of the practical activities' (Postema 1987: 303-4). Instead, a law that is fundamentally improvisational, to borrow from Postema in another context, 'displays a sophisticated awareness of the practice as a whole, its structuring elements and its concrete detail' (303). Yet, it also 'involves innovation, a kind of creativity, which not only fills in the interstices of the practice, but can visibly transform them' (303). Without a thorough grasp of both these dimensions, law 'blunders and fails' (303). Without failure, though, law would remain forever the same and there would be no need for law. Thus, if one takes anything from *Justice as Improvisation*, it is the following. A law that would not be a little bit wild and improvised would be no law at all (Derrida 1995a: 387).

Chapter 2

The rise and reform of the New York City cabaret laws

Jazz first gained popularity in New York City in the early 1900s as a 'naughty novelty' (Chevigny 1991: 40). White patrons would flock to a row of clubs in Harlem dubbed 'Jungle Alley' to listen to 'jass' bands (the word 'jass' referred to sexual intercourse (40) or orgasm[1] (Taylor 2000: 43)). They came to listen to the '"hot" and "barbaric" jazz', the 'risqué lyrics' and watch the '"junglelike" dancing' of the cabaret floorshows (Anderson 1981: 139). The 'legend of Harlem by night' – exhilarating and sensuous, throbbing to the beating of drums and the wailing of saxophones, cosmopolitan in its peculiar sophistications' (139–40) – beckoned white people Uptown 'with a shiver of adventure' (Chevigny 1991: 40–1). They perceived themselves to be abandoning the restraints of respectability, a perception intensified by the fact that Harlem clubs were some of the few places in the segregated United States where people of different races could mix (41).

Embodying the 'wild jazz-age spirit' (Ilma 1934: 2) of the time was NYC's Irish-American Mayor, James 'Jimmy' Walker. Variously and affectionately known as 'Duke of Jazzland' (Peretti 2007: 52), 'nightclub mayor' (55), 'Night Mayor of New York' (Mitgang 2003: 76), and 'Mayor of the Jazz Age' (Walsh 1974), Mayor Walker was notoriously nocturnal and displayed a 'well-known affinity for nightclubs' (Peretti 2007: 68).[2] In the words of Walsh (1974): 'no New Yorker would work so hard at having fun as Gentleman Jimmy' (59). It was undoubtedly quite surprising then when Mayor Walker, in 1926, 'led the crusade to regulate night clubs and impose the closing time' (Peretti 2007: 56).[3]

Mayor Walker's 'curfew bill' (*New York Times*, 20 November 1926[4]) was the city's 'first nightclub regulation of any kind' (Peretti 2007: 56). Introduced in the Municipal Assembly on 17 June 1926, its aim was to compel all nightclubs, cabarets and dance halls in the city to obtain licences and close between 3.00 a.m. and 8.00 a.m. (*NYT*, 18 June 1926; see also *NYT*, 30 June 1926: 1, 10; *NYT*, 20 November 1926). While NYC already licensed public dance halls, Mayor Walker's bill swept 'into the jurisdiction of the Commissioner of Licenses all places where any form of musical entertainment is given [with or without dancing]' (*NYT*, 18 June 1926).

According to the *New York Times* (20 November 1926), 'opponents of the restrictive law were outspoken and emphatic in its denunciation'. Alderman Murray Stand expressed his discontent, not as an Alderman, but as a private citizen:

> I am opposed to this bill ... because it is a piece of discriminatory legislation. It permits certain persons to do things and denies that right to others. In our time we have condemned prohibition, but now we propose to tell the people when they shall go to bed and when they shall stop spending their money. When did we get the right to set ourselves up as censors of the morals of the people of this city? What right do we have to invoke the powers of the home rule law for that purpose?

The bill was deemed discriminatory by its detractors mainly because of its exemptions, that is, the places it did not regulate, such as hotels of more than fifty rooms, premises owned by a membership corporation, club, society or association and premises owned, occupied or used by a religious, charitable or educational corporation or institution (*NYT*, 18 June 1926). Stated one club owner: 'What would prevent hotels from putting in cabarets and getting our business if they are not included in the new ruling?' Also regarded as unfair was the fact that, while restaurants did not come under the curfew provisions, Chinese restaurants, for example, would undoubtedly have their hours restricted because 'nearly all of them are equipped with automatic pianos or other form of musical entertainment' – although '[t]hey could avoid the operation of the law by abandoning their music' (*NYT*, 18 June 1926).

Despite the holding of two public meetings on the curfew bill, not a single voice came out in its favour (*NYT*, 20 November 1926; *NYT*, 30 November 1926). Friends of Mayor Walker were very dismayed by the lack of support, complaining that he had introduced the 'curfew bill' at the urging of local citizens, none of whom spoke out in its favour at the public hearings (*NYT*, 3 December 1926). At a third public meeting held on 3 December 1926, notwithstanding continued opposition, the Local Laws Committee of the Board of Aldermen, in an eight to three vote, passed the 'curfew bill', without modification or amendment, and sent it to the Aldermanic branch of the Municipal Assembly for further action. The vote in favour followed 'pleas for its passage by Police Commissioner McLaughlin, License Commissioner William F. Quigley, several clergymen of Catholic and Protestant churches and other proponents' (*NYT*, 4 December 1926).

On 7 December 1926, the Aldermanic Branch of the Municipal Assembly passed the 'curfew bill' by a vote of 58 to 2 (*NYT*, 8 December 1926: 1). Prior to voting, a report was submitted by the Committee on Local Laws, which gave the following reasons for the necessity of the cabaret laws:

> These night clubs or cabarets are simply dance halls, where food is served at exorbitant prices to the tune of jazz and tabloid entertainments.

> A very frank opposition was voiced by one of the licensees, on the ground that when strangers came to New York they wanted to 'run Wild'. Well, there has been altogether too much running 'wild' in some of these nightclubs and, in the judgment of your Committee, the 'wild' stranger and the foolish native should have the check-rein applied a little bit. It is well known that the 'wild' strangers are not all interested in our great museums of art and history, in our magnificent churches and public libraries, our splendid parks and public monuments. They are interested in speak-easies and dance halls and return to their native heaths to slander New York.
>
> Your committee believes that those 'wild' people should not be tumbling out of these resorts at six or seven o'clock in the morning to the scandal and annoyance of decent residents on their way to daily employment.
>
> Favorable action is recommended.
>
> (Municipal Assembly 1926: 572; see also Chevigny 1991: 55–6)

Coming into effect on 1 January 1927, Local Law No. 12, 'A Local Law to Regulate Dance Hall and Cabaret, and Providing for Licensing the Same', was passed on 16 December 1926, following a final public hearing, as prescribed by statute, and Mayor Walker's signature (*NYT*, 17 December 1926). At the behest of Mayor Walker, the new law was not enforced on New Year's Eve 1926. According to the *New York Times* (18 December 1926: 36), Mayor Walker, not desiring 'to be thought a "spoilsport"', sent a letter to License Commissioner Quigley on 17 December 1926, urging him to exercise his authority under section 5 of the law to issue special permits to licensed night clubs and cabarets whose owners wished to keep them open after 3.00 a.m. on New Year's morning.[5] Quigley, in turn, notified Police Commissioner McLaughlin on 22 December 1926 that 'permission had been extended to all licensed dance halls and cabarets to remain open New Year's morning until 8 o'clock'. The reason for this suspension of law, according to Commissioner Quigley, was 'the shortness of time allowed for preparation to enforce the provisions of the act' (*NYT*, 23 December 1926: 3).

Interestingly, according to Paul Chevigny, by the time the city got around to regulating 'cabarets', 'they were gone, destroyed by Prohibition' (Chevigny 1991: 55). What the cabaret laws were actually regulating were 'speakeasies' or illicit liquor shops or drinking clubs, which opened up during Prohibition. Thus, writes Chevigny, '[i]n the cabaret law, the City was seeking to apply its regulation to a genre that was already out of date' (55). Republican Ruth Pratt, the lone woman on the Board of Estate and a local laws committee member, made a similar point in 1926. What the city sought to regulate were 'illegal facilities that had no right to be open at all' (quoted in Peretti 2007: 70). In fact, as Peretti notes, during the initial period of regulation 'most nightclubs simply avoided licensing to elude city enforcement' (71). An amusing report in the *New York Times* (19 May 1927), for example, tells of Jack Bugler, the manager of the Footlight Club in NYC, who was arraigned on 18 May 1927 and charged with operating a cabaret without a licence. When Bugler denied that the place was a cabaret and therefore did not require licensing, the judge asked what the 'Club' was. Bugler replied, 'It's a speak-easy, your Honor' to which '[l]aughter filled the courtroom' (no page).

Out of date or not, ineffective or not, regulation of these places was viewed as necessary in light of the 'social evils that may flow from nonsupervised and unlicensed cabaret and dance halls' (*The People v. Greenberg and Slevin* 1958: 400). As pointed out by City Magistrate Scopas, in his retrospective examination of the laws in the 1958 case of *The People v. Greenberg and Slevin*, '[t]he public morals, health and safety can only be protected and safeguarded through proper supervision and licensing as prescribed by law' (401). According to Chevigny, the legislative concern over these 'social evils' had to have been directed at the 'black music and dance that was performed in the Harlem clubs' (Chevigny 1991: 57), along with the 'social mixing of races' (57; see also Vitullo-Martin 2003). It was mainly in Harlem that musicians played the jazz about which the Aldermen complained in the 7 December 1926 report (see above) (Chevigny 1991: 57). The cabaret laws thereby reinforced the view, 'then widely received throughout the country, that the origin of jazz music and dance in black culture was a source of moral degradation' (57).

In early 1931, Mayor Walker proposed a new curfew bill, a virtual redraft of the 1926 Local Law 12. One 'drastic change' (*NYT*, 16 May 1931) proposed under the terms of the new bill was that the NYPD (New York Police Department) Division of Licenses would take over control of the cabaret licensing from the NYC Licensing Bureau (*NYT*, 6 February 1931).[6] The power to extend the 3.00 a.m. curfew on special occasions, or to revoke licences in instances of violations, would now lie with the Police Commissioner.[7]

The proposed change was justified in terms of efficiency and changing conditions in the city. The current system, as explained by Mayor Walker in the *New York Times* (13 June 1931), required a complaint to be made by a police officer, which would then be examined by the License Commissioner and handed over to a police inspector, who would report back to the Commissioner before action could be taken. Under the new system, 'the police can go right in and salutary action is taken immediately'. Police Commissioner Mulrooney supported this action, adding in the same newspaper article that 'many so-called "clubs" were little better than gangster resorts' (no page).

The transfer of authority from the Department of Licenses to the Police Department was quite 'farcical', to quote Cohen (1993: 18). To begin with, although Prohibition was still the 'law of the land', cabarets that sold drinks to the public 'had to qualify and pay license fees to the Police Commissioner, the very official whose function it presumably was to apprehend and prosecute the law breaker' (18). This transfer was even more farcical when viewed in light of the Seabury Commission findings of 1930–1932. This investigation, headed by retired judge Samuel Seabury, probed suspected corruption in all levels of NYC government, including alleged misconduct by the city's magistrates,[8] the District Attorney,[9] the NYPD and Mayor Walker himself (Peretti 2007: 123).

An in-depth investigation into the findings of this Commission is beyond the scope of this chapter.[10] Suffice it to say, Seabury's 'most disturbing revelations' (Peretti 2007: 131) involved members of the NYPD, along with lawyers and bail bondsmen in the Women's Court, who 'systematically framed' (131) hundreds of innocent women on prostitution charges for financial gain. Seabury exposed the complicity of NYPD officers in this 'framing ring'[11] in early 1931, contemporaneous with Walker's transfer of power over the cabaret laws to the police department. The framing ring operated as follows:

> ... vice squad officers created the cases themselves. In a typical situation, the officers began by locating a woman with means and a reputation to protect. They then enlisted a male 'stool pigeon' to lure the victim to a hotel room. After he entered the room with the woman, the man planted marked currency at a predetermined spot. Policemen then burst in and questioned the man. Officers 'discovered' the currency, pretended to eject the man by force (he was not subject to arrest) and took the woman to the police station for booking. Bail was set at five hundred dollars. A bondsman pretending to be at the station by chance then offered to take her case. He obtained the keys to her home, retrieved her bankbook and attached himself to her account. He posted bail for the stunned woman, who was released. A few days later, before the trial, the bondsman introduced the woman to a lawyer. The attorney instructed her to plead not guilty. At the trial, if the woman's account held enough money to pay everyone's fees, the lawyer whispered to a complicit prosecutor, 'This one is OK'. An officer testified that no incriminating evidence existed after all; the prosecutor moved for dismissal, and the swindled woman was set free. If the defendant could not pay the fees, the officer testified to her guilt and she would be sentenced – usually for sixty days – to the Welfare Island jail.
>
> (Peretti 2007: 132–3)

Seabury's inquiry, and the ensuing departmental trials of the participating police officers ('police trials'), disclosed that not only was the NYPD involved in operating speakeasies (*NYT*, 24 February 1931), many police officers and 'higher-ups' actually 'benefited from the speakeasy collections and other forms of police graft' (*NYT*, 18 February 1931: 1). Harry Levey, for example, testified before Judge Seabury on 16 February 1931 that, in 1927–8, he collected monthly totals of approximately $7,500 from the proprietors of 125 speakeasies on the upper west side, which he turned over to two plainclothes police officers, James J. Quinlivan and William M. O'Connor (*NYT*, 17 February 1931: 1). This investigation ultimately left the NYPD in disrepute[12] and led to the resignation of Walker as Mayor in September 1932 (Peretti 2007: 123). Accordingly, the transfer of authority to the Police Commissioner, concurrent with an investigation into corruption and graft in the NYPD and NYC government, including the Mayor's office, was nothing less than absurd.

This transfer of authority from the Licensing Bureau to the NYPD was justified in terms of the 'certain evils that flourished in and followed the prohibition era' (*Friedman v. Valentine* 1941: 439). In order to control these so-called 'evils', police began fingerprinting applicants for cabaret licences (i.e. owners). However, according to Justice Pecora in the 1941 case of *Friedman v. Valentine*, 'simply fingerprinting such applicants did not give the police the adequate means to prevent crimes by and with employees, steerers and operators of so-called "clip joints," nor to apprehend the perpetrators' (440). Further restrictions were required. These came in the form of the NYC 'police cards'.

On 20 June 1940, the Police Commissioner created – '*not* by statute or by ordinance or by legislative authority' (Cohen 1993: 18, emphasis in original) – the NYPD Cabaret Rules and Regulations, which provided 'control over *employees* by means of the unlawful and oppressive Cabaret Employee's Identification Card' (18, emphasis in original). This 'discriminatory and harmful' (Peretti 1997: 138) system of legal regulation enabled police to fingerprint[13] and photograph people who worked in licensed places and to issue identification cards,[14] 'denying the cards to people they thought were not of good character' (Chevigny 1991: 58).[15]

The official rationale behind the Cabaret Employee's Identification Card was that Police Commissioner Valentine was 'responding to a series of complaints of major and minor law violations in and about night clubs and cabarets' (*NYT*, 15 August 1940: 1). However, many argue that the 'police cards', as they were otherwise known, came into existence for 'completely different reasons not related to crime prevention and control' (Cohen 1993: 18). First, for reasons unclear, the cards initially applied solely to chefs and waiters, and did not cover musicians until about two years later (19). This has led some to contend that the cards were 'directed as a political weapon at the presumed [Communist] leadership of the Joint Board of Waiters and Chefs Union' (Cohen 1961: 13; see also; Cohen 1993: 19–20 Nicholson 1995: 167; Peretti 1997: 115). Maxwell Cohen explains in his book *The Police Card Discord*:

> A study of strikes and labor difficulties of that period is revealing. The Brass Rail Restaurants in 1940 had a waiters' strike in progress for almost four continuous years ... The restaurants serving visitors at the World's Fair were threatened with strikes.
>
> It was believed, and evidently with some accuracy, that the Joint Board of Waiters and Chefs was Communist-dominated.
>
> (Cohen 1993: 19)

On 4 December 1940, Samuel Friedman, President of the New York Joint Board of the Hotel and Restaurant Employees International Alliance and Bartenders International League of America, brought an application to the Supreme Court of New York for an order to restrain enforcement of police regulations requiring the fingerprinting of cabaret employees (*NYT*, 5 December 1940). The pleadings indicated that the primary concern of the unions was the issue of fingerprinting, along with certain violations of labour rights. Inferentially, argues Cohen, 'due to the climate of that time (1939–1941)' (Cohen 1993: 19), there must also have been concern that the police department's new rules and regulations regarding cabaret employees were 'politically undemocratic procedures' (19). In petitioner Friedman's Brief, it stated:

> ... we respectfully urge upon the Court the fact that fingerprinting and identification cards are part of an internal passport system which does not comport with the American way of life, and which infringes upon the fundamental rights of liberty which only the sovereign state, acting under the police power, may abrogate for good cause shown.
>
> (Cohen 1993: 19)

Also inferred was that these rules and regulations were simply 'a ruse to prepare a labor black-list and a means to bar union organizers from the field of operations' (20). They were, in other words, viewed as being 'politically motivated and not a crime deterrent' (20).

Justice Pecora, deciding the case solely on affidavit evidence, held that the cabaret card system was necessary to 'purg[e] the business of unfit elements' (*Friedman v. Valentine* 1941: 440) and 'aid effectively in the solution of crimes or offenses peculiarly connected with the operation of cabarets' (440). He found that the 'Petitioners have failed to show that the regulations under attack are not justified by conditions existing in the cabaret industry' (441).[16] Moreover, the judge maintained that 'positive and convincing reasons for such regulations' (441) were in fact 'common knowledge' (441).

The court found untenable the argument made by Friedman that employees have a right to pursue employment without interference from the police commissioner (441). Justice Pecora held that '[a]ny occupation may be reasonably regulated if others may be exposed to danger or misfortune by such calling' (441). Of particular interest is the justification he gave for upholding the constitutionality of the fingerprint requirement: 'The test of constitutionality is whether an evil exists and whether there is a logical relation between the eradication of the evil and the enactment of regulations intended to cure the condition' (441). The evil of which Pecora J. was most concerned involved the 'favorable opportunities' (441) cabaret employees had 'to victimize patrons of such establishments' (441). Those employees without criminal records were viewed as 'less likely to victimize patrons than … those with criminal records' (441). Thus, he found that 'the regulations extending the requirements of fingerprinting to employees of licensees of cabarets is a lawful and proper exercise of power' (441). Moreover, he noted that the regulation did not automatically disqualify from employment a person with a criminal record for it was in the police commissioner's discretion to accept an application for a cabaret card where he believed the applicant would not endanger public safety (442). This decision by Justice Pecora became the leading case on the issue and would 'haunt almost every attempt to fight the Card system' (Cohen 1993: 22).[17]

The year 1943 marked the addition of musicians and performers to those employees covered under the Cabaret Employee's Identification Card system of regulation (Hoefer 1961: 6).[18] The reason for their inclusion is unclear. Admittedly, there 'was some underworld involvement in running the clubs' (Chevigny 1991: 59). Nonetheless, the 'nexus between crime and the musicians and other entertainers was entirely symbolic' (59). Chevigny explains:

> Neither the news reports nor the cases reveal a single instance during the entire controversy when anyone, whether from the police or any other source, claimed that a musician, or any entertainer, was denied a card because he had committed a crime in or even close to a club. The cards were invariably denied because of a past criminal record, often for narcotics offenses.
>
> (Chevigny 1991: 59)

One possible explanation for the addition of musicians to the list of employees requiring cabaret cards is that it was a 'racist impulse to control the supposedly degrading abandon of black music' (59). Through the cards, the NYPD was attempting to 'stomp out the "threat" of the wild, rhythmic sounds of jazz, and to curtail the intermixing of blacks and whites in Harlem jazz clubs' (Miller 2000). The fact that cooks and dishwashers were deemed to no longer require regulation at the same time musicians were added (Cohen 1993: 19; see also Hoefer 1961: 6) supports this claim. The rationale for the removal of the former was that kitchen staff 'did not come into *direct* contact with the public' (Hoefer 1961: 6, emphasis in original). Thus, it appears the cabaret laws looked less to crime control and more to the regulation of intimacy and the prevention of 'any close contact between the audience and the seductive art [of jazz]' (Chevigny 1991: 60) and those musicians 'who practiced the abandoned arts of these nightclubs' (60). A Press Release offered by the Citizens Union on 12 December 1960 offers proof. It stated:

> Intimacy is encouraged by the crowding, the drinking, the music and the dim lights. In such surroundings, a shady character can make hay while the sun is not shining. Because of these special circumstances, it is fair to put cabarets and dance halls in a class by themselves for regulatory purposes.
>
> (Citizens Union 1960: 2–3; see also Chevigny 1991: 65)

Upon their inclusion in the Cabaret Employee's Identification Card system of regulation, jazz musicians became its 'most vulnerable victims'[19] (Cohen 1993: ix). Musicians were required to have their cards on file with the nightclub owners during the time they were employed at a cabaret club and the owners had to 'enter the card number into a book that [was] kept for police inspection' (Hoefer 1961: 7; Cohen 1993: xiv). It became unlawful for a club to hire a person who did not have a so-called 'police card' and anyone with a criminal record was denied a cabaret card, regardless of how petty or distant the crime (Nicholson 1995: 167).

Not only was the cabaret-card system extremely degrading to the musicians, it was also conducted in an atmosphere of 'petty graft, corruption and personal influence' (167). Musicians applying for a card were often sent next door to a photo studio to pay for an identification photo – even if they had brought their own picture. Musicians also complained that '[t]he police used the cabaret-card ruling in "a mean-spirited way"' (Gourse 1997: 91), as a means of 'harassing African American jazz musicians in particular' (91; 118). Some musicians denied cards at first, usually because of past drug offences, found they could hire a lawyer and eventually obtain a card (Chevigny 1991: 61). However, many had neither the money nor adequate knowledge of the system to fight the problem. Others, such as Billie Holiday (see below), were rumoured to have had their appeals continually denied because of their political commitment to desegregation (Gomez 1993: 197, n. 7). The irony of this system was that artists denied a cabaret card could still perform in theatres, Central Park and, as Holiday later demonstrated, the nation's foremost stage, Carnegie Hall (Nicholson 1995: 167).

When applying for a card, applicants were required to answer the following question:

> 7. (a) Were you ever arrested or summoned (except traffic violation)? (Yes or No) ________
> (b) If answer is yes, state how many times and give facts.

This question, argues Maxwell Cohen, violated 'all known and accepted constitutional and statutory laws' (Cohen 1993: 14) in that 'an arrest, which per se is no evidence of guilt, was improperly and unlawfully made equivalent to a conviction of crime by the Police Department' (14). If the applicant answered 'yes' to the question, he or she was advised *not* to submit the application by the officer on duty, 'for the consequence of such submission would be a denial' (15). If the applicant insisted upon submission, in spite of this advice, he or she would be required to supply 'corroborative evidence of rehabilitation and/or of good reputation and character, or a State Liquor Authority Employment permission' (15). The application would then be 'reviewed by a higher officer for denial or approval at a later date – often too late for the specific employment possibility – or for a scheduled hearing by the Division of Licenses' (15). These hearings, according to Cohen, 'were at first conducted alongside a desk, were very brisk and routine, and inevitably resulted in a denial' (15).

The police commissioner had the discretion to grant a 'police card' to an applicant with a criminal record. This discretionary power was of great consequence to jazz musicians and other cabaret performers. Having a criminal record (or even an arrest) for a narcotics or drunk charge was commonplace in the entertainment industry where there had always been a 'taint of drugs' (Nicholson 1995: 137) and musicians and writers had long consumed drugs and alcohol to help them relax and enhance their creative imagination (137).[20] In 1937, the use and possession of marijuana became a federal offence in the United States. The government argued that prohibition under federal law was necessary because marijuana was so dangerous. Interestingly, the campaign to criminalise marijuana coincided with proposed budget cuts to all federal agencies, including the Federal Commission of Narcotic Drugs. It has been speculated that the Federal Commissioner of Narcotic Drugs, Harry J. Anslinger, lead the campaign to criminalise marijuana in order to ensure his Department (and his job) was not eliminated in the cutbacks (Clarke 1994: 204). This campaign is particularly intriguing in light of the fact that the only people who really smoked marijuana at that time were people in show business – and 'Mexicans or Indians' (Bryant, quoted 204).[21] Ironically, in response to, or for protection from, this criminalization, entertainers started to drink more: "cause before, if you were smoking pot you weren't drinking' (Bryant, quoted 204). This criminalization meant that the price of a marijuana cigarette increased from five cents to a dollar. It also meant that, when heroin hit town shortly after this criminalization, it was welcomed with open arms (205).

By the mid-1940s, heroin had become particularly fashionable with the young musicians in the burgeoning bebop music scene (Nicholson 1995: 137) and '[a] great number of musicians began using heroin in the early bebop era' (Gourse 1997: 98). Writes Gitler (1985): 'In the minds of many, bop and drugs were inextricable linked' (318). It was during this era that the idea of 'hip' developed (Monson 1995: 397). Beboppers 'created a language, a dress, a music, and a high which were closed unto themselves and allowed them to one-up the rest of the world' (Spellman 1985: 193). Heroin became 'the thing that made [bop musicians] different from the rest of the world ... It was the thing that gave [them] membership in a unique club' (Rodney, quoted in Blackburn 2005: 198). According to Spellman (1985), '[t]he bebop era was the first time that the black ego was expressed in America with self-assurance, and heroin, because its effect blocks out all doubt, is a drug that facilitates the self-assurance' (193). People in the jazz scene, especially black musicians and singers, worked in a society largely controlled by people who were extremely prejudiced against them. Getting high helped black performers cope with racism; insults could be effectively ignored when on heroin, argues Clarke (1994: 265–6). Stuart Nicholson (1995) writes that '[s]ome 50–75 per cent of the bop players had experience of the drug, a quarter to a third were seriously addicted, and as many as 20 per cent were killed by their addiction' (137).[22]

'Dizzy' Gillespie, in a chapter of his autobiography entitled 'Beboppers ... The Cult', explains the close relationship between bebop and drugs:

> Dope, heroin abuse, really got to be a major problem during the bebop era, especially in the late forties, and a lotta guys died from it. Cats were always getting 'busted' with drugs by the police, and they had a saying, 'To get the best band, go to KY.' That meant the 'best band' was in Lexington, Kentucky, at the federal narcotics hospital. Why did it happen? The style of life moved so fast, and cats were struggling to keep up. It was wartime, everybody was uptight. They probably wanted something to take their minds off all the killing and dying and the cares of this world.
>
> (Gillespie 1979: 283)

With the 'drug scourge of the forties' (284), heroin hit the jazz scene 'before it was on the street' (Jackie McLean, quoted in Spellman 1985: 193). Jazz musicians, in turn, became the target of much public attention and police surveillance. Billie Holiday, for instance, was 'regularly tailed by the narcotics police' (O'Brien 1996: 79). Due to their race and notoriety, jazz musicians were far more likely to be arrested than others in NYC for narcotics offences and these arrests effectively barred them from obtaining a cabaret card and thus from working in any NYC club (Nicholson 1995: 167). As Annie Ross says of Billie Holiday: 'I'm sure there were many people in America then of a different class and colour able to take drugs and lead relatively normal lives – but her livelihood was taken away when they denied her cabaret card' (quoted in O'Brien 1996: 79).

For applicants of the Cabaret Employee's Identification Card, who were also required to state their 'Race (Color)' on the form, being labelled as

'White' or 'Colored' had significant social consequences. Becoming a Muslim during segregation in the United States thus carried a bonus:

> [It was] a ticket out of the racial caste system of America. A Moslem [sic] was no longer treated as a 'colored person' but as a foreigner. Upon adopting a Moslem name, one was received by whites as an Arab, and one could be served in whites-only restaurants.
>
> (Gerard 1995)

In an attempt to avoid such labels 'a large number of modern jazz musicians did begin to turn toward Islam during the forties, a movement completely in line with the idea of freedom of religion' (Gillespie 1979: 291).[23] Gillespie points out that this move seemed more politically or socially, rather than religiously, motivated:

> 'Man, if you join the Muslim faith, you ain't colored no more, you'll be white,' they'd say. 'You get a new name and you don't have to be a nigger no more.' So everyone started joining because they considered it a big advantage not to be black during the time of segregation.
>
> (Gillespie 1979: 291)

Of relevance to the cabaret-card system of regulation was that musicians who converted to Islam were able to have printed on their police cards, under where it said 'Race', 'W' for white. Drummer Kenny Clarke had just such a card, which he showed to 'Dizzy' Gillespie: '[Clarke] said, "See, nigger, I ain't no spook; I'm white, 'W'." He changed his name to Arabic, Liaqat Ali Salaam' (Gillespie 1979: 291). Gillespie, himself, did not convert to Islam, though he considered doing so. Instead, he left the race question on the application blank and would not 'allow the police to type anything in that spot under race' (292):

> When the cop started to type something in there, I asked him 'What are you gonna put down there, C for me?'
>
> 'You're colored, ain't you?'
>
> 'Colored … ? No.'
>
> 'Well, what are you, white?'
>
> 'No, don't put nothing on there,' I said. 'Just give me the card.' They left it open. I wouldn't let them type me in W for white nor C for colored; just made them leave it blank. WC is a toilet in Europe.
>
> (Gillespie 1979: 292)

Billie Holiday's[24] relationship with the NYPD (and the 'police card' system of regulation) is perhaps the '[m]ost notorious' (Chevigny 1991: 59). Convicted in 1947 of narcotics possession (to which she actually pleaded guilty and requested medical treatment for her addiction), Holiday served a nine and a half month prison term at the Federal Reformatory for Women in Alderson, Virginia (Nicholson 1995: 158; Chilton 1975: 118). Upon her release, Holiday was denied a cabaret card when she returned to NYC in 1948 (Blackburn 2005: 136). After at least three further unsuccessful attempts to have her card reinstated (199–200), Holiday discovered the hard way that 'an entertainer exiled from New York suffers extensive career damage' (Hentoff 1972: 18). Without her cabaret card, Holiday had limited options. When offered a job by John Levy, co-manager of the Ebony Club (later to become Birdland), with the promise that action would not be taken against her by the police, Holiday had little choice but to take Levy up on his offer (Chilton 1975: 122). Holiday sang at the club undisturbed by the police[25] and with great success (122). She had become the '"in figure" with a vociferous crowd of New York sophisticates, whose interest was stimulated by the publicity concerning her past misdemeanours' (122). As her biographer, John Chilton, explains, '[t]hey had sensed that Billie, by law, should not be appearing at the club, and this added to the thrill of hearing her' (122).

Without a cabaret card, Holiday had no choice but to go back on the road in order to make enough money (Blackburn 2005: 136). She got a gig in San Francisco, California where, in 1949, federal narcotics agents arrested her for possession (Nicholson 1995: 173). During the time between this arrest and her trial,[26] Holiday returned to NYC. While back east, she was delivered another huge blow. Denied, once again, a cabaret card, it cost her an engagement at the Royal Roost in NYC (at $3,000 a week). According to *Down Beat* (6 May 1949) magazine, at her appeal against the card ruling, Justice Aaron Levy commended the police department for refusing to issue Holiday a card (see also Chilton 1975: 133; Nicholson 1995: 175; Blackburn 2005: 200). Holiday spent the rest of her short life trying to get her cabaret card back, dying of cirrhosis of the liver in 1959 at age 44 following another arrest for narcotics possession while in hospital (Griffin 2001: 27).

Holiday's death followed closely on from that of another famous musician, alto saxophonist Charlie 'Yardbird'[27] Parker, who also did not escape legal regulation by the NYPD during his all too brief life and career. Bird was 'celebrated as the most original, the most brilliant and the most influential jazzman of our time' (Shaw 1957: 246). His 'rhythmic invention and use of chromatic harmony changed the basic vocabulary of improvisation' (Coleman 1987: 33) and he became known as one of the originators of bebop jazz music (33).[28] In 1951, however, Parker lost his cabaret card. Legend has it that it was Parker's notoriety as a heroin addict, and not any arrest or conviction, which led to his card being revoked 'at the recommendation of the narcotics squad' (Ross 1972: 304). Woideck (1998: 43), however, argues that Parker was arrested at least once for possession of drugs and received a three-month suspended sentence. Without a card, Parker had to go on the road outside of New York State in order to get work. Eventually he was able to get his card back in 1953 through a police hearing (Chevigny 1991: 60), but '[h]aving his card taken also gave him a reputation of being unreliable and unpredictable' (Peterson 1999) and no clubs wanted to employ him even with the reinstatement of his 'police card' (Peterson 1999). Due in part to his employment problems, Parker attempted suicide in 1954 and voluntarily committed himself to New York's Bellevue Hospital (Gitler 1985: 297). His last public appearance was on 4 March 1955 – at Birdland, the club named in his honour (298). Eight days later, he was dead. He died on 12 March 1955 from 'a combination of cirrhosis of the liver, stomach ulcers, pneumonia and, quite possibly, a heart attack' (Nicholson 2005: 29).

Attorney Maxwell Cohen, who would become one of the strongest opponents of the 'police cards', first heard about this requirement in 1951, after bebop pianist and composer Bud Powell was arrested, along with Thelonious Monk,[29] on a narcotics charge, which was subsequently dismissed. Following the arrest, Powell was committed to a state psychiatric hospital, where he was neglected and ignored for months by hospital authorities. If it had not been for a sympathetic nurse who encouraged Powell to play the hospital piano, his 'deterioration and vegetation threatened to become that inevitable termination of what had once been a promising career in music' (Cohen 1993: xiii). Upon his release from the hospital, Powell applied for his cabaret card, but was denied because of two previous convictions. Cohen, referred to Powell by Alan Morrison, editor of *Jet* and *Ebony* magazines (xiv), appealed against this decision on Powell's behalf and explained in court the circumstances of the arrest and conviction (xiii–xiv). The deputy police commissioner, who Morrison knew, granted a temporary card, but only for a limited engagement at the world-famous jazz club Birdland (xiii–xiv).

In the late 1950s, the 'clamor' (Chevigny 1991: 61) against the 'police cards' increased. Maxwell Cohen brought a test suit in the Supreme Court of New York County, using bandleader Johnny Richards and two of his side musicians, pianist Bill Rubenstein and trombonist J.J. Johnson, as plaintiffs (61). According to Chevigny:

> The facts presented sobering examples of the arbitrariness of the regulations. Once convicted of a marijuana offense, Rubenstein had been twice denied a card after police hearings. From an artistic point of view, the denial to J.J. Johnson was even more dismaying. The indispensable master of the modern-jazz trombone, without whose work the City was much poorer artistically, Johnson had been once caught with a hypodermic thirteen years earlier.
>
> (Chevigny 1991: 61–2)

According to the *New York Times* (15 May 1959), Johnson had been denied a cabaret card due to a suspended 60-day sentence in 1946 for 'possessing a hypodermic needle although he said he had never been a narcotics addict' (24). He testified at trial that the police had denied his applications for many years, without ever providing a reason for the denial.

Cohen argued in court that the police department had 'no explicit authority with regard to the Police Cards and for the imposition of fees and the deposit of such funds in the Police Pension Fund' (Cohen 1993: 24). The police admitted this to be the case in their answer. However, they argued that 'the authority was implied in the power of the Police Commissioner to make reasonable rules and regulations' (24). A 'bargain' was eventually struck in chambers in which it was agreed that police cards would be issued to Rubenstein and Johnson if Cohen withdrew the other causes of action (without prejudice to his rights to institute other actions in the future) (50). As such, the court did not get a chance to comment on the legality of the cabaret cards and 'the system remained undisturbed' (Chevigny 1991: 62).

In April 1959, the musicians' union, Local 802, 'successfully lobbied for a state bill that deprived the New York City police of the power to deny a card if the person was acceptable under the standards of the State Liquor Authority' (Chevigny 1991: 62; *NYT*, 24 April 1959). Unfortunately, Governor Rockefeller vetoed the bill 'after the mayor appealed to him to do so because of what the police commissioner called the "peculiar problems in New York City concerning cabarets"' (Chevigny 1991: 62).

In November 1960, an incident occurred from which the cabaret-card system never really recovered. Its downfall began when comedian Lord Buckley – 'the jazz philosopher who jammed with Charlie Parker' (Cruickshank 2002: 1) – began performing at NYC's Jazz Gallery in October 1960. In the middle of his 19 October performance, Buckley was forced off the stage by the NYPD and relieved of his cabaret card (Chevigny 1991: 62) – 'without prior notice or hearing' (Nichols 1960: 3) as is required by section 6 of the Regulations. Buckley it seems had been convicted of a drunk charge in Reno, Nevada 19 years prior and was arrested in Indianapolis, Indiana 17 years earlier for assault and possession of marijuana. He had neglected to list these arrests and conviction on his cabaret-card application, arguing later that he thought he only had to list his convictions, not his arrests, and that he had forgotten about his conviction as it was so long ago. Upon discovering these 'priors' during the requisite fingerprint check, the police revoked Buckley's card (Chevigny 1991: 62). When Buckley went down to the police department hoping to get it back, the police officer in charge 'referred to the fact that there was very little difference between a performer and a criminal anyway' (Ullman 1980: 33).

Maxwell Cohen arranged for a hearing to reinstate Lord Buckley's card before deputy chief inspector Francis W. Lent on 3 November 1960. However, due to the lateness of the hearing and the large number of witnesses who had come to speak on Buckley's behalf, the hearing was adjourned first until 7 November 1960 and then until 14 November 1960. With the card withdrawn on 19 October 1960, Lord Buckley had been unable to work for three weeks. On Saturday 12 November 1960, two days before the scheduled hearing, Buckley died tragically of a stroke brought on by malnutrition and a kidney ailment precipitated allegedly by his inability to afford food for the two days prior to his death (Cohen 1993: xvi, 62).

Following Buckley's untimely death, his friend and renowned novelist Harold Humes organized a number of prominent writers and entertainers into a Citizens' Emergency Committee (CEC)[30] in order to put an end to the card system once and for all (Chevigny 1991: 62). The CEC charged the NYPD with corruption and argued that 'many performers were forced to pay bribes to maintain the cabaret cards, without which they are not supposed to work' (Carr 1960: 1). It came to light that Buckley himself had been told that he could get into the police department's good graces if he performed for free at an Honor Legion dinner, an unofficial police function (Chevigny 1991: 62). During this function, a theatrical agent allegedly approached Buckley and told him that he could get a card from a deputy police commissioner if Buckley paid $100 (63). After Buckley's death, the CEC tried to prove that this proposed bribe took place, but the suspected booking agent, Al Wintner, denied the charge (Carr 1960: 1; Robinson 1960: 32).

Lord Buckley's family and friends were adamant that Cohen should appear at the 14 November 1960 hearing and obtain the card for Buckley posthumously. They believed Buckley 'deserved at least the recognition that he was a worthy citizen of good repute' (Cohen 1993: 75). Cohen made certain that only three character witnesses would be available to testify at this hearing (so as not to anger Deputy Chief Inspector Lent). Harry Sedgwick and Harold Humes would attend with Cohen; Ed Sullivan would be available to testify if needed. In attendance for the police, on the other hand, were the police commissioner, a number of police officials, television-camera operators, photographers and reporters. Police Commissioner Kennedy immediately took charge of the hearing, ordering on record the names of everyone present. Cohen objected to the commissioner's conduct on the ground that he had not attended the original hearing. He argued that Lent should conduct the investigation because he was familiar with the facts (78).

The commissioner relinquished the hearing to Lent and Cohen presented his case for the reinstatement of Lord Buckley's cabaret card. Lent was about to make a decision when he was passed a note by Kennedy. It is uncertain whether this note had any bearing on his decision, but Lent denied Buckley's application (xvi, 78). When Cohen demanded to see the note, Kennedy deliberately tore it up (78). The police commissioner then turned on Harry Sedgwick and started yelling at him: '"Who are the Citizens?" "What is the emergency," and "Were you ever known by any other name?"' (quoted 78–9). A battle of words ensued, all captured by the attending press. That night, newscasts were extended by an extra 15 minutes to report on this event (79).

After the failed hearing, the CEC decided to draft a petition to Governor Rockefeller, which it sent by telegram on 15 November 1960, asking for an overall investigation of the NYPD. The committee asked the governor to 'appoint a special authority to examine "the effect of any illegal activity" among the department's "present and former personnel"' (Gelb 1960a: 1; Gelb 1960b: 1; Gelb 1960c: 44). Governor Rockefeller directed that a report be filed by Mayor Wagner; Wagner, in turn, directed Louis I. Kaplan, Commissioner of Investigation, to conduct a 'sweeping investigation of charges of police corruption' (Gelb 1960b: 1). He was ordered to '"check every phase" of the situation' (1), focusing first and foremost on the NYPD's licensing of cabaret employees (1).

The result of this investigation, reported *Down Beat* magazine (5 January 1961), was a 'commando type raid' by the police department on more than 1,200 cabarets in NYC: 'Far from becoming more lenient in the handling of the card cases, the New York police cracked down with severity, as if resenting the challenge to their rule over a major slice of the entertainment world' (11). The raids, staged on the weekend before Thanksgiving 1960, produced 114 violations; the police issued 20 court summonses (11). The punishment for any violation was a four-day suspension, which meant shutting down the violating clubs during the holiday weekend (11; see also Perlmutter 1960a: 21). For many, the raids were 'not based upon reason or violation of law but upon anger and retaliatory measures' (quoted in Peluso and Lee 1960: 3).

At the end of November 1960, Cohen brought yet another suit to the Supreme Court of the State of New York, this time on behalf of singer Nina Simone and musician Quincy Jones, among others (see *Simone v. Kennedy* 1961). The relief sought by the plaintiffs was as follows:

> (1) a judgment declaring unconstitutional and illegal regulations issued by the Police Commissioner, which require the fingerprinting of every employee of a cabaret who comes in contact or is likely to come in contact with patrons of such cabaret and which require all such employees to obtain identification cards; (2) an injunction against enforcement of said regulations; (3) a direction that the Police Commissioner account to plaintiffs for all the 'service' fees of $2 charged for the issuance of each identification card; (4) a direction that the Board of Trustees of the Police Pension Fund account to plaintiffs for the proceeds of the $2 fees which were received by the Fund from the Police Department, together with 'interest, earnings and profit'; (5) a judgment directing the repayment of all the $2 fees to the persons who paid them, and (6) an allowance to plaintiffs' attorney of a legal fee out of the total of the 'service' fees directed to be repaid with interest, etc.
>
> (*Simone v. Kennedy* 1961: 840)

Relying on the decision of *Friedman v. Valentine* (1943), Justice Fine held that the fingerprinting requirement and identification cards were constitutional and legal and the 'court is bound by the determination of the Appellate Division that the regulations are valid' (840). Moreover, the court found that '[t]he right to require the identification cards carries with it the implied authority to charge fees necessary to meet the costs of the service involved' (841).

Around the same time, Mayor Wagner introduced a bill in the City Council to 'transfer the licensing power from the Police Department to the Department of Licensing' (Maiorana 1961: 1). In his report to Governor Rockefeller, Mayor Wagner denied that there was any evidence of police corruption in the issuance of cabaret cards to entertainers and other employees. However, he did agree to have the regulations changed to permit permanent identification cards be awarded, provided the employee did not violate the law (Freeman 1960a: 1). Moreover, it was recommended that applicants be able to obtain their cards and be fingerprinted and photographed at a more convenient locality for musicians and entertainers (Chevigny 1991: 64; see also Freeman 1960a: 1) – the midtown theatrical area (Hoefer 1961: 20) – and 'at a place not associated with other police activities' (Perlmutter 1960b: 1). In light of these recommendations, identity cards were made permanent in 1961 and the administration of the system was transferred back to the Department of Licenses, away from the NYPD (Sibley 1961: 1).

Notwithstanding these changes, the cabaret-card system remained in place – at least until John Lindsay came into office as mayor of NYC on 1 January 1966. According to Chevigny, '[Lindsay] and his cohorts sought to make New York "Fun City," partly no doubt to encourage the tourist trade, but also because they were less suspicious of fun, and of the diversity of the city' (Chevigny 1991: 67). As early as 19 January 1966, Mayor Lindsay announced that 'he would support any effort to abolish the city's generation-old requirements that cabaret entertainers and employees be fingerprinted and licensed' (Zion 1966: 24). In fact, during his mayoral campaign, a letter Lindsay had written to Art D'Lugoff, owner of the Village Gate nightclub and pioneer crusader against the cabaret laws, was made public, which stated the following: 'I cannot understand a law which would regulate practically everyone associated with an entirely legal form of business. In my opinion, finger printing of cabaret owners is sufficient to prevent shady and underworld characters from invading the cabarets' (24).

Will Lissner of the *New York Times* (29 August 1966) reported that, on 28 August 1966, Mayor Lindsay directed the License Department to end the fingerprinting of cabaret entertainers and other employees (Lissner 1966: 1). The License Commissioner Joel J. Tyler announced concurrently that

> ... the fingerprinting was required only by a departmental regulation and therefore could be suspended. The licensing of cabaret employees and the issuance of identification cards to them was required by law ... and

> could not be suspended. The employes [sic] will receive licenses and cards without fingerprinting.
>
> (Lissner 1966: 24)

Thus, the elimination of the fingerprinting requirement proved unexpectedly easy, as Chevigny explains:

> After trying to get the City Council to pass a bill to abolish fingerprinting, the administration realized that none was needed. The fingerprinting had begun as the result of an administrative decision in 1940, and could be ended the same way; Mayor Lindsay simply ordered it to be ended. That somehow broke the spell of fear of wicked comedians and musicians; the rest was simple.
>
> (Chevigny 1991: 67)

The *New York Times* lauded this move as a 'victory for performers' organizations and restaurant trade unions, which have been fighting the fingerprinting rule since it was adopted a generation ago' (Lissner 1966: 1). As 'one small but welcome victory for individual dignity against Big Brother supervision' (*NYT*, 30 August 1966), no longer would the fingerprinting requirement keep entertainers from working in NYC.[31]

On 7 September 1967, the Special Committee on Fingerprinting held a public hearing 'to consider elimination of the requirement that employes [sic] of public dance halls and cabarets carry identification cards' (Bennett 1967a: 16). An executive session of this committee followed the hearing to discuss the possibility of reporting the bill out for early action by the NYC Council (16). The committee voted unanimously to recommend its adoption by the council. The cabaret law was labelled by the License Commissioner as 'nothing more than a carryover from the Prohibition Era' and no longer relevant in 1967 (Callahan 1967: 31).

In a vote of 35 to 1, the City Council repealed the 36-year-old law requiring cabaret entertainers to carry identification cards on 12 September 1967 (Bennett 1967b: 31). According to Chevigny:

> When the bill to ratify the mayor's action by eliminating the licensing of club employees came up in the City Council, the License Commissioner scoffed at the notion ' ... that the safety of the public is served by a system which presupposes a need to be suspicious of everyone, from top-flight artists [to] go-go girls and bartenders, and require them to submit to the indignity of a police-like check.'
>
> (Chevigny 1991: 67)

Mayor Lindsay signed the amendment to the Administrative Code on 25 September 1967, ending the practice of requiring identification cards for cabaret entertainers and other employees (Perlmutter 1967: 53).

The 'police cards' may be gone, but the cabaret laws remain. Having lain dormant for years, they experienced a revival in the mid-1990s as part of Mayor Rudolph Giuliani's 'Quality of Life' campaign. In 2005, NYU Law professor Paul Chevigny[32] and former New York Civil Liberties Union Executive Director Norman Siegel filed a lawsuit, which:

> ... challenges the constitutionality of the New York City's cabaret law and provisions of the New York City Zoning Resolution which, taken together, regulate the circumstances under which participatory social dancing may be permitted in eating and drinking establishments, and the location of those establishments throughout New York City.[33]
>
> (*Festa v NYC* 2006: 455; see also Arden 2005: 1; Petersson 2005; Whitney 2005; O'Rourke 2006)

Judge Michael D. Stallman dismissed the case 'for lack of any viable constitutional claim' (*Festa v NYC* 2006: 467). On appeal, the New York Supreme Court, Appellate Division, upheld the decision, ruling 5 to 0 that the NYC cabaret laws 'were rationally related to permissible governmental objectives' (*Festa v NYC* 2007: par. 1).

The story of the NYC cabaret laws, and, specifically the 'police cards', tell of a generalized law, in opposition to the wild singularity of jazz and improvisation. Yet, this positioning was never incontrovertible or beyond challenge. The NYC 'police cards' instead united municipal law and bebop jazz in a very unstable and conflicted relationship, one that will be further explored throughout this book as it pertains to law and improvisation more generally. Legal reform, although slow in coming, was only possible through the introduction of singularity and unpredictability into law. In this sense, all attempts by law to rein in wildness and singularity contain the seeds of their own demise. To understand this inherent instability or irresolution as between singularity and generality, improvisation and law, the guidance of Jacques Derrida is key.

Chapter 3

Deconstructive legal improvisation[1]

Paris, July 1997. Famed jazz saxophonist Ornette Coleman[2] has just invited French philosopher Jacques Derrida to share the stage with him at the Paris La Villette Jazz Festival for an improvised jazz–text collaboration (Nettelbeck 2004: 198).[3] Coleman 'blows' while Derrida 'read[s]'[4] (Stein 2002). The audience members, 'intolerant of this unaccustomed form' (Nettelbeck 2004: 198), drive Derrida off the stage before he can 'get into his stride' (198; see also Wills 2006: 31).[5] His contribution to the event is 'pathetically foreshortened' (198) and Derrida is left shaken by the 'painful experience' (quoted in Stein 2002).[6] Reflecting on the event in *Counterpath* (with Catherine Malabou), Derrida writes:

> It was Paris, but no voyage will ever have taken me so far away, myself and my body and my words, onto an unknown stage, without any possible rehearsal or repetition. Music always travels 'further closer' than words. The brief 'rehearsal' that preceded the improvisation, Coleman's or my own, in no way resembled what took place before the audience. … [T]he event comes, as always, after the event.
>
> (Malabou and Derrida 2004: 97)

Of particular intrigue to this chapter (and book) is the willingness of Derrida to collaborate with Coleman in this manner – especially when his arguments against the possibility of 'spontaneity, improvisation and unmediated expression' (quoted in O'Reilly 1999) are often cited to critique jazz and jazz improvisation (O'Reilly 1999). Coleman, in contrast, attempts everything Derrida says is impossible in relation to improvisation: 'dispens[ing] with harmonic, formal and metric conventions' (Demsey 2000: 797) and resisting 'hierarchical distinctions between improvisation and inscription' (Nettelbeck 2004: 200). His 'harmolodic'[7] musical form taunts the laws governing musicality, 'encourag[ing] the improviser to be freer, and not obey a pre-conceived chord-pattern according to set ideas of "proper" harmony and tonality' (Williams 1961: 3).[8] Throughout his performances, 'harmony becomes melody becomes harmony' (Goldman (n.d.)) and the law that orders the division of the two concepts[9] is effectively ignored, transgressed. As Coleman is quoted as saying in the liner notes of his *Free Jazz* album: 'Let's try to play the music and not the background'[10] (quoted in Williams 1961: 3).

Driving this chapter is a deep scepticism, fuelled by Derrida, as to whether jazz improvisation can actually transgress or ignore the 'background' of which Coleman speaks.[11] Can it, borrowing from Haldar (2004), 'properly' (7) escape jazz's law, the law of jazz, which 'hums in the background' (1)? Or, far from 'bring[ing] down the law' (5), is improvisation 'nothing more than the law of the law' (5), 'nothing more than the repetition of man's vertical aspirations' (5)?[12]

Before addressing these questions, it is necessary to engage briefly with the question of whether Derrida's thoughts can in fact be applied to the musical genre of jazz improvisation. The philosopher himself is of little assistance here for, despite being an avid jazz fan (O'Reilly 1999; Stein 2002; Gallope 2011: 4),[13] nowhere in his discussions on invention does Derrida mention jazz or jazz improvisation (or any form of musical invention to be exact).[14] This omission, of course, does not negate the possibility of deconstructing music. In fact, Derrida himself reportedly endorsed the attempt, remarking to Rose Subotnik that he 'would be interested to see what resulted' (Subotnik 1996: 39) from her deconstruction of a Chopin prelude (39–147). Notwithstanding this endorsement, however, a brief exploration into whether one can apply a deconstructive framework to the topic of jazz improvisation needs to be undertaken.

For this inquiry, we return to Paris. The exact date is uncertain.[15] Pop star Green Gartside, lead singer and composer for the pop band Scritti Politti, has just been invited to meet with the philosopher after writing a song entitled 'Jacques Derrida' (1982), which Derrida's students played for him (O'Reilly 1999). Asked years later what he and Derrida spoke about at that meeting, Gartside answered:

> Oh, music! ... As I remember, he likes jazz, which was pretty neat 'cause I had it in me to ask him some things. Half-jokingly, I said, 'Well, isn't it true that jazz is valued for its spontaneity and improvisation, the idea that it represents the moment of self-present expression and meaning? But isn't that all somewhat suspect?'
>
> (Quoted in Chang (n.d.))

Derrida's reply to this query remains undocumented. However, Gartside plays an important role in this discussion for, despite being well-versed in deconstructive theory, he remains convinced that there is something unique to music, which positions it 'outside the limits of language and logocentrism' (quoted in Hoskyns 1981). Its 'meaning or its sense', in other words, is not 'determined by language' and cannot be found 'innately residing within four beats to the bar' (ibid.).

Gartside is nonetheless not blind to the metaphysical limits of music: 'no one musical phenomenon is ever going to transcend beat or repetition, nor is it ever going to transcend the history of criticism and the industry' (ibid.). Despite this admission, however, he does believe that '[i]t *is* possible, but again only in a metaphysical way, to think and talk about music as something that undoes' (quoted in Toop 1988, emphasis in original). Quoting Gartside:

> When I met Derrida he said that what I was doing was part of the same project of undoing and unsettling that he's engaged in. He's written that what sets the musician apart is the possibility of meaninglessness. That unsettling has always been my experience of pop, from the earliest moments – pop is the abuse of language.
>
> (Quoted in Reynolds 1988)

In his attempt to work through this statement by Gartside, Marcel Cobussen (2002f) writes: 'Of course (pop) music has meaning; it has political, economic, social, cultural and psychological meaning (and I am not only referring to its lyrics here). In this sense, we can approach music through language, through all kinds of discourses on music' (par. 5). That said, he admits that Gartside 'points to something, a non-localizable place, where music transgresses the power of language' (par. 5). Again, quoting Cobussen:

> We cannot understand music the same way we understand language. Music is a language, music is text, but it is not the same as a spoken or written language. Because something in music always escapes comprehension, understanding. Language fails to make music completely transparent. Music appeals to something that exceeds the semantic part of language; it appeals to non-discursive sonority.
>
> (Cobussen 2002f: par. 5)

Unfortunately, we are unable to look to Derrida for answers to this dilemma. As noted above, he never really engaged with the topic of music in his work. When asked by Gartside why he never wrote a book expressly on the subject, Derrida replied that to do so was 'the most difficult thing' (quoted in O'Reilly 1999). Instead, his 'loftiest aim' was to give his texts 'the condition of musicality' (quoted in O'Reilly 1999; see also Roberts 1991). In one interview, he is quoted as saying: 'music is the object of my strongest desire, and yet at the same time it remains completely forbidden. I don't have the competence. ... I am even more afraid of speaking nonsense in this area than in any other' (Brunette and Wills 1994: 21).

Derrida's silence on the subject has led some theorists to argue that he simply 'stays closely connected to the philosophers he criticizes' (Cobussen 2002c: par. 4) and that '[h]is deconstructive practices do not reach the sonorous domain, the domain of music' (par. 4). Cobussen (2002d) criticizes this characterization of Derrida and notes that he touches on the idea of sonority in his treatment of 'words', which he likens to 'non-discursive sonority' (par. 6). As Derrida himself asserts in an interview with Brunette and Wills:

> And if I love words it is also because of their ability to escape their proper form, whether they interest me as visible things, letters representing the spatial visibility of the word, or as something musical or audible. That is to say, I am also interested in words, paradoxically, to the extent that they are nondiscursive, for that's how they can be used to explode discourse.
>
> (Brunette and Wills 1994: 20)

His treatment of 'words' in this manner, argues Cobussen (2002d), 'opens a way to connect Derrida's thoughts to music'[16] (par. 6) and it is on this note that I begin my discussion of deconstructive legal improvisation.

Four *aporias* will frame this discussion of Derrida, law and improvisation. They include the aporia of singularity, the aporia of originality, the aporia of performative immediacy, and the aporia of the extempore. All four present or display a certain 'logic' or 'tension', which can be found equally in law and improvisation. An aporia, stated rather crudely, is a productive or creative paradox, or what Derrida (1999) terms 'the *non-way* [that] is the condition of walking' (73, emphasis in original). Elaborating further, he writes: 'if there was no aporia, we wouldn't walk, we wouldn't find our way; path-breaking implies aporia' (73). This will become clearer as the material unfolds below. For now, it is enough to say that these shared aporias point to essential similarities between law and improvisation and thus are central to this study.

The aporia of singularity

Never addressing the subject directly, Derrida instead chose to write *around* musical improvisation, commencing in the middle: 'every beginning has always already begun' (Cobussen 2008b: 10).[17] So too, here, I start *in medias res*, writing around the topic of legal improvisation, wondering whether it is ever possible or possible not to start anew (10; see also Snow 2004: 45). Roaming in the middle (Cobussen 2008b: 11) with improvisation (Manderson 2000: 31), Derrida's texts on law and justice[18] are read in tandem with his views on invention[19] in order to confront the extemporary in improvisation as purely free and singular in relation to a more generalised structure or law. While improvisation[20] and invention[21] are by no means identical, they do share certain qualities that become extremely relevant when explored through a deconstructive framework. As will be illuminated below, both concepts describe 'event[s] without precedent' (Derrida 1989: 43), 'unique situation[s]' (60), which are constituted in their 'singularity' (28). This singularity, albeit contested, can be starkly contrasted to the dominant conception of law, which privileges generality and universality over unpredictability and arbitrariness.

Perhaps unsurprisingly, deconstructive legal improvisation requires an initial attentiveness to Derrida's 'legal philosophy' (Goodrich et al. 2008).[22] Of particular relevance to this discussion is the consideration Derrida gives in his essay 'Force of Law: The "Mystical Foundation of Authority"' (2002b), and elsewhere (Derrida 1992a), to the 'difficult and unstable distinction between justice and law' (Derrida 2002b: 250). This distinction can be likened to the 'problematic relation between the singular and the general' (Attridge 1992a: 181; Beardsworth 1996: 25; Derrida 1992a: 187), or the 'antinomy between the general and the particular' (Belay 1996: 125). I am here calling this problematic or paradoxical relation the 'aporia of singularity'.

In a move that mirrors their dominant (albeit overly-simplified) conceptualisation, Derrida positions justice as singularity in opposition to a more generalised law. For Derrida, 'justice' – 'infinite, incalculable, rebellious to rule and foreign to symmetry, heterogeneous and heterotropic' (Derrida 2002b: 250) – 'always addresses itself to singularity, to the singularity of the other, despite or even because it pretends to universality' (248). Law, in contrast, is described as 'a *system* of regulated and coded prescriptions' (250, emphasis added). Constituted solely in terms of its 'generality' (245) and 'universality' (245), as that which always follows pre-existing and 'given' (253) rules. For Derrida, the issue then becomes how to reconcile the 'event' or 'act of justice' (245) with the rules, norms or imperatives that 'necessarily have a general form, even if this generality prescribes a singular application in each case' (245).

Upon setting up the dichotomy between law and justice, Derrida proceeds to dismantle it: 'Everything would still be simple if this distinction between justice and law were a true distinction' (250). He makes evident that not only does law claim to 'exercise itself in the name of justice' (251), but 'justice demands for itself that it be established in the name of a law' (251). Justice, in other words, exists solely as 'an experience of the *impossible*' (Derrida 2002b: 244, emphasis added). Derrida unpacks the impossibility of justice through three aporias. In the first aporia, 'The *Epokhē* of the Rule', he highlights the importance of singularity and improvisation for justice:

> To be just, the decision of the judge, for example, must not only follow a rule of law or a general law but must also assume it, approve it, confirm its value, by a reinstating act of interpretation, as if, at the limit, the law did not exist previously – as if the judge himself invented it in

> each case. Each exercise of justice as law can be just only if it is a 'fresh judgment'. ...
>
> (Derrida 2002b: 251)

Phrased slightly differently, as '[e]ach case is other, each decision is different and requires an absolutely unique interpretation, which no existing, coded rule can or ought to guarantee absolutely' (251), the judge improvises on rules and principles in every event of decision. This, however, as Derrida points out, is not improvisation outside 'all rules, all principles' (252). We shall return to this below.

The second aporia of justice, that of 'The Haunting of the Undecidable', presents justice as possible only *through* law, thereby emphasizing the importance of generality and law. Derrida writes: 'No justice is exercised, no justice is rendered, no justice becomes effective nor does it determine itself in the form of law, without a decision that cuts and divides' (Derrida 2002b: 252). The 'undecidable', like justice, is that which, 'though foreign and heterogeneous to the order of the calculable and the rule, must nonetheless ... deliver itself over to the impossible decision while taking account of law and rules' (252). Not only then is law necessary for justice (see First Aporia), so too is justice, as the 'undecideable' (253), necessary for law. As Derrida remarks, '[t]he undecideable remains caught, lodged, as a ghost at least, but an *essential* ghost, in every decision, in every event of decision' (Derrida 2002b: 253, emphasis added).

In the third aporia, 'The Urgency That Obstructs the Horizon of Knowledge', Derrida relates the problematic between singularity and generality (and thus law and improvisation) to *time*:

> ... a just decision is always required *immediately*, right away, as quickly as possible. It cannot provide itself with the infinite information and the unlimited knowledge of conditions, rules, or hypothetical imperatives that could justify it. And even if it did have all that at its disposal, even if it did give itself the time, all the time and all the necessary knowledge about the matter, well then, the moment of *decision as such*, what must be just, *must* always remain a finite moment of urgency and precipitation; it must not be the consequence or the effect of this theoretical or historical knowledge, of this reflection or this deliberation, since the decision always marks the interruption of the juridico-, ethico-, or politico-cognitive deliberation that precedes it, that *must* precede it. The instant of decision is a madness, says Kierkegaard. This is particularly true of the instant of the *just* decision that must rend time and defy dialectics.
>
> (Derrida 2002b: 255, emphasis in original)

All three aporias point to a certain relationship between singularity and generality, which is shared by law and improvisation. Focusing on law for the moment, legal theorist Peter Fitzpatrick (2005a) assists. Law, he writes, 'cannot be … enduringly ordered and predictable' (8). If it were, 'there could be no call for decision, for determination, for law' (9). Instead, for law to endure, it requires a simultaneous 'responsiveness' (9), an 'attunement and attentiveness to what is beyond' (9). Law, argues Fitzpatrick, must be able to 'change and adapt to such other things as "society" or "history"' (9; see also Fitzpatrick 2005c: 464). Moreover, this responsiveness to the other of law is '*essential* for law' (Fitzpatrick 2005a: 9, emphasis added). Once again quoting Fitzpatrick:

> Of course the rule of law is usually typified in terms of an enduring determinacy, in terms of providing some assured stability of expectation, some definite normative hold on futurity. But to hold a determinacy invariant is impossible since that would entail a totalized comprehension of all that may ever come to and affect it. Yet for law to rule, it has also to be quite contrary to those standard attributes. It must be utterly responsive and ever capable of being other that what it determinately may be. If it failed to do so, it would cease to rule situations inexorably changing around it.
>
> (Fitzpatrick 2011: 72)

A similar irresolution between singularity and generality exists in relation to invention and this is important for improvisation, as we shall see below. In 'Psyche: Inventions of the Other' (1989), Derrida critiques the 'traditional and dominant value of invention' (44), which must, 'by definition' (41), 'break with convention' (41); it must 'overflow, overlook, transgress, negate' (41) that from which it comes. So too must it transgress (41) or break with *law*. As Derrida writes, 'every invention should make fun of the statutory' (45); and every invention 'always presupposes some illegality, the breaking of an implicit contract' (25). 'True' invention, or what Derrida calls the 'invention of the other' (55), is impossible because there can be no invention 'without a prevailing statutory context' (45). Stated differently, invention exists solely on the condition that it transgresses the 'status' (41) with which it is supposed to comply. This status, like law, is constituted as 'stable, established, and legitimated by a social or symbolic order in an institutionalizable code, discourse, or text' (45).

Concentrating on the paradoxical relation between the singular and the general, or the aporia of singularity, the singular event of invention demands its simultaneous capture within a system of conventions that will ensure its position more generally in culture and society (Derrida 1989: 28). Thus, whilst the event of invention 'can take place only once' (51), invention more generally must be 'essentially repeatable, transmissible, and transposable' (51). 'To invent', writes Derrida, 'is to produce iterability' (51), that is, repetition of the originary inventive event. It is therefore a paradox or aporia that invention is founded solely on singularity and uniqueness and yet can only be recognized as inventive by compromising its singularity in 'repetition' (51) and 'generality' (51). Wholly dependent on generality for recognition and legitimation, invention remains forever lodged within the 'order of the calculable' (Derrida 1989: 55), the 'order of the same' (55), which is, for Derrida, the order of law (Derrida 2002b: 244). To be otherwise would make its recognition *as* invention impossible.

Invention thus needs to *be with* law to *be* inventive. Its originality can only be 'display[ed]' (Derrida 1989: 27), can only be brought into presence or made present, *through* law, through the 'values of form and composition' (27). Law is therefore necessary not only for invention to be 'recognized, identified, legitimized' *as* invention, but also for it 'even to occur, or, let us say, for it to *come about*' (44, emphasis in original). Equally, and as importantly, just as invention needs law, so too does law need invention to remain properly commanding in society. As revealed by Derrida's First Aporia which is mentioned above, but bears repeating:

> To be just, the decision of the judge, for example, must not only follow a rule of law or a general law but must also assume it, approve it, confirm its value, by a reinstituting act of interpretation, as if, at the limit, the law did not exist previously – as if the judge himself *invented* it in each case. Each exercise of justice as law can be just only if it is a '*fresh judgment.*'
>
> (Derrida 2002b: 251, emphasis added)

The necessary albeit impossible singularity of invention consequently becomes the 'undecideable' (Derrida 2002b: 253), which haunts the legal decision and ensures transformation and change are possible (257). In its concern for the other, invention effectively sustains the need for decision, the need for law.

In their deconstruction of 'absolute singularity' (Derrida 2001d: 90), Derrida's writings on law and invention become extremely relevant to this study of improvisation for it is the 'ideal of singularity' (Maras 1999), which most often activates notions of improvisation in society. A deconstructive reading of improvisation exposes the undecidable relation between singularity and generality and reads improvisation likewise as aporia. To help explain, the singularity of the improvised act must be an 'inaugural event' (Derrida 1989: 28), a 'first time ever' (quoted 28). Yet, this 'first time', in order to be a completely original and 'unique moment' (29), must also be a 'last time' (29; see also Derrida 2005e: 2). It must be singular, complete and containable. To be so purely present, however, would erase all relation with that which is outside and recognition as improvisation would be impossible. Thus, as with invention and justice noted above, the singularity of improvisation must be understood as 'iterability' (Derrida 1989: 51), in which, as Birmingham (1997) explains, the 'instituting act' only gains meaning through 'the repetition of an origin with which it cannot coincide, since it is of the very essence of the origin to be pure anteriority' (131). The 'singular, creative event' (131) is accordingly 'marked by the lack of self-presence' (131) and it is this iterability, this repetition and alteration, which makes the originality of improvisation possible in the first place (Birmingham 1997: 131).

Law and improvisation thus coalesce in the irresolution of the extemporary act. The aporetic relation between generality and singularity provides some commonality between the singularity that is privileged in improvisation and the generality deemed essential to law. Borrowing from Fitzpatrick (2001b) in another context, law cannot subsist without a responsive 'opening onto all that lies beyond' (59) just as improvisation requires 'some' determinacy in order to endure as a 'contained, distinct being' (59), to endure *as* improvisation. It is therefore 'the necessity yet impossibility' (Fitzpatrick 2005c: 464) of both pure determinacy in law and pure responsiveness in improvisation, which 'iteratively impel[s]' (464) both concepts 'into existence' (464). The originary repetition of improvisation becomes its law and without such improvisation could not exist.

Improvisation is therefore far from the extempore event it is often deemed to be. To appreciate the extemporary nature of improvisation, it must instead be captured within a 'system of *conventions*' (Derrida 1989: 28, emphasis in original), which will ensure its position more generally in culture and society (28). The improvised act, in other words, can only be analysed or understood through pre-existing or prevailing laws of language and music; it can never be completely beyond or outside the law of the musical text and exists only in relation to an original melody, theme or musical tradition. In the words of Charles Mingus, '[y]ou gotta improvise on *somethin*'' (quoted in Kernfeld 1995: 119, emphasis added). To do otherwise would make its recognition *as* improvisation impossible. Equally, if improvisation was completely determined by the prevailing musical laws or tradition, it would cease to be improvisation and would instead become 'predictable, calculable, and programmable' (Derrida 1995a: 387). If improvisation remained forever the same, there would be no need for improvisation. Improvisation thus must, at least in some limited sense, signal the possibility of an 'other side of nowhere'[23] (Fischlin and Heble 2004). Which is why the skill or talent of an improvising soloist is often judged not only by her ability to depart from the original melody, but also her safe return, to 'somehow [return] to *sense* when he seemed to have unleashed mere *chaos*' (Jones 2004: 64, emphasis added). This is the music of the aporia of singularity.

The aporia of originality

Law and improvisation, as delineated above, share the same aporetic 'logic' or tension as between singularity and generality, and this shared tension becomes all the more acute when applied to the paradox of *originality* or the *origin*. The link between improvisation and originality is often taken for granted. Improvisation is supposed to produce 'the singular and new' (Landgraf 2011: 27). Landgraf cautions, though, that this is actually a 'particularly *modern* understanding of improvisation' (6, emphasis added):

> As Western society's understanding of art changed fundamentally in the second half of the eighteenth century, the meaning and expectations for improvisation also changed. Central, of course, is the modern emphasis on inventiveness. Before the eighteenth century, inventiveness was not a major concern, neither for art in general, nor for improvisation in particular.
>
> (Landgraf 2011: 6)

The modern understanding of improvisation as original and inventive in turn rests on the 'particularly modern understanding' of invention, which Derrida (1989) reveals. With modernity came a 'new regime of invention' (54), he writes. Originally, two competing meanings co-existed. First, there was the notion of invention as *discovery*, of 'invention of what was already there and came into view as an existence or as meaning and truth' (49). This meaning was overtaken in the seventeenth century (49) by 'the productive invention of a technical apparatus that was not already there as such' (49), that is, as Landgraf (2011) explains, the understanding of invention as 'a mode of producing the singular and new' (27). The modern understanding conceives invention extemporaneously as that which offers 'a *place* upon *finding* it' (Derrida 1989: 49, emphasis in original). Prior to this reinvention of invention, 'its place was found there where it was already *located*' (49, emphasis in original).[24]

The paradox of originality in modernity belongs also to law. Modernity, notes Fitzpatrick (2005b), 'is supposed to have taken us away from the world of myth' (64), that is, from an existence that 'has a responsive regard for what is beyond it' (64), the unknown, singular. And yet,

> [m]ythology has not gone away. It remains operative in various entities too readily labeled 'secular.' Law is one of those: law is one way in which we give recognition and effect to something about us that is both mundane *and* mysterious. That something is our ability to take our present existence and orient it beyond itself.
>
> (Fitzpatrick 2005b: 64, emphasis in original)

Modern law thus subsists as paradox in that it cannot, yet cannot but, look beyond itself for the origins of its legitimacy and force. While Derrida was not the first to question whence law's power and authority comes, his approach to the issue, in contrast to others, is 'slightly to the side of manifest determination', as Peter Goodrich explains:

> He asked what comes *before* the law? What precedes the rush to determination? How do we understand law in terms of whence it came? In his essay on the force of law Derrida held up the institutional site of legal judgement to scrutiny. He argued that before law there has to be a moment of suspension, an instance of inattention to law, a hearing of the particular, person and event, prior to rule or determination.
>
> (Goodrich 2005: 23, emphasis added)

The question of law, for Derrida, is *always* one of origin: 'what comes prior to judgement and law'? (22). An origin, like modern conceptions of improvisation and invention above, must, by nature, be both a first and a last time, at one and the same time (Derrida 1989: 28). As Derrida explains in relation to invention, 'to be *unique* (even if the uniqueness has to be repeatable), it is also necessary for the first time, this unique moment of origin, to be a last time' (29, emphasis in the original). How, then, can we speak of an origin, of a completely unique moment, a moment that begins and ends simultaneously? For this question, we need to understand the role that *narration* plays in creating or sustaining a relation between the singularity of the origin and its more generalized recognition as unique and original. Blanchot, more than Derrida, assists in this regard and his description of the 'logic' of the 'tale' is invaluable to understanding Derrida's subsequent deconstruction of law's origin.

Typically, origins are advanced or referenced through stories or tales of their emergence. The 'tale', commonly conceived, is regarded as a 'true telling of an exceptional event which has taken place and which someone is trying to report' (Blanchot 1999: 447). For Blanchot, however, a tale is not the narration or the reporting of an exceptional event; it is instead 'that event itself, the approach to that event, the place where the event is made to happen – an event which is yet to come and through whose power of attraction the tale can hope to come into being, too' (447). Put more simply, it is the iterant re-telling of the tale that brings us into a relation with the singular event such that we can say something about it, such that we can 'report' on it.

This rendering of the event as both proximate and distant is what Blanchot calls the 'secret law of the tale' (447). For our purposes here, it is actually the secret tale of law. It is a 'movement towards a point' (447), which is 'unknown, obscure, foreign' (447). Devoid of this movement, the tale seems to have no real prior existence. The aporia of the secret law of the tale (of law) is that the tale must derive its power of attraction only from this point-which-is-unknown, so that 'it cannot even "begin" before reaching it' (447). Yet, 'only the tale and the unpredictable movement of the tale create the space where the point becomes real, powerful, and alluring' (447). This is the tale's pretension, as Blanchot explains:

> It only 'narrates' itself, and in the same moment that this narration comes into being it creates what it is narrating; it cannot exist as a narration unless it creates what is happening in that narration, because then it contains the point or the plane where the reality 'described' by the story can keep uniting with its reality as a tale, can secure this reality and be secured by it.
>
> (Blanchot 1999: 447)

The secret law of the tale is admittedly obscure. Blanchot likens such to 'the embarrassment the first man would have felt if, in order to be created, he himself had had to pronounce in a completely human way the divine *Fiat lux* ["Let there be light"] that would actually cause his eyes to open' (448). Peter Fitzpatrick (2001b) assists with this perplexity. If the origin is the 'true' origin, and not simply the 'tale' of the origin, it would have to be 'not the same' (43) and 'completely different to us' (43). The origin, as singular, complete and containable, would have to stand 'opposite the universal in its completeness' (63). If this were so, asserts Fitzpatrick, 'there would be no possibility of adequate relation to it in order for us to know it' (43). Phrased slightly differently, '[t]he antithesis of the universal can only be utterly antithetical. It has to be of a totally different kind of existence' (Fitzpatrick 2005b: 69).

Such is the paradox of the origin. It 'has to "be" before and after the point of origination' (Fitzpatrick 2003: 48) – but not *completely* before or after. This 'first time' is thus unknowable as 'a unique fact' (Birmingham 1997: 130) or 'totally present' (131); instead, the 'singularity of the instituting act' (130) can only be understood as 'originary repetition' (131) or as an iteration of 'an origin with which it cannot coincide, since it is of the very essence of the origin to be pure anteriority' (131). In Birmingham's words:

> If it were not, it would be fully and always present and no activity of repetition would be necessary. The present contains the alterity of an absolute origin. Indeed, Derrida's celebrated notion of 'differance' must be understood in terms of this anteriority at the very origin of the historical; that is, at the very heart of Being. Thus, the singular, creative event is marked by the lack of self-presence. Furthermore, this original repetition is the condition for re-production, re-citation, representation.
>
> (Birmingham 1997: 131)

Quoting Gasché (1986), 'original repetition gives the possibility of citation and must be inscribed in any entity, sign or act of speech in order for an entity or speech act to be possible in its singularity in the first place' (215, quoted in Birmingham 1997: 131).

The secret tale of law, the tale of law's founding, can now be described thus: 'Everything happens in relation to an originary given, to the law of the law: I exist' (Cixous 1991: 19). This naming *of* law *by* law is of particular intrigue to Derrida (1992a: 189) and goes to the very core of the 'jurisprudential problematic' which Davies (2001: 213), among other legal theorists (see, for example, Fitzpatrick 1992, 2001b, 2002, 2003), are concerned:

> Self-entitlement of the law is nothing more than a parental 'because I say so' translated into a constitutional mandate, and – as the guardian and apologist for legitimacy – mainstream legal philosophy has struggled to escape the arbitrariness by attempting to discover or describe an absolute source of legitimacy. This 'law of law' or 'source of authority' not only preoccupies legal philosophers, it is presumed to have real force for citizens and legal officials alike, and for those who do not accept a particular legal regime, it represents a refusal to negotiate, compromise, or reconcile on the part of those who uphold and administer the law.
>
> (Davies 2001: 213)

The preoccupation warrants some discussion. As Derrida makes evident, the 'law of the law' unfolds in the form of the following imperative: 'law must be without history, genesis, or any possible derivation' (Derrida 1992a: 191). It comes to us in the form of Kant's 'Categorical Imperative' in which pure morality, pure moral law, has 'no intrinsic history' (191). Notwithstanding this imperative, however, we continue to spend innumerable hours trying to trace law's history and resolve once and for all the question of its origin. Derrida explains:

> The question and the quest are ineluctable, rendering irresistible the journey toward the place and the origin of law. The law yields by withholding itself, without imparting its provenance and its site. This silence and discontinuity constitute the phenomenon of the law. To enter into relations with the law which says 'you must' and 'you must not' is to act as if it had no history or at any rate as if no longer depended on its historical presentation. At the same time, it is to let oneself be enticed, provoked, and hailed by the history of this non-history. It is to let oneself be tempted by the impossible: a theory of the origin of law, and therefore of its non-origin, for example, of moral law.
>
> (Derrida 1992a: 192)

And elsewhere, he writes:

> ... there would be no importation, no simply assignable origin for the history of law, only a reflecting apparatus, with projections of images,

> inversions of paths, interior duplications, and effects of history for a law whose structure and whose 'history' consist in taking away the origin.
>
> (Derrida 1987: 22)

The dilemma is made manifest through Derrida's comments and the preoccupation becomes understandable. If law is to be without history, or, at the very least, if its authority is seen to 'exclude all historicity' (Derrida 1992a: 190), then any origin posited regarding law is in fact a 'fiction',[25] a story recounted by the only one with the authority to tell it: 'law: I exist' (Cixous 1991: 19). The story of law's founding is thus not actually 'original', but is instead a 'tale' that must be repeatedly evoked and brought to bear on new situations in order to reinforce law's power and authority.

One specific 'tale' of origin, which has invoked comment by Derrida (1992a), is that in Sigmund Freud's *Totem and Taboo* (1918) of the primal parricide, which led to the emergence of modern law and society. Briefly stated, for Freud (1918), 'civilization' allegedly began when the sons, or the 'primal horde' (182), killed and ate the 'violent, jealous father' (182–83) in order to put an end to his reign and to his exclusive access over the women of the community (182). The sons, all equal in strength (186), made a pact ('social contract') that no one would be deemed superior and that the '*brother clan*' (188, emphasis in original) would instead all be governed by certain rules or prohibitions so as to ensure that the primal violence, which led to the murder of the father, never occurred again (186, 188). Freud's tale of origin thus has both law and society emerging out of, and in opposition to, wildness, violence and savagery.

In Derrida's deconstruction of Freud's tale (1992a), he focuses on the 'remorse' (Freud, quoted 198) supposedly felt by the sons over killing their father, which led to the decision that 'it should never be repeated' (quoted 198). Law and morality consequently emerged out of the murderous event and the sons' 'remorse for the deed' (quoted 198). Derrida questions in his essay 'Before the Law', though, how and why the sons can experience remorse 'if this is *before* morality, *before* law?' (198, emphasis in original). Beardsworth elaborates on Derrida's meaning:

> For the brothers to feel guilty for the murder of their father, the moral law would *already* have to be in place prior to the crime. To have felt remorse the brothers must have already transgressed a prior law, not produced it; otherwise their remorse is incomprehensible.
>
> (Beardsworth 1996: 31, emphasis in original)

Thus, Freud's attempt to make guilt comprehensible ends up simply 'repeat[ing] the incomprehensibility of law' (31). The tale of law's origin, as that which escaped the wildness and savagery of the state of nature, thus becomes an 'impossible' (31) tale.

The 'philosophical project of discovering the source, nature, or law of law', notes Davies (2001), 'has been plagued by some unresolvable contradictions and paradoxes' (213). Derrida does not try and resolve these 'theoretical difficulties', nor does he completely reject traditional legal theory 'for failing to develop a conceptually unified or coherent picture of law' (213). Instead, again relying on Davies:

> Derrida's work in relation to law allows us to see the contradictions and paradoxes of legal thought not as conceptual failures (except, perhaps, as a failure in self-reflectiveness), but rather as systemic philosophical matters which go to the heart of any question of meaning (and thus normality, authority, and understanding). In other words, the gaps and contradictions of legal philosophy and legal systems are also the gaps and contradictions of philosophical systems generally.
>
> (Davies 2001: 213–14)

The aporia of performative immediacy

The paradox of originality, which unites law and improvisation, is most clearly visible when explored through the originary event or the performance of *becoming* law or improvisation. As mentioned previously, the dominant conceptions of law and improvisation position them as planned and prescribed (law) in relation to an immediate, extempore event (improvisation). Chapter 5 troubles the extemporary conceptualization of improvisation through the application of CSI theory. Here, though, focusing on the insights of Derrida, the concept of performance or performativity in relation to both law and improvisation is shown to be irresolute and aporetic.

For this discussion, two pre-'Force of Law' texts written by Derrida on legal themes, namely 'The Laws of Reflection: Nelson Mandela, In Admiration' (1987) and 'Declarations of Independence' (1986), are of particular value. Writing about the creation of the Charter of Freedom in South Africa and the Declaration of Independence in the United States of America, Derrida interrogates the originary paradox that lies at the heart of law in which the 'founding act of the law', 'necessarily alegal in itself', only becomes legal 'after the fact' (Derrida 1987: 21). To explain, the inauguration of any fundamental law, such as a first constitution or a charter of rights and freedoms, 'cannot, either in law or in fact, simply precede that which at once initiates it and nevertheless supposes it: projecting and reflecting it!' (20). The law, in other words, which is signed into existence by the signature attached to the constitutional document, must retrospectively authorize the original signature or the originary act of signing. Remarks Derrida, 'a signature authorizes itself to sign, in a word, legalizes itself on its own without the guarantee of a pre-existing law' (20).

Looking specifically at the American Declaration of Independence, it is generally assumed – although not without contest (Tyler 2012: 956) – that the signing[26] of the 1776 Declaration formally renounced the English legal system and created a new nation and laws, that of the United States of America (956; Cross 2012: 1238; House 2008: 755). The question Derrida asks in his analysis of this document is whether independence is *stated* or *produced* by this declarative act of freedom from British rule. In other words, are the 'good people' of America already free and simply stating the fact of this freedom in the Declaration, or does the signing of the Declaration produce their liberty? Derrida elaborates:

> It is not a question here of an obscurity or of a difficulty of interpretation, of a problematic on the way to its (re)solution. It is not a question of a difficult analysis which would fail in the face of the structure of the acts involved or the overdetermined temporality of the events. This obscurity, this undecideability between, let's say, a performative structure and a constative structure, is *required* in order to produce the sought-after effect. It is essential to the very positing or position of a right as such, whether one is speaking here of hypocrisy, of equivocation, of undecideability, or of fiction. I would even go so far as to say that every signature finds itself thus affected.
>
> (Derrida 1986: 9–10, emphasis in original)

The 'good people' of the United States of America do not exist prior to the signing of the Declaration, at least not '*as such*' (10, emphasis in original). Instead, they are born in the act of signature. 'The signature invents the signer' (10), says Derrida. This is what is meant by the phrase, 'a sort of fabulous retroactivity': 'There was no signer, by right, before the text of the Declaration which itself remains the producer and guarantor of its own signature' (10). So, too, the dissolution with Britain, with 'the links of colonial paternity or maternity' (11), 'involves both constation and performance, indissociably mixed. The signature of every American citizen today depends, in fact and by right, on this indispensible confusion' (11). In the end, the question remains: 'How is a State made or founded, how does a State make or found itself? And an independence? And the autonomy of one which both gives itself, and signs, its own law? Who signs all these authorizations to sign?' (13).

What Derrida's texts make evident is that the signature, as the origin or inventor of law, encounters similar paradoxes and contradictions to those outlined above. As with Blanchot's 'tale', '[t]he signature maintains a link with the instituting act, as an act of language and of writing, a link which has absolutely nothing of the empirical accident about it' (Derrida 1986: 8). Conceived another way, the 'signature' is governed by the 'structure of the mark' (Derrida 1982a: 316), by 'iterability' (*iter* comes from *itera*, *other* in

Sanskrit) (315; Derrida 2005d: 136), which 'links repetition to alterity' (Derrida 1982a: 315) and ensures structural legibility 'beyond the death of the addressee' (315). Derrida elaborates:

> ... there is no code – an organon of iterability – that is structurally secret. The possibility of repeating, and therefore of identifying, marks is implied in every code, making of it a communicable, transmittable, decipherable grid that is iterable for a third party, and thus for any possible user in general. All writing [and by 'writing' Derrida means 'the disruption of presence in the mark' (327)], therefore, in order to be what it is, must be able to function in the radical absence of every empirically determined addressee in general. And this absence is not a continuous modification of presence; it is a break in presence, 'death,' or the possibility of the 'death' of the addressee, inscribed in the structure of the mark.
>
> (Derrida 1982a: 315–16)

The 'absolute singularity of the event of the signature' (Derrida 1982a: 328) must thus 'have a repeatable, iterable, imitable form; it must be able to detach itself from the present and singular intention of its production' (328). Bennington (1993) further elaborates on Derrida's meaning. The signature can only exist *as* signature on the condition that 'it be repeatable as the same signature, in several copies' (155). The signature is thus always '*already* contaminated' (162, emphasis in original) by alterity; it is 'already in some sense the other's signature' (162). Bennington explains:

> This is why a text is never closed upon itself, in spite of the effort of the signatory who wants to appropriate it. This desire is also paradoxical: for to make one's text absolutely proper to oneself, absolutely idiomatic, would be to bar all reading of it, even by oneself, and so the totally signed text, proper to its signatory, appropriated by him, would no longer be a text.
>
> (Bennington 1993: 163)

At the origin (signature, signing) is a suspension of authority. It is as if the law improvised itself into existence in the act of performance. In 'Declarations of Independence' (1986), Derrida interrogates the undecidability between the constative and the performative, between a speech act that typically describes what exists and one that actually performs an action (de Ville 2008: 102). Says Derrida:

> ... there's an utterance that is called constative, a theoretical speech that consists in saying what it is, describing or noting what is, and there's an utterance that is called *performative* and that does in speaking. For

> instance, when I make a promise, I'm not saying an event; I'm pronouncing it by my commitment.
>
> (Derrida 2007: 446, emphasis in original)

By establishing that the American Declaration of Independence, typically viewed as a constative speech act, actually performs or 'does what it says it does' (Derrida 1986: 8), Derrida, once again, unveils the performance of 'pure event' as an impossibility, as de Ville explains in relation to Derrida's concept of iterability:

> Because of its inscription within iterability a performative speech act can never be a pure event, in other words absolutely singular, a present and singular intervention, or 'something' that happens for the first and last time – it is always split, dissociated from itself. Iterability necessarily limits what it makes possible, rendering its rigor and purity impossible.
>
> (de Ville 2008: 103)

The undecidability between the performative and the constative in law belongs also to improvisation. In his performance of 'Play – The First Name' (2004a), the text Derrida reads on stage with Ornette Coleman on that (in)famous night in Paris, 1997, the difficulty in determining what constitutes the performance of improvisation becomes remarkably decidable in its undecidability. Landgraf's analysis of both the text and the event are of value here:

> Acknowledging the unpredictability of the future (and how the future will come to define the present), the delivery of the speech plays with its own fallibility, its openness toward the advent of something unexpected, unplanned, unforeseen. Reflecting on the status of his performance (really on the performative aspect of any delivery of text), Derrida unsettles the distinction between a planned, textually prescribed act and improvised doings. The apparent reading of a text, a seemingly fixed, pre-composed, pre-articulated artefact, remains in a strict sense an improvisational exercise. The reader can never fully control what is happening, nor foresee what will happen.
>
> (Landgraf 2011: 20–21)

Derrida's text at once announces and invokes its own unpredictability (and the 'unpredictability of the future' (20)):

> Qu'est-ce qui arrive? What's happening? What's going to happen, Ornette, now, right now?
>
> What's happening to me, here, now, with Ornette Coleman? With you? Who?

> It is indeed necessary to improvise, it is necessary to improvise *well*. ... I knew that Ornette was going to call on me to join him tonight, he told me so when we met to talk one afternoon last week. This chance frightens me, I have no idea what is going to happen.
>
> (Derrida 2004a: 331–32, emphasis in the original)

As dialogic and self-referential (not accidentally so, as these are important features of jazz improvisation[27]), the text, again relying on Landgraf (2011), 'playfully marks its openness' (21) by making obvious its 'own process of composition, blurring the line between composition and presentation' (21), and mischievously questioning its 'pragmatic status' (21). 'Play' is read, performed as a 'written score', but is also authorized to be published (21).[28] It is as if, Landgraf provocatively adds, Derrida 'wants to be caught in a lie' (21).

The admissions of the text completely contradict what is most apparent to the audience or reader (21–22). Derrida speaks the following: 'As all of you see, I have here a sort of written score, you think that I am not improvising, well, you are wrong. I am pretending not to improvise, I just pretend, I play at reading, but by improvising' (Derrida 2004a: 331). Paradox ensues: 'If he is lying, he is saying the truth (he is indeed reading); if, however, he is saying the truth, then what we perceive, namely Derrida reading a text, would indeed be a lie' (Landgraf 2011: 22). The unpredictability of the text's meaning is no accident. It is instead 'a structural mark of communication, a precondition for the possibility of communication in the first place' (22). In the words of Landgraf, '[c]ommunication works *because* the meaning of signs, words, text, and language can never be fully controlled or anticipated' (22, emphasis in original).

In 'Play – The First Name', writes Wills (2006), further elaborating on the text, Derrida plays with the singularity of the proper name, a name that must be performed 'as a signatory repetition' (39) in order to be understood properly. In so doing, Derrida highlights the 'structural' similarities between iterability and improvisation, performance and writing, language and music. As Wills remarks, 'Derrida is inviting Coleman to pretend to speak just as Derrida has been pretending to improvise between language and music, to create a new language or a new music or both' (43). The fact that much of Derrida's text was not actually performed on stage at La Villette, as he was compelled to leave before he could finish, confirms that '[p]erformance alone does not constitute an event' (42):

> Yet as we read what we didn't hear, and as we read it beyond the jeers and insults, something remains of Derrida's 'performance.' That something is this: the Derrida who would not permit himself to write on jazz ... nevertheless raises a set of profound questions that go to the heart of the project of jazz, namely its sense of the event of improvisation as invention.
>
> (Wills 2006: 42)

The aporia of the extempore

The extempore as pure singularity is supposed to make 'what is not yet here come to be' (Derrida 2007: 450) and invent the wholly new. Yet, as Derrida points out, '[i]f I can invent what I invent, if I have the ability to invent what I invent, that means that invention follows a potentiality, an ability that is in me, and thus brings nothing new' (450). It lacks singularity, in other words, 'simply because it comes after and it loses the singularity in generality' (446). The purely extemporaneous event of improvisation is therefore impossible, '[i]t merely develops and unfolds a possibility, a potentiality that is already present and therefore it is not an event' (450).

The singular (extempore) in both improvisation and law is better understood as 'a mode of affirmation, indeed as a mode of double affirmation' (Grosz 2003: 239), a '*yes, yes*' (Derrida 1992c: 257, emphasis in original) or '*oui, oui*' (257). This double affirmation both affirms the self-same, the 'I am here' (Attridge 1992c: 254), while simultaneously reaching out and engaging with the other, with alterity. The extempore as 'absolute singularity' (Edkins 2005: 380), may be the impossible itself, but in its 'apprehension of *otherness*' (Attridge 2004: 67, emphasis in original), it glances towards the unknown, helping prepare us for the impossible coming of the invention (or the improvisation) of the other.

The other is always singular for Derrida, as J. Hillis Miller (2007) explains. With Lévinas, Derrida 'assume[s] the singularity and absolute alterity of the other' (258). However, against Lévinas, Derrida maintains that the other remains 'always wholly other' (258). Thus, it is only by affirming the same that we can even speak to or about the other. The other as 'the monstrous *arrivant*', the monstrous to-come, whose arrival we can only prepare ourselves to welcome (Derrida 1995a: 387). To say 'monstrous' is deliberate for this coming arrival or arrival 'to come' always carries with it both promise and trauma.[29] Derrida explains:

> The absolute *arrivant* must not be merely an invited guest, someone I'm prepared to welcome, whom I have the ability to welcome. It must be someone whose unexpected, unforeseeable arrival, whose *visitation* – and here I'm opposing visitation to invitation – is such an irruption that I'm not prepared to receive the person. … .The absolute guest [*hôte*] is this *arrivant* for whom there is not even a horizon of expectation, who bursts onto my horizon of expectation when I am not even prepared to receive the one who I'll be receiving. That's hospitality.
>
> (Derrida 2007: 451, emphasis in original)

Hospitality thus becomes a '[w]elcoming beyond my capacity to welcome' (451). It means 'receiving precisely when I cannot receive, when the coming of the other overwhelms me, seems bigger than my house, and I can't know beforehand if he or she will behave well in my home, in my city, in my state, in my nation' (451).

Like the *arrivant*, the extempore 'can only seem to me to be impossible before it occurs [*arriver*]' (452). This does not mean that it does not or can not occur, but instead that there is no way to talk about such in 'theoretical terms' (452) or to 'pre-dict it either' (452). While this impossibility may lead us to conclude that bewilderment and negativity is inevitable when faced with the extemporary, according to Derrida, our disarmament is 'never pure or absolute' (452). The extemporary event 'presuppose[s] some sort of inevitable neutralization ... by its iterability' (452), presupposes repetition. This is the 'logic' of the dual affirmative, as Bennington (1993) explains: letting the first 'yes' 'be in its singularity' (188) 'implies that in some sense one says "yes" to the law of the thing' (188), to generality. The originary 'yes' opens itself to 'the repetition whose trace is already inscribed in its "first" time, thus inaugurating time in finitude' (202). Conversely, repetition needs this 'first' time in order to take place (202). Thus, repetition of the 'yes' not only 'opens memory, in mourning for this impossible "first" time' (202–3), it also 'fictionalizes [the "yes"] in the possibility of its repetition' (203). This dual affirmation recognises a '*certain* inevitable complicity' (203, emphasis in original), which 'immediately places' (203) us 'within an *economy of violence*' (Derrida 2001c: 400, n. 21, emphasis in original) whereby our only ethical, resistant or democratic choice is that of 'the lesser violence' (400, n. 21).[30]

In summary, Derrida exposes law and improvisation as sharing the same 'structural tension' (Landgraf 2011: 25), the same aporias, which challenge, yet are also subject to, the law of iterability, as that which 'ties repetition to alterity and, vice versa, ties alterity, singularity, and uniqueness to the general, to rules, laws, and repetition' (25). The chapters to follow probe further the consequences of uniting law and improvisation in this manner. What does it mean to say that law is fundamentally improvisational? What does improvisation bring to law? And, perhaps most importantly, what does it mean to improvise *well*, to achieve *just* unpredictability in law? This last question is a lesson only CSI scholars can teach. Echoing Derrida's sentiments on stage with Ornette Coleman at the 1997 La Villette Jazz Festival: 'It is indeed necessary to improvise, it is necessary to improvise but *well*, this is already a *music lesson*, your lesson, Ornette, that unsettles our old idea of improvisation. ... ' (Derrida 2004a: 332, emphasis in original).

Chapter 4

The 'wildness' of jazz improvisation

> It was the music. ... It made you do unwise disorderly things. Just hearing it was like violating the law.
>
> (Morrison 1992: 58)

'Wild' origins

To the white socialites who lived downtown, Harlem, the hub of jazz in NYC, embodied 'primitive and thrilling qualities' (Haskins 1977: 20), representing 'a blend of danger and excitement'[1] (20). Deemed 'wild and immoral' (Chevigny, quoted in Weinberg 1999), many saw jazz as a 'reversion to savagery' (Leonard 1962: inside flap). Contributing to this perception was its racialized conceptualisation and supposed lineage to African tribal music and ritual[2] (Finkelstein 1948: 12, 13; Hadler 1995: 252; Leonard 1962: 39). The so-called 'exotic jungle rhythms' further provided 'intimations of sensuality beyond the wildest fantasies of the sons and daughters of proper New York society'[3] (20). Writes Haskins (1977): 'Harlem was an adventure; Harlem was the unknown; and Harlem became a fad' (21). Citing Langston Hughes, he further elaborates:

> The Negro was in vogue, and in Harlem the speakeasy took on a new dimension. White downtowners invaded Harlem to observe the blacks at play, 'flooding the little cabarets and bars where formerly only colored people laughed and sang, and where now the strangers were given the best ringside tables to sit and stare at the Negro customers – like amusing animals in a zoo'.
>
> (Quoted in Haskins 1977: 21)

Dubbed the 'Montmartre of America' (Erenberg 1981: 256), Harlem became the place to visit '[i]f one were looking "to go on moral vacation," or wished to soften the "asperities of a Puritan conscience"' (Osofsky 1963: 185).

Jazz was conceptually linked to wild sexuality and the 'primitive rhythms which excite the basic human instincts' (Sousa, quoted in Leonard 1962: 33);

it was branded a music of 'man's "lower nature," the carnal'[4] (33). Freud was at least partly to blame for this, claims Ogren (1989: 146). In keeping with the 'Freudian underpinnings of the cult of primitivism' (156), many 1920s artists and intellectuals 'invested primitive cultures with "uncivilized" virtues – particularly sexual freedom' (146). Harlem jazz, in its supposed reproduction of the 'marvellous syncopation of the African jungle' (quoted 146), led 'curious whites' (Ostransky 1978: 218) uptown to 'safely watch the primitives perform their rites in their native habitat' (218), hoping that 'by merely looking on they could revitalize their own sexually pale lives' (218).

The 'White celebration of "primitivism"' (Ogren 1989: 146) was reflected in the decor of many Harlem clubs, especially those that catered specifically to white downtowners, or 'slummers' (Haskins 1977: 57), as they were called. The Cotton Club,[5] for example, had a 'jungle décor' (33), complete with 'numerous artificial palm trees' (33). Its floor shows, recalls singer Lena Horne:

> ... had a primitive, naked quality that was supposed to make a civilized audience lose its inhibitions. The music had an intensive, pervasive rhythm – sometimes loud and brassy, often weird and wild. The dances were eloquently provocative; and if they were occasionally stately, that stateliness served only to heighten their abandon.
>
> (Quoted in Anderson 1981: 175; also quoted in Chevigny 1991: 40)

For the white audience,[6] the music had the desired effect of 'conjuring up tribal warriors and man-eating tigers and war dances' (Haskins 1977: 50). Haskins explains: 'Watching and listening to the spectacle, the Cotton Club patrons could have no doubt that they were witnessing firsthand the emergence of the primal African from beneath the sequined costumes and tan skins of the performers' (50, 53). Befitting this image, the house band, originally known as the Washingtonians, soon became 'Duke Ellington's Jungle Band' and many of Ellington's compositions during this time reflected the jungle motif: 'Jungle Jamboree,' 'Jungle Blues,' 'Jungle Nights in Harlem' and 'Echoes of the Jungle' (53).

The expectation of the audience at the Cotton Club in relation to Ellington's 'jungle music' was to encounter 'sounds they could not predict, sounds that would seem to them strange, exotic, primitive, guttural' (Ostransky 1978: 216). According to Ostransky, this gave Ellington 'the licence to try unusual chords, timbres, sonorities (unusual, that is, in the jazz of the time)' (216–17). However, listeners (both white and black) unfamiliar 'with the rhythms or the exchange of ideas in an improvised art, experienced this as "abandonment"' (Chevigny 1991: 41–42).[7] And, as Chevigny points out:

> It turned out to be a historic misfortune that the forces of respectability identified the music with sexual abandon in a crude sense and that the purveyors capitalized on it; they played into the hands of early critics who condemned jazz as cacophonous on the one hand and insidiously immoral on the other.
>
> (Chevigny 1991: 42)

Thus, whether or not Ellington took his 'jungle music' seriously or considered it to be a 'private joke' (Ostransky 1978: 216), played with 'considerable tongue-in-cheek, a high degree of put-on' (216), this music worked to reproduce and reinforce the image of jazz as wild and savage and would go on to 'influence the work of jazzmen everywhere' (217).

By the late 1930s, Harlem nightclubs were visibly in decline. Following the race riots on 19 March 1935, which were sparked by a rumour that a black teenager was being beaten, New Yorkers no longer viewed Harlem as the 'center of exotic nightlife' (DeVeaux 1997: 229), but saw it instead as 'a dangerous slum' (229). Large clubs, such as the Cotton Club, either closed or relocated downtown in and around 52nd Street (dubbed 'Swing Street'). This movement downtown prompted some black musicians to 'wonder whether the widely publicized dangers of wandering through Harlem at night were simply a ruse to frighten white customers away from Harlem after-hours clubs to a more convenient midtown location' (229). Whatever the reason for the change in location, by the mid-1940s 'the center of gravity had gradually shifted away from Harlem to 52nd Street' (229). During that time, some Harlem clubs 'remained in operation to provide the adventurous with late-night entertainment and musicians with sporadic employment' (229). It was in these after-hours clubs that a new, even 'wilder',[8] brand of jazz was being developed: a music, later labelled bop or bebop,[9] which would cause much furore in US society.

Bebop's sonic and social wildness

After an evening of playing in a large orchestral swing band, musicians would gather at jam sessions in Harlem venues such as Minton's and Monroe's (Gioia 1997: 213) to 'learn new techniques or to hear a new melodic sequence (or "lick")' (Belgrad 1998: 180). Daniel Belgrad (1998) argues that the most important function of the bebop jam session was to give musicians the opportunity to practice solo improvisation, a musical technique that had little place in the performances of large swing bands (180). Characterised by an extremely fast tempo, dissonant notes, 'polyrhythmic complexity' and 'irregular phrasings' (187), bebop emerged as 'an aggressive, esoteric music, difficult to understand or to play, and deliberately so' (Chevigny 1991: 45; Hebdige 1999 [1979]: 47).[10] Considered 'revolutionary' (45; see also Ellison 1953: 201; Green 1966: 39; Ross 1972: 257; Szwed 2002: 34), bebop became defined ideologically as 'a music of revolt, revolt against big bands, arrangers, vertical harmonies, soggy rhythms, non-playing orchestra leaders and Tin Pan Alley; against commercialised music in general' (Allsop 1961–62: 33). Bebop 'burst through the formal confines of swing', to borrow from Ross (2008), 'and made music of ricocheting freedom and imperturbable cool' (476). A 'rejection of the Western cultural norms encoded in the symphony orchestra' (Belgrad 1998: 185) and 'a reaction against big-band swing' (185), bebop, argues Belgrad, 'embodied spontaneity's challenge to America's wartime corporate-liberal culture'[11] (185).

Kofsky, among others (for example, Gioia 1997: 202–3 and Muyumba 2009: 26), have noted that 'the invention of bebop in the 1930s was by no means beyond the scope of existing musical knowledge in jazz, inasmuch as the procedure for improvising a solo on a set of chords' (Kofsky 1998a: 106). He cites Martin Williams's *The Jazz Tradition* (1970) as evidence for this claim:

> … one can find choruses of non-thematic improvisation in the recordings of players who were leaders in the 'twenties and earlier. …
>
> The practices are, basically, as old as the blues. … One might say that jazz musicians spent the late 'twenties and the 'thirties discovering that they could 'play the blues' on chords of [the numerous popular songs of the period].
>
> (Quoted in Kofsky 1998a: 106)

Baraka[12] makes a similar point, citing an interview with Williams in Nat Hentoff's *The Jazz Life* (1961: 195):

> The boppers were tired of the same old chords and explored new ones. But essentially, most of them were still playing a riff style;[13] it is just their kind of riffs were built on a new approach to harmony – but not really so new as one thought. Again the best of them leaned on the melodic background of the blues for a melodic form and unity of mood.
>
> (Quoted in Baraka 1963: 226)[14]

Kofsky (1998a) goes so far to say that Charlie 'Bird' Parker, one of the key bebop innovators, 'did not so much invent his music from scratch as he did recast material that was already present in jazz' (106).[15] He concludes that '[c]onsidered strictly as a *musical problem*, it does indeed seem as if bebop could have been perfected several years before its actual arrival in the 1940s' (107, emphasis in original).

Insofar as 'all the strictly musical techniques and devices that formed the foundation of bebop were already well known prior to the musical revolution of the 1940s' (110), Kofsky confidently claims that the delay in the advent of bebop was 'less a matter of musical development than of extra-musical considerations' (107).[16] This statement led to a very heated exchange between Kofsky and (white) jazz critics, such as Ira Gitler and Leonard Feather, regarding the relation between 'the sounds produced' by bebop musicians and 'the brutal {social} conditions that persisted through the bebop years'[17] (Leonard, quoted in Kofsky 1998b: 82). I have no desire to engage with this, quite dated,[18] debate here. That said, I must agree with Kofsky that 'there were social as well as purely musical forces underlying the attempt of bebop artists to overturn the reigning swing style' (80; see also DeVeaux 1997). Quoting George Lewis:

> For African-American improvisers … sonic symbolism is often constructed with a view toward social instrumentality as well as form. New improvisative and compositional styles are often identified with ideals of race advancement and, more important, as resistive ripostes to perceived opposition to black social expression and economic advancement by the dominant white American culture.
>
> Ebullient, incisive, and transgressive, the so-called bebop movement brought this theme of resistance to international attention. Influencing musicality worldwide, the movement posed both implicit and explicit challenges to Western notions of structure, form, and expression.
>
> (Lewis 2004b: 134)

As Belgrad (1998) points out, one of the best methodological ways to identify the content of any music is to compare it with that from which 'it immediately derives' (185). In the case of bebop, that would be big band swing music. How better to formally contrast bebop and swing than through 'the specific differences distinguishing two versions of the same tune' (185), as Belgrad explains:

> In 1939, Charlie Barnet's big band recorded a popular rendition of the standard 'Cherokee'. 'Cherokee' is built on a basic 64-bar structure of four 16-bar phrases in a AABA sequence (the first phrase is played three times, twice before the 'bridge' and once after). Late in 1945, Charlie Parker's Repoppers recorded a bebop version of 'Cherokee' that they renamed 'KoKo'. 'Koko' was created from 'Cherokee' in two phases: first, modern chord changes were substituted for the conventional harmonies of the standard; then a completely new melody was improvised to accompany the new changes. Therefore it is possible to hum the melody of 'Cherokee' – at a faster tempo – over the harmonic changes of 'KoKo', though the original melody is nowhere in evidence.
>
> (Belgrad 1998: 185, footnotes omitted)

'KoKo' was, according to Gary Giddens, 'the seminal point of departure for jazz in the postwar era' (quoted in DeVeaux 1997: 365) and its

26 November 1945 recording 'still stands as a milestone in jazz history' (Gitler 2001: 27).

Epitomizing the bebop sound, the November 1945 recording of 'KoKo' contains a 'lengthy, jittery, mysterious introduction and ending' (Kernfeld 1995: 53). Max Roach (drums) provides the only accompaniment during the 32-bar introduction; the bassist (Curly Russell) and pianist ('Dizzy' Gillespie) are both silent. Parker (alto saxophone) and Gillespie (trumpet/piano) play in octaves at a tempo of 300 beats per minute. Gillespie improvises, then Parker; and finally they come together in parallel thirds and then in octaves again. Roach ends the piece with a drum solo (taken at an even faster tempo), followed by a reprise of the introduction (minus the last three bars). Russell 'jumps in on the last beat' (53), ending with the 'trademark *be-bop* figure: a pair of eighth notes landing on a dissonant flatted fifth' (DeVeaux 1997: 426, emphasis in original).

To anyone who has listened to this recording of 'Ko-Ko', it is obvious that '[t]he fast tempo and high energy level of bebop restricted it to a skilled coterie of musicians' (Belgrad 1998: 187). Indeed, even the immensely talented Miles Davis is said to have had difficulties tackling the speed and intensity of bebop when he first began playing it and was unable to perform on the recording of 'KoKo' despite being Parker's sideman at the time.[19] This musical genre encouraged musicians to 'take creative risks' (187) and, in stark contrast to both European concert music[20] and swing-era big bands, '[i]n bebop, the spontaneous articulation of new musical ideas was valued above precision or accuracy' (187).

Bebop differed from the music that came before it in terms of its sonic 'unpredictability', as DeVeaux elucidates:

> Within its brief confines, bop musicians concentrated all that was most novel and disorienting in their new musical language. By placing it *first* – before the listener could situate the improvisation within some recognizable context – the beboppers made it impossible to hear their music as a version, a 'jazzing,' of some other repertory.
>
> (DeVeaux 1997: 425, emphasis in original)

John Szwed, Miles Davis's biographer, concurs:

> … it was the rhythm of bebop where the giddiness of creation was most strongly felt. Just as the melodies of bop seemed broken up, so was the rhythm, such that on a first hearing of this music, both rhythm and melody seemed erratic and disorganized. Even the rests – the brief moments of silence in bop melody lines – were used rhythmically. These pauses sprang up in surprising places, not at the moments of quiet usually left at the ends of phrases in pop songs and the blues. When this kind of staggered use of silence occurred along with offbeat accents and

> sudden shifts of speed in the melody, at the same time as it was played over the steady beat of the bass and the jagged snare drum accents and erratic 'bombs' dropped on the bass drum, fleeting moments of polymeter, or multiple rhythms, could be heard.
>
> (Szwed 2002: 36)

The effect was unnerving, even to fellow professional musicians. As drummer Dave Tough explains regarding his reaction to hearing Parker and Gillespie play for the first time on 52nd Street:

> As we walked in, see, these cats snatched up their horns and blew crazy stuff. One would stop all of a sudden and another would start for no reason at all. We never could tell when a solo was supposed to begin or end. Then they all quit at once and walked off the stage. *It scared us.*[21]
>
> (Quoted in DeVeaux 1997: 425, emphasis added)

Thus, compared to the large orchestral performances of the swing-era big bands or any other music that was 'planned and familiar' (Chevigny 1991: 50), bebop's perceived sonic 'wildness' unsettled all those who were listening to it for the first time.

Gioia details other aspects of bebop's supposed sonic 'wildness', such as its furious tempo and 'off-balance quality':

> The 2/4 rhythmic feeling of New Orleans and Chicago was now completely replaced by the streamlined &4/4; sound favored by the Kansas City bands. But even more important, phrases often began and ended on the weak beats (two and four) or, increasingly, between beats. This gave the music a querulous, incisive tone, imparting a slightly off-balance quality to each phrase and providing momentum for a solo as a whole. Above all, these crystalline improvisations were made vibrant by the breathless speed with which they were executed. Never before had instrumental technique been so central to the music's sound. Rarely had jazz tempos been so fast. Or, for that matter, so slow – the boppers were not afraid of even the most languid ballad tempos, but even in those instances their solos frequently implied a doubling of the stated time, staying true to the ethos of speed at all costs. The onomatopoeia of its nickname – at first 'rebop' or 'bebop,' eventually shortened further to a simple 'bop' – was all too fitting. This was music built out of small jabs and feints, rather than the sucker-punch haymakers, driven by straightforward syncopations.
>
> (Gioia 1997: 202)

These sentiments are shared by Peretti (1997) who writes: 'While Parker and Gillespie were also masters of the ballad improvisation, their signature innovation was to make many improvisations more intricately swinging, tighter, faster, and more intense' (101).

In addition to its furious tempo,[22] bebop introduced a 'newfound complexity' to the music (Gioia 1997: 202). That, along with 'the sheer virtuosity of its players', writes Szwed (2002: 36), 'made bop feel even wilder and more of a break with the past'. Referring back to 'KoKo', although the chords were 'anything but new, having been borrowed wholesale from the swing standard "Cherokee"' (203), 'before Parker, few dared to solo on this rapid romp through the circle of fifths, and the hearty souls who did would never have tried it at the tempos that the boppers preferred' (203). Although the bebop style appeared free and natural, it actually 'required a great deal of technical study' (Gillespie 1996: 562). Its 'nonsense-syllable' (Ellison 1996: 548) name, 'bop', often betrayed its technical complexity, as Ellison explains:

> A most inadequate word. ... A word which throws up its hands in clownish self-deprecation before all the complexity of sound and rhythm and self-assertive passion which it pretends to name; a mask-word for the charged ambiguities of the new sound, hiding the serious face of art.
>
> (Ellison 1996: 548)

Despite its complexity and speed, the early reactions against bop in the mainstream media 'were almost uniformly negative', as Gioia explains:

> An article in *Collier's* proclaimed, 'you can't sing it. You can't dance to it. Maybe you can't even stand it. It's bebop.' *Time* magazine, struggling to define bebop for its readers, explained that it was 'hot jazz overheated, with overdone lyrics full of bawdiness, references to narcotics and double-talk'. Prominent musicians of the 'old school' also chimed in with invective: Cab Calloway denounced modern jazz as 'Chinese music'; Louis Armstrong lambasted 'all them weird chords that don't mean nothing ... you got no melody to remember and no beat to dance to'; Benny Goodman complained that modern jazz players were 'not real musicians', they were 'just faking'. Traditional cornetist Doc Evans went so far as to hold a 'mock' funeral for bebop. *Down Beat*, which delighted in the controversy, ran a photo commemorating the event.
>
> (Gioia 1997: 217)

As is evidenced by the above comments, it is obvious that the sonic techniques employed by bebop musicians translated, for many listeners, into a 'wild', 'crazy' and lawless music. However, as Gioia (1997) aptly notes, 'musicological analysis only takes us so far. Bebop was defined by its social context as much as by the flats and sharps of its altered chords' (204).

Many other factors contributed to bebop's wild and revolutionary reputation, which had little to do with the actual music. Perhaps the most significant was the 'black character of the revolution'[23] (DeVeaux 1997: 18). The lawless and transgressive image of bebop, in other words, cannot be divorced from its almost universally accepted representation as 'an unassailably African-American phenomenon' (18). Even James Lincoln Collier, a strident opponent of those who automatically identify jazz with African-American culture, 'readily concedes the black character of the [bop] revolution' (18). He writes:

> ... black musicians dominated bop in a way that they had not dominated other forms of jazz since the early days in New Orleans. Black musicians devised the music without any help from whites, and they were its stars for a considerable period thereafter: Parker, Gillespie, Thelonious Monk, Bud Powell, and somewhat later, Fats Navarro, Clifford Brown, and Sonny Stitt were the quintessential boppers and they were all black.
>
> (Collier 1993: 209–10)

Many argue that black musicians developed bop to prevent the parasitic appropriation and exploitation of jazz by white musicians, musicians who had, in the past, 'stole' swing (and ragtime) and who were then offered all the best recording contracts and live performances (Ellison 1953: 212; Hentoff 1959: 73; Allsop 1961–62: 33; Green 1966: 39; Hore 1993).[24] It has also been suggested that bop began as 'a militant demonstration against "Uncle Tomism"'[25] (Allsop 1961–62: 33; see also Beyer 2000: 542) and was a 'political' attempt to turn jazz into an art music (Green 1966: 39), to make it 'a music meant for listening and not for dancing'[26] (Belgrad 1998: 187).

No matter what the reason for bebop's emergence, in their refusal to cultivate a stage persona or to entertain (white) audiences, bebop musicians were met with much racial antagonism. As one observer remarked, having seen the Parker–Gillespie quintet perform:

> That [bebop] sounded arrogant, uppity. ... [When I] saw Bird's combo, what struck me even more than the music was the *attitude* coming off the bandstand – self-confident, aggressive. It was something I'd never seen from black musicians before.[27]
>
> (Quoted in DeVeaux 1997: 435, emphasis in original)

This so-called 'attitude' coming off the bandstand was derived in part from the musicians' political opposition to racism and it manifested itself in a withdrawal 'from the conventions of popular American culture' (Beyer 2000: 542) and an adoption of 'distinctive patterns of dress and speech to further separate themselves from dominant American society' (542). Beyer argues that '[i]n its musical and cultural separatism, bebop replaced dominant norms with dissonant expression. Through cultural disengagement, bebop challenged contemporary styles in the same way black militancy attacked conventional politics' (542).[28]

Bebop musicians – with their ethos of 'nonconformity' (Baraka 1963: 190), their 'rather "radical" social attitudes' (191) and their creation of a dress (190) and a '"secret" … language' (202) (both musical and otherwise) all of their own – were seen to pose a danger sonically to wartime musical culture, but also to liberal law and society more generally. Bebop's so-called sonic 'wildness' seeped out, beyond the jam session and performance stage, into the non-musical (and even non-African-American) population. Amiri Baraka explains:

> Socially, even the term bebop, which began merely as an onomatopoeic way of characterizing a rhythmic element of the music, came to denote some kind of social nonconformity attributable to the *general* American scene, and not merely to the Negro.
>
> (Baraka 1963: 190, emphasis in original)

Bebop became synonymous with nonconformity (190), lawlessness, delinquency and immorality.[29] Its identification with 'crime, vice and greater sexual freedom' (Berger, quoted in Merriam and Mack 1960: 213) led to a 'basic rejection' (214) of the 'jazz community' in the wider society (214; see also Gitler 1985: 5), making bebop 'a public target for the sort of prim resentment that jazz had attracted in its early brothel-confined days' (Allsop 1961–62: 34). Allsop explains:

> There was hostile reaction both to the bewildering 'out of tuneness' of the music and to the *outré* uniform of the bopper: the beret, sunglasses and goatee made modish by Dizzy Gillespie. The word 'bop' became a handily snappy headline word, a portmanteau label for viciousness, neurosis, delinquency, dope and hazily unspecified war-time treason.
>
> (Allsop 1961–62: 34)

Either as 'arrant foolishness, a farrago of nonsense syllables and noisy, incomprehensible music' (DeVeaux 1997: 440) or 'an underground of drug users, antisocial deviants, and racial militants' (440; see also Allsop 1961–62: 34), this is how bebop was characterized. 'Both impressions', notes DeVeaux, 'were informed by racially grounded stereotypes' (DeVeaux 1997: 440).

As a result, bebop was wedged into a 'difficult-to-escape marginal status defined by the racial stereotype of social deviance' (398). The bebop musician replaced 'stripteasers and wife murderers as a thing to have Sunday supplement pieces on' (Hentoff, quoted in Adderley et al. 1960). This association between bebop and alterity fed into its wild and lawless image, as pianist Hampton Hawes recalls:

> We were the first generation to rebel. … Playing bebop, trying to be different, going through a lot of changes and getting strung out in the

process. *What these crazy niggers doin' playin' that crazy music?* Wild. Out of the jungle.

(Quoted in DeVeaux 1997: 6, emphasis in original)

Whether or not bebop deserved its wild and rebellious label,[30] it did give to the post-war generation a brave new sound, one that irrevocably changed the way that the West viewed jazz.

Improvisation, wildness, invention

Both musically and socially, the brave new sound of bebop owed much to the Harlem jamming culture in 1940s NYC, especially those jam sessions at Monroe's Uptown House and Minton's Playhouse[31] (Belgrad 1998: 180; Ward and Burns 2001: 291; Muyumba 2009: 26), from which bebop emerged (Gioia 1997: 213; Muyumba 2009: 26). In those sessions, the art of the improvising solo was practised and honed, thereby giving bebop its improvisational focus. As will be charted below, not only did the Harlem jam session influence the image of bebop as wild and lawless, it also helped shape the conception of jazz and improvisation more generally as wildly inventive, in the modern sense of the word as *newness* (Derrida 1989: 49). Many argue that the jamming culture of the 1930s and 1940s determined the nature of jazz from the Second World War onwards and legitimized jazz as a contemporary art form. As DeVeaux (1997) writes, '[t]he jam session, in short, underlies all claims for the legitimacy of bebop – not simply as a jazz idiom, but as the decisive step towards jazz as art' (202–3).

One of the factors contributing to the conceptualisation of the jam session (and thus bebop improvisation) as wild and lawless stemmed from the fact that '[a]n incidental but variable feature of jam-session culture was a degree of racial mixing'[32] (Townsend 2000: 51). Townsend elaborates:

> To a large extent the racial composition of sessions reflected the demographics of the city districts, so that the population of an after-hours club in Harlem, for example, would be predominantly black. But it is apparent that a good deal of meeting and playing together went on between black and white players, at a time when it was still unacceptable for players of both groups to appear together on a theatre stage or in a conventional music job.
>
> (Townsend 2000: 51)

Green shares this view: 'Mixed groups were taboo even in the recording studios. But though the two races were never employed together, they mingled freely after hours, forming a brotherhood of artists exchanging ideas, the traffic almost exclusively from black to white' (Green 1966: 33, 35; see also Dugan and Hammond 1938: 4).

The inter-race mixing in jam sessions arose because the 'bebop pioneers seemed unmotivated by racial exclusivity' (DeVeaux 1997: 18). Both 'Dizzy' Gillespie and Charlie Parker 'made a point of hiring white musicians for some of the earliest bop bands' (19). While many of these white musicians remained peripheral to the bebop movement, 'their very presence in otherwise all-black bands was a powerful statement – a deliberate breaching of the artificial barriers imposed by segregation' (19). In the words of DeVeaux:

> By admitting whites into the inner circle, Parker and Gillespie affirmed music to be a meritocracy rather than a racial privilege. If the initial creative impulse for bebop was rooted in an ethnic sensibility, musicians of both races quickly mastered the style, making it possible for Leonard Feather, writing in 1960, to assert the ultimate irrelevance of race: 'As soon as the rigid segregation under which [black jazz musicians] had lived began to relax, it became clear that given a freer interchange of ideas anyone could play jazz, according to his environment, his ability and his value as an individual, not as white or Negro.'
>
> (DeVeaux 1997: 19)[33]

As one of the only places in segregated United Stated in which musicians of different races could mix, the bebop jam sessions in NYC, along with the music they produced, were viewed to be all the more transgressive and wild because of this.

Further contributing to this wild image was the fact that, as a product of the jam session, bebop was considered as 'structure-less or chaotic' (Alterhaug 2004: 103) as the sessions themselves. The dominant perception of the jam session as eschewing all law is influenced to a large degree by the fact that it offers 'few clues to the uncontexted outsider' (DeVeaux 1997: 203) regarding its nature and structure. No written music is evident and there is 'certainly no rehearsal' (203). No stable or definitive 'house band' exists and musicians 'come and go as they please, even during the middle of the number' (203). The performances are without 'frame' and there are 'no spoken introductions or attention-getting silences' (203). Indeed, during the performances, '[h]ardly a word is exchanged beyond a few cryptic phrases – "blues in B-flat", "rhythm changes", a quick countdown to set the tempo – and they are off, into a performance that may last anywhere from a few minutes to an hour' (203). All the musicians in the jam session seem to 'know what to do without being told' (203) and '[t]he listener is left face to face with the *mystery of improvisation* – an alchemy that creates music out of nothingness' (203, emphasis added).

It is this 'mystery of improvisation'[34] that perhaps most inspired the characterization of bebop as not only wild, but also wildly inventive. As unique and 'unforeseen'[35] (Lewis 2004b: 145), improvisation is meant to eschew all law, convention, structure or form. It is constituted as 'pure spontaneity' (148) to the exclusion of 'history or memory' (147; see also Panish 1997: 120). Borrowing from the format of the jam session, bebop's improvised focus[36] propelled its understanding as wildly inventive. This, in turn, prompted a change in the way jazz music more generally was conceived. The 'string of solos'[37] (Townsend 2000: 37) jam-session format of the bebop era paved the way for the modern day understanding of jazz, in which improvisation is 'often taken to be a defining and unique feature of jazz' (7) (whether or not this is actually the case (Martin 2002: 133)).[38] James Lincoln Collier agrees:

> So much is the improvised solo seen as the essence of the music that listeners feel cheated when they discover that a solo is not the sudden outpouring of an open heart but has been memorized and repeated night after night, or even written out and played from sheet music. Most jazz fans do not feel a solo with the same force if they believe it is not spontaneous, even though the music itself would be no different. Clearly, the circumstances surrounding the music have much to do with how we perceive it; for the jazz fan, it *must* be seen as *spontaneous* – 'improvised'.
>
> (Collier 1993: 25–26, emphasis added)

No longer would jazz be offered as a form of popular entertainment; it was now 'a creative expression of unassailable integrity' (DeVeaux 1997: 443), 'a music to be listened to' (Williams, quoted 443; see also Belgrad 1998: 187). As DeVeaux (1997) explains, '[i]n its wake, *all* of jazz must be properly understood as an autonomous art, governed by its own laws and judgeable only by its own criteria' (443, emphasis in original).[39] Thus, in the end, the close connection between jazz and improvisation, made all the more compellingly by bebop's focus on the improvised solo, influenced a reciprocal association between improvisation, wildness and inventiveness.

Emphasizing the inventive potential of the association between bebop, wildness and improvisation were writers and theorists in the 1940s and 1950s, such as the beat poets. Wild, 'mad' or 'ludicrous' associations were seen to be revealed through the unconscious mind and bebop improvisation supposedly involved just such a lack of (self-)consciousness (Belgrad 1998: 212; cf. Finkelstein 1948: 15, 17, 71, 72). Kerouac, for example, developed his technique of 'spontaneous writing' ('spontaneous bop prosody') to mirror his interpretation of the bebop performance. For him, it was a revolutionary style of writing and 'the only possible literature of the future' (Kerouac, quoted in Charters 1995: 481).

Describing his technique of spontaneous bop prosody,[40] Kerouac writes:

> If possible write 'without consciousness' in semi-trance (as Yeats' later 'trance writing') allowing subconscious to admit in own uninhibited interesting necessary and so 'modern' language what conscious art would

> censor, and write excitedly, swiftly, with writing-or-typing cramps, in accordance (as from center to periphery) with laws of orgasm, Reigh's 'beclouding of consciousness'. *Come* from within, out-to relaxed and said.
>
> (Kerouac 1995a: 485, emphasis in original)[41]

These descriptions of bebop subculture by Kerouac, not always welcomed by the musicians themselves,[42] simply reinforced and reproduced taken for granted assumptions about the relationship between bebop improvisation and wild invention.

The belief in the wild inventiveness of improvisation was further nourished by popular notions of the bebop improviser, most notably Charlie 'Yardbird' Parker, as 'genius' (M. Davis 1996: 577). Geniuses are 'godlike individuals quite unlike ordinary people, possessing marvellous and practically boundless capabilities that the common run of men and women could never dream of'[43] (Howe 1999: vii). With an essential characteristic of genius being novelty and originality (Kant 1951: 150), a link thereby exists 'between the quality of being a genius and the unpredictability of the event, the "it just so happens" aspect of it' (Derrida 2006: 62). Genius 'appears to be a mystery'; it 'defies analysis' (Howe 1999: 1). Originality, argues Edward Young (1930: 319), 'rises *spontaneously* from the vital roots of genius; it grows, it is not made' (emphasis added).[44]

Landgraf (2011) notes the 'proximity of improvisation to the aesthetics of genius' (8):

> Historically, the belief that art exceeds the providence of what can be planned and fully comprehended is rooted in a very long tradition that has linked art to divine inspiration. Well into the eighteenth century, inspiration is understood in religious terms, as the expression of a higher voice (god or the Muses) that spoke through the artist. In the second half of the eighteenth century, the idea of divine intervention is internalized and the artist-genius endowed with godlike qualities.
>
> (Landgraf 2011: 81–82)

Citing examples from the period, Landgraf posits the image of 'inspired genius' as that which enables and authenticates 'successful improvisation' (82).

The notion of the 'mystical "improvisational genius"' (Finkelstein 1948: 73) is both sustained by, and, in turn, sustains, the conception of improvisation as 'extempore' (OERD 1996: 710), that is, 'without preparation' (494) or 'on the spur of the moment' (494; see also Landgraf 2011: 74). The 'mystery of improvisation', charted above, envisions a creative music 'made up out of nothing, invented out of thin air' (Perlman and Greenblatt 1981: 169). Sonic creations erupt via 'divine intervention' (Demsey 2000: 788); with improvising musicians deemed 'displaced bards, shamen, or griots'

(Jarrett 2004: 320). Chapter 5 trades mystery for method, revealing how the improvising jazz solo, as that which is supposedly impromptu or 'invent[ed] during the act of performance' (Panish 1997: 79), is never created *ex nihilo* (319). Those working in the emerging interdisciplinary field of Critical Studies in Improvisation (CSI) know all too well that 'creativity without artifice' (DeVeaux 1997: 203) is simply not possible (Perlman and Greenblatt 1981: 169; Jarrett 2004: 319) and that 'improvising – in any domain – implies creation from preexisting material' (Lussier 2011: 1). CSI scholars will therefore navigate us through the 'laws' of improvisation and the workings of the 'jazz form' (Finkelstein 1948: 79) in the exploration to follow.

Chapter 5

Demystifying improvisation

> When you're just learning jazz, everything is mystical.
>
> (Wynton Marsalis, quoted in Berliner 1994: 2)

Myths and misconceptions abound when contemplating the art of jazz improvisation and these views are 'held as often by nonjazz musicians as by the general public' (Demsey 2000: 788). Fundamental to the Western conception of improvisation are two underlying misunderstandings:

1 *Improvisation is formless*, i.e. 'that improvisation involves adherence to neither convention nor protocol, that it tolerates no system of constraint, requires no prior thought' (Fischlin and Heble 2004: 23; see also Demsey 2000: 788–89).
2 *Improvisation is individualistic*, i.e. 'the assumption that improvisation is, first and foremost, about unblocking the obstacles that impede access to forms of individual self-expression' (Fischlin and Heble 2004: 23).

Improvising musicians and critical improvisation theorists alike know that both misconceptions are 'simply not so' (Perlman and Greenblatt 1981: 169). Not only is the improvising solo 'constructed according to specific harmonic and melodic constraints' (169), but accounts that regard improvisation as:

> … expressions of individuality, originality and creativity … fail to account for the ways in which jazz improvisation and creative improvised music have always … been about community building (rather than individual self-expression), about fostering new ways of thinking about, and participating in, human relationships.
>
> (Fischlin and Heble 2004: 23)

This chapter aims to debunk the above myths surrounding jazz improvisation. Before commencing, it is of note that it is not only non-improvising musicians and laypersons who are responsible for the continued mystique surrounding improvisation. Collier (1993) claims that jazz musicians are themselves partially to blame. Musicians, he says, tend to avoid many of the technical improvisation schemes to which they could have recourse for fear that 'too much conscious control will inhibit the free expression of feeling they are supposed to be exhibiting' (59). The notion that one should not talk or even think about the improvisational method has been, argues Collier, 'endemic to jazz for a long time' (59). He investigates why musicians are so loath to discuss their own creative process and concludes that it is because 'they are afraid analysis will kill the spirit of the music' (60). 'Jazz', he writes, 'is supposed to be spontaneous, supposed to be a product of the feeling of the moment' (60). Thus, it is assumed, albeit incorrectly, that 'if you deliberately set out to impose some sort of scheme on the music' (60–61), it will 'interfere with the direct expression of feeling' (61).[1] Perhaps best evidencing this is Charlie Parker's advice to Sonny Criss in 1947: 'Don't think. Quit thinking' (Belgrad 1998: 184).

That said, the art and process of improvisation has become the focus of exploration for many musicians, musicologists and critical improvisation theorists. Paul Berliner (1994), for example, has written a 900-page ethnomusicology on this exact topic and Derek Bailey (1992) has examined not only improvisation in jazz, but also in Indian music, flamenco, baroque, church organ music and rock-and-roll. Kernfeld's *What to Listen for in Jazz* (1995) is also instructive on the topic of improvisation, as is Ingrid Monson's book, *Saying Something: Jazz Improvisation and Interaction* (1996).

Dispelling the myth of the individual nature of improvisation has become a preoccupation of many working in the field of CSI. One brilliant collection of work on the relationship between subjectivity, community and the 'jazz form' is Fischlin and Heble's edited collection *The Other Side of Nowhere: Jazz, Improvisation, and Communities in Dialogue* (2004). Three other forthcoming publications, which will undoubtedly add much to this discussion, are highly anticipated, namely Heble and Wallace's collection of essays entitled *People Get Ready: The Future of Jazz is Now!*; Fischlin, Heble and Lipsitz's The Fierce Urgency of Now: Improvisation, Rights, and the Ethics of Co-creation; and Waterman and Siddal's *Sounding the Body: Improvisation, Representation and Subjectivity*. All these sources challenge the extemporary and individual nature of improvisation and confirm that 'there is far more to improvisation than meets the ear' (Berliner 1994: 3).

Improvisation and the 'jazz form'

The 'jazz form' references an improvisation that is not 'structure-less or chaotic' (Alterhaug 2004: 103), but instead requires some sort of framework or pre-determined form or structure (Coleman and Derrida 2004: 321). Improvisation is *not*, in other words, 'unfettered freedom' (Demsey 2000: 789; see also Coleman and Derrida 2004: 320); it is instead 'made up of several elements' (Demsey 2000: 789), many of which are found in composed pieces of music, such as harmony and melody, rhythm and time (789–91; see also Berliner 1994: 63). Barrett provides a detailed explanation:

> Jazz improvisation involves creating music on the spot without a prescribed score or plan. However, jazz is guided by a non-negotiable framework that constrains what the soloist can play. This structure provides the necessary backdrop to coordinate action and organize choice of notes. To quote the bassist Charles Mingus, 'You can't improvise on nothin'. You gotta have somethin'.' The 'something' that provides the resources players draw upon are songs that are made up of chords and corresponding chords.
>
> Songs are divided into bars, phrases, and sections. Each bar is assigned one or more chords that complement and give context to the melody. When jazz musicians improvise they are 'following the chord changes' that outline the song. These chord changes, or chord progressions, as they are sometimes called, follow familiar rule bound patterns and customs not unlike the rules of grammar and syntax that guide proper speech.
>
> (Barrett and Peplowski 1998: 558)

One needs a superior grasp of these elements to improvise well, requiring enormous hard work and discipline (Lewis 2004b: 153). All these components – harmonic and melodic constraints, rhythm and time, and discipline and hard work – are essential to the 'jazz form'. Improvisation could not exist without such, as Postema (1987) stresses: 'Improvisation is free creative energy made possible by recognized forms – made possible not just by providing a contrast, but supplying improvisation its necessary material and the structure of its meaning' (303).

In their consideration of the jazz form, Perlman and Greenblatt (1981) describe harmony as the 'deep structure' of a piece of music (170). Expressed by 'the chord symbols found on all sheet music', harmony 'constitute[s] a universal structural basis for improvisation' and is among one of the first topics covered in any introduction to improvisation (170; Berliner 1994: 72). Perlman and Greenblatt explain:

> 'Playing the changes', that is, improvising on the predetermined harmonic pattern of a song, is the sine qua non of jazz competence. To play the changes is to involve oneself in the collaborative effort of a jazz performance. Not to do so is to sound horribly discordant, even to the most untrained ear.
>
> (Perlman and Greenblatt 1981: 170)

The same chord sequence can become the deep structure for numerous songs. As just one example, by following the 'changes' of the well-known standard 'How High is the Moon' Charlie Parker created a new melody, 'Ornithology' (170).

Of course, the 'implicit goal' of any improvising soloist in jazz is to 'create an impromptu melody' (175) – one that 'sounds like jazz and has such coherence and fluency that it appears to have been written beforehand and rehearsed' (175). To accomplish such requires 'mastery of and spontaneous resort to a basic vocabulary of musical figures' (175). While more will be offered below on improvisation as language or conversation, these musical figures, or 'licks' as they are called, when played on the correct scale and chord-tones, are what give an improvised solo its distinctive sound (175). In jazz, the basic lexicon of 'licks' is not large – according to Perlman and Greenblatt, 'there are perhaps two or three dozen that most players rely on' (176). However, because 'any lick can be played over any chord, beginning with any scale/chord-tone and repeated indefinitely up and down the entire range of an instrument, the improvisational possibilities becomes enormous' (176).

The melody of a piece of music or song, as its 'most recognizable feature', 'far more accessible than its abstract chord sequence' (Demsey 2000: 791), is invaluable to the improvising solo. Writes Berliner:

> Composed pieces or tunes, consisting of a melody and an accompanying harmonic progression, have provided the structure for improvisations throughout most of the history of jazz. Enjoying favour to varying degrees from one period to the next, spirituals, marches, rags, and popular songs have all contributed to the artists' repertory of established compositions or standards. Performers commonly refer to the melody or theme as the head, and to the progression as chord changes or simple changes. It has become the convention for musicians to perform the melody and its accompaniment at the opening and closing of a performance's piece. In between, they take turns improvising solos within the piece's cyclical rhythmic form.
>
> (Berliner 1994: 63)

Thus, the improvising soloist will 'keep the melody in their mind's ear as their reference point as they glide through the harmonies; they may refer to it in brief, coded bits during their solos as a marker of the form' (Demsey 2000: 791). The improvised solo, in other words, can only be analysed or understood in relation to the melodic head. Again quoting Charles Mingus, '[y]ou gotta improvise on *somethin*'' (quoted in Kernfeld 1995: 119, emphasis added). To do otherwise would make its recognition *as* improvisation impossible. Moreover, the skill or talent of a jazz soloist is often judged by his or her ability to return, after a period of 'wild' improvisation, to the original melody, to 'somehow [return] to *sense* when he seemed to have unleashed mere *chaos*' (Jones 2004: 64, emphasis added).

Also of importance to providing improvisation with presence and form are the elements of rhythm and time. Time and rhythm are intricately linked in jazz improvisation and Monson writes that 'the primary function of the rhythm section is ... to provide the timeline against which the soloist can interact and build' (Monson 1996: 82–83). This timeline produces a 'dynamic tension between the relatively fixed and variable elements of the ensemble' (83), which Samuel Floyd calls 'Signifying on the timeline' (quoted 83). While the rhythm section must 'provide the timeline' (82), it is also the case that there is 'a considerable degree of flexibility even in the relatively fixed instrumental roles of the jazz rhythm section' (82). Soloists, in other words, 'often change the character of what they play from chorus to chorus, and sensitive rhythm sections change the character of accompaniment in response' (83). Thus, rhythm section members must always be listening and reacting to the 'continuous changes in an improviser's solo' (83). The timeline is accordingly not fixed and constant, but is instead responsive to change and adapts accordingly.

The improvised solo, in contrast, typically conceived as full of illimitable possibility and freedom – notes picked out of the thin air (Berliner 1994: 1) or brought to life by divine intervention (Demsey 2000: 789) – is positioned as timeless, or free from the constraints of time. However, quite paradoxically, the rhythmic 'timeline' bestows on the improvising solo its being and presence. The story of Frederic Rzewski's reunion with fellow musician Steve Lacy on the street in Rome illustrates this paradox of improvisational time. According to Rzewski, upon meeting Lacy, he took out his pocket tape recorder and asked him to 'describe in fifteen seconds the difference between composition and improvisation' (quoted in Bailey 1992: 141). Lacy's reply: 'In fifteen seconds the difference between composition and improvisation is that in composition you have all the time you want to think about what to say in fifteen seconds, while in improvisation you have only fifteen seconds' (quoted in Rzewski 2002: 378; quoted in Bailey 1992: 141). For Rzewski, this answer, which 'took exactly fifteen seconds' (Rzewski 2002: 378), remains 'the best formulation of the question' (quoted in Bailey 1992: 141) he has ever heard.

For our purposes, Lacy's response is most telling in its divergence from the dominant conception of jazz improvisation as formless and thus devoid of structure and time. As he explains, it is the time given to the composer, which offers unlimited possibility in relation to creation and originality. The fifteen seconds given to the improviser, in contrast, constrains the improvisation and places limits on its possibility. Spontaneity, in other words, must, in the 'fifteen second improvisation', be paradoxically projected into a 'carefully staged moment' (DeVeaux 1997: 372) and the improviser must 'mak[e] the most of his [or her] brief time in the spotlight – concentrated gesture instead of cumulative intensity' (372). It is this quality of improvised time to which, I believe, Charlie Parker was referring when he boasted, 'I can play all

I know in eight bars' (quoted 372). The fifteen seconds of time in Rzewski's anecdote both enables the presence of improvisation and orients it beyond itself. Without these two dimensions, the 'fifteen second improvisation' would not exist.

The necessity of all these elements – harmony, melody, rhythm and time – has led Finkelstein (1948) to view jazz improvisation as 'a form of composition' (71). 'It is the height of superficiality', he writes, 'to imagine that a hot solo emerges directly from a performer's "unconscious"' (72). Jazz musicians 'simply cannot create on a consistent level this way' (72). Instead, an improvised solo is 'generally worked up from performance to performance, using the same material' (72). This becomes particularly evident if we follow the work of a particular performer, tracing the 'growth of these solos' (73). Finkelstein explains that when an improvised creation is arrived at, and is one that satisfies the creator, the improviser 'remembers it and repeats it' (73). Thus, while improvisation often sounds 'fresh and new' (73), musicians 'generally know what they are doing every step of the way' (73).

Collier (1993) makes a similar argument. He asserts that jazz musicians have either trained themselves, or learned from experience, how to play on an instrument more or less anything they hear – whether actual sound or that existing only in their heads (50). Thus, the 'jazz musician is not simply spilling unconsidered notes from an open psyche; instead he hears in his head the notes he is going to play before he plays them' (52). Charlie Parker echoes this in his description of his own 'invention' of bebop in 1939:

> I'd been getting bored with the stereotyped changes that were being used at the time, and I kept thinking there's bound to be something else. I could hear it sometimes but I couldn't play it. Well, that night I was working over 'Cherokee' and as I did I found that by using higher intervals of a chord as a melody line and backing them with appropriately related changes, I could play the thing I'd been hearing. I came alive.
>
> (Quoted in Belgrad 1998: 184)

If we understand jazz improvisation as 'consciously worked out and carefully built up from performance to performance' (Finkelstein 1948: 73), the 'mystery of improvisation' (DeVeaux 1997: 203) becomes less mysterious. Again, Finkelstein offers support:

> We can see why it is impossible to ask that a performance be wholly invented on the spur of the moment, wholly fresh and different in every phrase. A great improvised performance must necessarily be a combination of old and new, familiar and fresh material. If half of what is heard is truly new, the performance is miraculous.
>
> (Finkelstein 1948: 73)

It is therefore the case that the best improvised performances come about when a 'familiar number' (74) is improvised upon, as opposed to 'a wholly fresh melody' (74). Musicians in the former situation 'know all the nuances, the ins and outs of the old piece. They have worked it out many times, and have a base from which to go further' (74).

Musicians and critical improvisation scholars stress that jazz does not 'exist wholly by its own invented laws' (Finkelstein 1948: 71) and improvisation 'does not consist mainly in inventing new licks' (Belgrad 1998: 180); instead, it involves, amongst other techniques, 'stringing together learned licks and references in new and appropriate combinations' (180). Jazz improvisation, Finkelstein (1948) argues, 'follows old and familiar patterns of music, and is new only in that it follows these patterns in terms of its own rhythms, melodies and timbres' (71). The 'accomplished improviser' (Gabbard 2004: 315) will have 'learned the codes that connote freshness, looseness, and a feeling of spontaneity' (315). Such learned procedures 'create a pattern so complex that we get an illusion of randomness' (Nachmanovitch 1990: 27).

In light of the above, it is obvious that improvisation is neither spontaneous nor created instinctively or by divine intervention. Instead, it is hard work (Demsey 2000: 789) and 'there is no musical activity which requires greater skill and devotion, preparation, training and commitment' (Bailey 1992: xii). Musician Andy Laking[2] of the band Gráda backs this sentiment:

> One question I thought of is: why are so many listeners being fooled? Probably because they don't understand the music well enough (and who could blame them). Perhaps also because most people seem to think that jazz musicians are naturally talented, but certainly not hard working; it's something you do for fun. This belief would make it hard for people to realise that it's less about spontaneous creation and improvisation, but more about hard work and long term commitment.
>
> (Laking 2005)

Demsey (2000) posits that 'the crucial factor that ties together the careers of the great improvisers throughout the history of jazz', which audiences and listeners often forgot, or do not even consider, is the fact that 'they all possessed an unmatched work ethic' (797). He elaborates:

> Seemingly extemporaneous solos heard in performance are actually the tip of the musical iceberg, the result of countless hours of daily practice for years, to the point where the music becomes the primary language, spoken dialect the sound. …
>
> It is in the solitude of the practice room … where, for the most inexperienced student and the legendary jazz master alike, the basic elements of form and harmony are ingrained, new melodies or

> voice-leading pathways are learned, and experiments made in rhythmic manipulation. In the end, it is this constant state of learning, expanding, and practicing that achieves art and beauty.
>
> (Demsey 2000: 797–98)

The improvising jazz musician relies not on tricks, but on craft. Krin Gabbard (2004) explains: 'Although jazz musicians, like Method actors, have been constructed as more in touch with their unconscious minds than the rest of us, it is not at all accurate to say that jazz musicians simply dig into their ids during a solo' (314). Instead, as has been mentioned above, 'accomplished jazz artists have large bodies of music under their fingers and can insert favorite motifs, bits of scales learned in practicing, and fragments of familiar melodies into a performance' (314). Different strategies for deploying this material have been fleshed out in rehearsals and practice such that each performance is different than the last. Writes Gabbard, '[t]his model of improvisation is a long way from the one in which jazz artists simply get in touch with their inner selves' (314).

On the discipline and hard work that goes into preparing to improvise, a few anecdotes from the biographies of accomplished jazz improvisers are worth relaying. First, as Charlie Parker tells Paul Desmond in 1953,

> I put quite a bit of study into the horn, that's true. In fact, the neighbors threatened to ask my mother to move once when I was living out West. They said I was driving them crazy with the horn. I used to put in at least eleven to fifteen hours a day. I did that for over a period of three or four years.
>
> (Quoted in Crouch 1996: 1029)

Miles Davis also explains the commitment and hard work that went into playing bebop:

> We really studied … If a door squeaked, we would call out the exact pitch. And every time I heard the chord of G, for example, my fingers automatically took the position for C-sharp on the horn – the flatted fifth – whether I was playing or not.
>
> Freddie Webster and I used to go down every night to hear Diz. If we missed a night, we missed something. … Stand up at the bar, throw up a quarter, and name the note that it came down on. That shit be going so fast; and we'd be testing ourselves.
>
> (Quoted in Szwed 2002: 40–41)

Saxophonist Gerry Mulligan further testifies to Davis's studious approach to improvisation:

> Miles and I used to spend a lot of time talking about ... the mechanics of music. He was particularly interested in chord progressions. He loved to make alterations ... loved to make changes in chord progressions and try different things, you know, then how to apply that to a line so that the line flowed. And how to deal with it melodically.
>
> (Quoted in Szwed 2002: 41)

Tradition of improvisation

Improvisation requires not only deep understanding of the 'jazz form', but also 'thorough attention to the background, history, and culture' (Lewis 2004b: 153) and a comprehensive knowledge of the *tradition* within which she or he is working.

Both George Lewis and John Panish have written on the different ways of conceiving improvisation in relation to tradition. In his book, *The Color of Jazz: Race and Representation in Postwar American Culture* (1997), Panish argues that African-Americans see the tradition embedded within improvisation while white Americans simply see individualised spontaneity devoid of collectivity and context. Similarly, but slightly less racially essentialized, George Lewis adopts the terms 'Eurological' and 'Afrological' to 'refer *metaphorically* to musical beliefs and behavior that ... exemplify particular kinds of musical "logic"' (Lewis 2004b: 133, emphasis added). For Lewis, the 'Eurological' perspective conceives improvisation as 'pure spontaneity' (148), unmediated by 'history or memory' (147). In contrast, the 'Afrological' approach emphasises the discipline, technical knowledge, and 'thorough attention to the background, history, and culture' (153), which is necessary for the creation of 'good' improvisation. What both authors make evident, albeit in slightly different ways, is that individually oriented Western society is unable or unwilling to view jazz improvisation as 'something informed by tradition and mastery of its techniques' (Jones 1991: 91).

In contrast to the Eurological, or dominant, view of improvisation, the 'structural and thematic unities that inhere in African American culture' (Panish 1997: xvii) are emphasised by Panish through the work of Henry Louis Gates, Jr. in *The Signifying Monkey: A Theory of African-American Literary Criticism* (1988), Gates posits the following conception of improvisation:

> Improvisation, of course, so fundamental to the very idea of jazz, is 'nothing more' than repetition and revision. In this sort of revision, again where meaning is fixed, it is the realignment of the signifier that is the straight trait of expressive genius. The more mundane the fixed text ('April in Paris' by Charlie Parker, 'My Favorite Things' by John Coltrane), the more dramatic is the Signifyin(g) revision. It is this principle of repetition and difference, this practice of intertextuality,

> which has been so crucial to the black vernacular forms of Signifyin(g), jazz—and even its antecedents, the blues, the spirituals, and ragtime—and which is the source of my trope for black intertextuality in the Afro-American formal literary tradition.
>
> (Gates 1988: 63–64)

Thus, instead of privileging the individualistic elements of jazz improvisation, Gates points to the 'repetition and revision' of tradition itself (Panish 1997: 81), or what Lewis would call '[t]he changing same' (Lewis 2004a: 163).

The work of Jack Kerouac and John Clellon Holmes is cited as proof by Panish (1997) that dominant (white) society conceives improvisation as a 'universal experimental technique' (120), disengaged from any particular cultural tradition; as something that can be adopted and modified for anyone's own purposes (120). He compares the use of jazz by white writers to that of African-American writers of the same era and argues that the latter 'incorporated elements of jazz into the structure of their work' (120) and 'saw improvisation as part of a specific cultural lineage' (120). Far from being a 'universal experimental technique' which is disengaged from any particular cultural tradition and which can be adopted and modified for one's own purposes, improvisation, for Panish, is actually 'part of a specific cultural lineage' (120). In other words, improvisation is 'not only a process of creation that emphasizes freedom and spontaneity', it is also 'a culturally specific concept that is ineluctably connected to historical and contemporary social contexts' (123). As such, improvisation 'is connected to more than simply a single person's unconscious, emotional life or creative genius' (123).

The context in which jazz improvisation takes place includes the existing musical material, which 'constitutes the jazz tradition and comprises such diverse forms as blues songs, variations on pop melodies, chord progressions, intervals, scales, rhythmic patterns, and other performers' improvised solos' (125). A jazz musician puts these elements 'together in different ways' (125) in order to take his or her 'place within the jazz tradition' (125) and 'establish his [or her] unique voice' (125). As Panish highlights, '[i]n this sense, jazz playing is as much a traditional approach as it is an individual one' (125).

Tradition is often located in opposition to innovation, as that which excludes or limits pure invention. Applied to jazz, tradition, as 'a closed and elite collection of "classic" works' (Tomlinson, quoted in Bucholtz 2003: 450), is said to determine 'what is and isn't jazz' (quoted 450). A paradox ensues, however, when one conceives jazz as 'largely improvisational in nature' (Finkelstein 1948: 71; Hall 1999: 1599). If the jazz tradition comprises almost solely of innovation, then the dichotomy between the two concepts, tradition and innovation, is effectively disrupted and destabilised. It is thus the case, to quote Steve Lacy, that jazz improvisation sits 'on the *edge* – in between the known and the unknown' (quoted in Bailey

1992: 54, emphasis added), in between tradition and innovation, 'and you have to keep pushing it towards the unknown otherwise it and you die' (quoted 54).

The 'edge' or divide between tradition and innovation highlights another paradox of jazz improvisation: 'the importance of tradition to the uniqueness of individual spontaneous expression' (Soules 2004: 276). Innovation is impossible without tradition. Lacy explains how the innovative elements of improvisation arise from a 'leap into the unknown' (quoted in Bailey 1992: 57–58). However, *before* the leap, required are 'years of preparation and all your sensibilities and your prepared means' (quoted 57). Even if a 'higher value' (quoted 58) is placed on what is found in the leap rather than on what is prepared (58), the leap would not be possible without 'what you can prepare, especially in the way that it can take you to the edge' (quoted 58). Musical tradition and preparation thus 'take you to the edge safely so that you can go out there and find the other stuff' (quoted 58).

Tradition both limits and enables innovation. On the one hand, guardians of the canon may resist 'outsider incursions' (Bucholtz 2003: 451) by 'deploying elitist and formalistic standards against the innovations of the other' (452). Innovation in this sense is outside tradition, as that which threatens and disrupts the pre-existent. One must simply recall the violent reaction to bebop music, both from jazz musicians themselves and from the wider public, in order to understand the fear that such innovation can generate. However, as with the metaphysical tradition more generally, eventually the other is assimilated into the same (Bernasconi 1993: 119) and innovation is absorbed into the canon, 'thereby expanding and refining our understanding and appreciation of the reach and depth of the jazz idiom' (Bucholtz 2003: 452). Again, the invention of bebop is telling: once the initial panic died down, it stopped being regarded as an 'outsider incursion' and began to enjoy greater commercial success in 52nd Street jazz clubs and is now seen as having determined the shape of jazz from the 1940s onwards (Townsend 2000: 36).

The canon – 'our received wisdom' (Bucholtz 2003: 457) – is 'where we begin' (457). Innovation 'presupposes intensive training' (454) and 'assume[s] and demand[s] a mastery of the existing canon' (454). Much improvisation and invention in jazz accordingly 'does not challenge or transcend the limits of the canon' (457), but instead 'seeks to develop or view its possibilities in different ways' (457). This innovation operates both outside and 'within the canon' (457), through the '"idiosyncratic embellishments" jazz artists invent to "exploit" the limits of the canon in "richly inventive and strikingly original ways"' (Meyer 2000: 190–91, quoted in Bucholtz 2003: 457). In this sense, '[j]azz is [a] paradox. … [It is] both conservative and radical, reactionary and revolutionary at the same time' (Metzer 1999: xiii, quoted in Bucholtz 2003: 457). Moreover, just as innovation would be impossible without a canon or tradition from which to 'reach beyond' (Bucholtz 2003: 454), tradition needs innovation to survive and endure.

To help explain this latter point, Fitzpatrick and Joyce (2007) trace the etymology of the word 'tradition' in order to unpack its contradictory nature. Tradition, from the Latin *tradere*, means both 'to transmit and to betray' (Zartaloudis 2005: 391). Moreover, as discovered by Fitzpatrick and Joyce, '"tradition" as betrayal was once the name of a crime' (Fitzpatrick and Joyce 2007: 172), a transgression that compelled the 'surrender of sacred books in times of persecution' (quoted 172). The authors focus on 'tradition's self-transgressive quality' (172) in order to argue that '"tradition" is itself the very *failure* to protect both text and life from inimical forces' (172–73, emphasis in original).

This reading of '"tradition" as betrayal' (172) contradicts 'the standard view' (171), which positions tradition as 'fixed and static' (171), as 'hav[ing] some positioned, some determinately enduring existence' (173), which can be handed over, delivered or entrusted. Tradition, as Fitzpatrick and Joyce reveal, 'can never be fully determined or stilled' (171); 'in this very positioning and enduring, tradition constantly orients present existence beyond itself' (173). Accordingly, '[i]n this relating integrally to the illimitable contingencies of our being-with each other, tradition must be capable of *being* utterly responsive, comprehensively self-transgressive' (173, emphasis in original). It is important to note, however, that tradition 'cannot exist as either of its two dimensions' (173). If determinately invariant or static, it would not endure; conversely, if 'merely responsive, it would dissipate entirely' (173). Thus, in the words of Fitzpatrick and Joyce, 'this intrinsic responsiveness of tradition, its attentiveness and attunement to what is ever beyond the determinate, makes impossible the reduction of tradition to what invariably "is"' (173).

Tradition thereby exists as 'a mode of our being-with each other' (173) or as a 'manifestation of our being-with' (175). It can only 'be' insofar as it exists *between* the two dimensions of determinacy and responsiveness. Applied to jazz improvisation, it can be said that, just as the jazz tradition cannot be perfectly stilled or static, musical innovation can never be completely open or responsive. Innovation needs to be 'with' tradition in order to 'be'. Improvisation not only utilizes those materials that comprise the jazz tradition in order to transform an 'existing melody' (Bucholtz 2003: 454), but 'by gradually reaching beyond existing boundaries and current understandings of the idiom' (454), it transforms the jazz canon and brings new melodies into being. Thus, while the jazz idiom can only be 'revitalized and sustained' (457) by 'giving space to canonoclastic voice' (457), the canon itself is of value (457). For it is only through the 'implied structures of categories and classes' (457) that we can 'make sense of experience' (457) and 'provide a framework for exploring the possibilities of other interpretations and other aspects of experience' (457) in order to 'shape and foster cultural continuity' (457).

Perhaps Ralph Ellison expresses it best:

> I had learned too that the end of all this discipline and technical mastery was the desire to express an affirmative way of life through its musical tradition and that this tradition insisted that each artist achieve his creativity within its frame. He must learn the best of the past, and add to it his personal vision.
>
> (Ellison 1953: 189)

Collective individuality[3]

The second misconception about improvisation is that it is solely 'an individual matter', taking place in 'a social vacuum' with the presence of other musicians, listeners, etc. being 'at best an irrelevance and at worse an interference in the individual's contemplation of the musical work' (Small 1998: 6).[4] This myth is founded primarily on the notion that improvisational creativity 'is a burst of inspiration from a lone genius; that a person working alone is always more creative than a group; and that social conventions and expectations always interfere with creativity' (Sawyer 2006: 259). The relationship between the individual and the collective or community within which creation occurs has occupied the work of many critical improvisation theorists.[5] Sawyer's work on 'creative group performance', for instance, posits improvisation as 'fundamentally social and collaborative' (257), involving 'preparation, training, and hard work' (257), the 'process' being 'more important than the product or the personality' (257).

Jazz aficionados will be familiar with the term 'jamming' as another formulation of creative group performance (Sawyer 2006: 3). Detailed in Chapter 4 was the importance of the after-hours jam session to the polishing and perfecting of the improvised solo. Often portrayed as a 'solo art' (Green 1966: 40), 'merely the expression of individual freedom' (Stewart 2003: 96) or something musicians 'do "off the top of their heads"' (96), improvisation as creative group performance is, in actual fact, a communal effort and is judged in relation to the collective performance as a whole.

This is one of the paradoxes of improvised creativity. The improvising performer 'works with and against the group at the same time' (Jones 1991: 48; Szwed 2002: 51). It involves a 'delicate balance' being struck 'between [a] strong individual personality and the group' (Ellison 1953: 189). Ralph Ellison describes the jam session as 'a marvel of social organization' (189). It is a 'cruel contradiction' (234), he writes, that an improviser must 'lose his identity even as he finds it' (234) and 'each solo flight, or improvisation, represents … a definition of his identity: as an individual, as a member of the collectivity and as a link in the chain of tradition' (234). The creativity of any improviser, then, instead of being illimitably free and unconstrained, depends on the group and the community within which he or she is improvising for meaning.

Marshall Soules (2004) writes on the violent contradiction of jamming:

> The complex negotiation of identity within a performance context – whether the art be music, acting, writing, or performance of self in everyday life – pits individual freedoms against the constraints and opportunities of society.
>
> (Soules 2004: 268)

Each assertion of individuality is challenged by the collective and requires much 'commitment, courage, and risk-taking' (268) by the improvising performer. The violence or cruelty done to the individual, however, is simultaneously marked by an 'affirmation … of … implacable necessity' (Derrida 2001b: 292; see also Soules 2004: 268). Violence, in other words, not only renders individual expression expressible, but also ensures the possibility of this expression being other than what it is. This 'cruel contradiction' (Soules 2004: 269), which 'threatens to erase the traces of identity' (269), also 'animates improvisation' (269) and enables it to thrive:

> … improvising musicians … must lose their identities even as they find them, but they do so within a framework of productive constraints – the protocols of improvisation. In a seeming paradox that threatens to erase the traces of identity, improvisation thrives when the performance of character is given latitude of expression within the framework of the ensemble.
>
> (Soules 2004: 269)

These protocols – the '"long established codes" determining "precedence and precisely correct procedure"' (270) – act as the 'laws' of improvisation, broadly conceived. Thus, while it 'may at first seem antithetical to popular notions of improvised creativity' (270), improvisation can only exist in relation to these 'voluntary constraints' (270).

This is even the case with performances as 'radically improvisational' (270) as Ornette Coleman's *Free Jazz*. Martin Williams's liner notes to the album outline the protocols or laws governing the music in this particular recording:

> Not only is the improvisation almost total, it is frequently collective, involving all eight men at once. And there were no preconceptions as to themes, chord patterns or chorus lengths. The guide for each soloist was a brief ensemble part which introduces him and which gave him an area of musical pitch.
>
> (Williams 1961: 2–3)

Improvisation is accordingly 'not typified by unrestrained freedom' (Soules 2004: 271) and instead requires a constant mindfulness as to how the individual improvisations are determining or influencing the performance as a whole. Ornette Coleman explains in relation to his *Free Jazz* recording:

> The most important thing … was for us to play together, all at the same time, without getting in each other's way, and also have enough room for each player to ad lib alone – and to follow this idea for the duration of the album.
>
> (Quoted in Williams 1961: 3)

Jazz entails a 'constant negotiation between the freedoms accorded to the individual improviser and those of the group as a whole' (Stewart 2003: 93)[6] and requires both 'individual responsibility for the sounds produced and collective responsibility for the overall performance' (Prévost 2004: 358). Jazz improvisation accordingly provides 'the means towards both individual self-fashioning *and* communal liberation' (Gilroy 2000a: 497, emphasis added).

The relationship between the individual and the collective is of crucial importance to improvisation. According to Marcel Cobussen (2008a), '[i]mprovisation is about interaction. Musicians do not improvise in isolation' (6). Integral to improvisation are the emotional bonds forged with others through a shared experience of 'risk, vulnerability and trust' (6). Improvisation is not simply a spontaneous action, but is, writes Cobussen quoting Stanyek, an 'empathetic, hermeneutic interaction that is constituted upon a recognition of the powerful synergy and responsibility that arises when humans with multiple perspectives come together' (quoted 7). Fischlin and Heble even go so far as to assert that 'improvisation is less about original acts of self-creation than about an ongoing process of community building' (Fischlin and Heble 2004: 17).

The concept of community is invaluable to any discussion of improvisation. Serving as a 'site for the negotiation of individuality and collectivity through the multiplicitious interactions of improviser to improviser, improviser to audience, as well as audiences to one another' (Smith 2004: 236), improvisation is 'predicated on the exploration of alternative (and alterative) modes of being in community' (Fischlin and Heble 2004: 13). In the words of Fischlin and Heble:

> … jazz has always been about animating civic space with the spirit of dialogue and collaboration, and … the innovative working models of improvisation and collaboration developed by its creative practitioners have helped to promote a dynamic exchange of cultural forms, and to develop new, socially responsive forms of community building across national, cultural, and artistic boundaries. Both improvisation and collaboration, in short, involve shared responsibility for participation in

> community life, an ability to negotiate differences, and a willingness to accept the challenges of risk and contingency.
>
> (Fischlin and Heble 2004: 24)

The concept 'musicking', coined by Christopher Small, posits music not as a 'thing', but as 'an activity, something that people do' (2). Both noun and verb:

> To music is to take part, in any capacity, in a musical performance, whether by performing, by listening, by rehearsing or practicing, by providing material for performance (which is called composing), or by dancing. We might at times even extend its meaning to what the person is doing who takes the tickets at the door or the hefty men who shift the piano and the drums or the roadies who set up the instruments and carry out the sound checks or the cleaners who clean up after everyone else has gone. They, too, are all contributing to the nature of the event that is a musical performance.
>
> (Small 1998: 9, emphasis omitted)

Viewed this way, a musical performance becomes 'an encounter between human beings that takes place through the medium of sounds organized in specific ways' (10).

Musicking recognizes that not all improvised music aligns itself 'with antihegemonic resistance or critical strategies of alternative community building' (Fischlin and Heble 2004: 2). However, there exists an 'identifiable and radical form of improvisational practices' (2), which activates 'critical modes of resistance and dialogue' (2). Improvisation as dialogue captures the 'immediate inventions' (Berliner 1994: 349) within a 'trail of sound' (quoted in Bucholtz 2003: 456) or 'the groove', i.e. 'a shared sense of the beat' (456). It enables 'an ongoing interchange or conversation between and among performers' (456), which 'underscores the collaborative and communicative quality of improvisation' (Monson 1996: 2).[7]

The dialogic features of improvisation are the focus of Ingrid Monson's book, *Saying Something: Jazz Improvisation and Interaction* (1996). In this study, Monson discovers that the existing material, of which the jazz tradition is comprised, is often referred to as the jazz players' 'vocabulary'[8] and many musicians use 'the metaphor of conversation to describe aspects of the improvisational process' (73; see also Hatch 1998: 565; Weick 1998: 543, 547–49; Iyer 2004: 398–99; Landgraf 2011: 106; cf. Snow 2004: 49).[9] Jazz entails a 'musical language' (Monson 1996: 73) and improvisation constitutes 'musical conversation' (73). Muyumba adds:

> Jazz musicians create and extend musical 'conversations' among themselves while in performance, largely by building improvised solos that

> 'tell stories'. The ability to 'say something' through one's play relies on a tight network of understanding jazz history and musicological theories, rigorously shaped personal aesthetic, and a willingness to interrogate personal identity through performance.
>
> (Muyumba 2009: 18)

Finkelstein similarly argues that improvisation 'requires not only the ability to invent, but a language in which to invent. … To improvise successfully he must have a musical language that has become part of his thought processes' (Finkelstein 1948: 74). It is 'only because this body of musical language exists' (75) that a jazz musician can be 'fresh and inventive' (75). Thus, jazz improvisation requires both a tradition, i.e. 'musical material' (73), and 'a *common language*' (73, emphasis added). Musician Andy Laking agrees:

> To play within be-bop's complicated framework one has to understand every aspect of it. I know too that if the entire band doesn't share this understanding, then the whole thing can easily fall apart. It's like a *language* in that respect.
>
> (Laking 2005, emphasis added)

The 'ideal bebop number'[10] (Belgrad 1998: 189) has been described as a 'musical conversation among the musicians' (198) and Demsey likens the performance of an improvised jazz solo to 'the delivery of a concise, eloquent answer to a question in conversation' (Demsey 2000: 788). Just as a spoken response 'requires knowledge of the issue at hand, a powerful vocabulary, and a quick mind' (788), so too the jazz improviser must have 'a working knowledge of harmony, an innate feel for form and melodic line, a strong technique, a quick, relaxed mind, and a deep sense of history' (789). 'Dizzy' Gillespie mirrors this in his description of the musicking taking place in the after-hours jam sessions of 1940s NYC:

> What we were doing at Minton's was playing, seriously, creating a new dialogue among ourselves, blending our ideas into a new style of music. You only have so many notes, and what makes a style is how you get from one note to the other. … We invented our own way of getting from one place to the next. … Musically, we were changing the way that we spoke, to reflect the way that we felt. New phrasing came in with the new accent. Our music had a new accent.
>
> (Gillespie 1996: 561–62)

Thus, as Belgrad (1998: 189) points out, '[o]nce a conversational dynamic is understood to be the structural model for bebop, it becomes clear that other bebop innovations developed to enhance the conversation'.

Musical interaction or conversation between improvising musicians typically takes the form of 'improvisational antiphony, or call-and-response' (Belgrad 1998: 187). This mode of interaction, focused upon and sharpened in the after-hours jam sessions of the bebop era, made for better improvisers; musicians 'further increased the expressiveness of their solo utterances by developing a larger vocabulary of rhythms, tones, and timbres' (189). It was in the jam session that participating musicians engaged in 'the competitive give-and-take of "cutting"' (180), a form of 'musical duelling', which was prevalent during that time (180). 'Cutting' tested the 'skill and creativity' (180) of the individual musicians and it was through these 'cutting contests' that 'musicians established and maintained a hierarchy of professional competence' (DeVeaux 1997: 209). Reputations were both made and broken in these sessions[11] and '[f]or younger musicians still learning their craft, the trial by fire of the jam session was as much a part of their training as practising scales' (211).[12]

The competition may have been fierce in the jam session, but 'the ultimate purpose was to raise the quality of performance all around' (211). Solo improvisation thus exists not in its singularity, but in relation to the collective performance. Argues Belgrad:

> As a vision of sociality, the antiphonal structure of bebop suggests an intersubjective dynamic, one in which the individual and community empower one another. Each presence enliven the others, creating a whole that is animated by a collective energy without which the individual expression would not itself exist
>
> (Belgrad 1998: 191)

One could even go further to argue that, without these cutting contests, bebop would not exist as a musical genre. Cutting contests of the bebop jam session cut into and made possible the collective 'saying something' (Monson 1996: 2) of bebop improvisation, even while denying their singular or 'immediate inventions' (Berliner 1994: 349). In other words, if jazz improvisation existed solely in its immediacy or singularity we would not be in a sufficient relation with it to 'hear' what it says. Alternatively, if such music was devoid of all innovation then it would cease to survive or attract listeners. Thus, as the 'cutting contests' make evident, jazz improvisation only 'say[s] something' (Monson 1996: 2), only communicates, through the being-with of the individual and the collective, tradition and innovation, competition and co-operation. Jazz improvisation consequently becomes '"controlled freedom" ... just like conversation' (Hancock, quoted in Monson 1996: 81). As with conversation, it communicates solely through this relation.[13]

Improvisation as dialogue or communication not only entails 'saying something', but also listening: '*to oneself* as well as to other people' (Weick

1998: 547, emphasis in original).[14] Notes one musician interviewed by Berliner: 'You have to listen to other people very closely. If you're not doing that, you're not playing jazz' (quoted in Berliner 1994: 7). Adds Wynton Marsalis, also in an interview with Berliner:

> Playing is like speaking … As we are talking now, I only know what I am going to say a second before I say it. People who don't do it like this can be the worse people to talk to. When you're talking, they're thinking about what they are going to tell you next, instead of listening to what you are saying.
>
> (Quoted in Berliner 1994: 401; see also Weick 1998: 549)

This is why Julie Lassonde, a movement improviser and performance artist – as well as a lawyer – lists listening as the 'grounding rule'[15] of improvisational practice. For her, 'improvisation is about being in the moment and listening' (Lassonde 2010: 1).[16]

Deep Listening ® is a philosophy and practice developed by 'improvising composer' Pauline Oliveros (2005: xix).[17] It entails an 'intense form of commitment and responsibility to – as well as interaction with – all that surrounds us: people, environments, nature, the sounds of daily life' (Fischlin and Heble 2004: 11). According to Oliveros,

> *Deep Listening* … is learning to expand the perception of sounds to include the whole space/time continuum of sound – encountering the vastness and complexities as much as possible. Simultaneously one ought to be able to target a sound or sequence of sounds as a focus within the space/time continuum and to perceive the detail or trajectory of the sound or the sequence of sounds. Such focus should always return to, or be within the whole of the space/time continuum.
>
> Such expansion means that one is connected to the whole of the environment and beyond.
>
> (Oliveros 2005: xxiii)

Deep Listening thus demands attunement, not only to the singularity of the situation, but also to the context and community within which music is made. From 'deep listening' springs compassion and understanding (xxv). 'In this way', she writes, 'discovery and exploration can take place. New fields of thought can be opened and the individual may be expanded and find opportunity to connect in new ways to communities of interest. Practice enhances openness' (xxv).

Whereas this chapter interrogated the structure of freedom in improvisation, the following chapter examines the freedom of structure in law. Although various legal theorists recognize instances of imprecision in relation to judicial precedent and discretion in law, common among all, as noted by Weick (1998) in another context, 'is that they attempt to acknowledge the existence of improvisation, but do so without giving up on the prior commitment to stability and order' (551). 'The result', argues Weick, 'when theorists graft mechanisms for improvisation onto concepts that basically are built to explain order, is a caricature of improvisation that ignores nuances highlighted [above]' (551). These caricatures, as will be detailed in the next chapter, continue to view improvisation as singular and extemporary breaches of law's order and control. Imagined in Chapter 3 was a more complex and layered vision of legal improvisation, one that does 'more with the simultaneous presence of seeming opposites' (551) than 'simply label them as paradoxes' (551). Using the structure–freedom paradox as a point of departure and applying it, first, to the doctrines of judicial precedent and discretion and then to the specific case of the NYC 'police cards', Chapter 6 shows legal improvisation to be an active ingredient in common-law judicial decision-making.

Chapter 6

The structure–freedom paradox[1] in law

Much has been written on the musical aspects of law or the relationship between law and music (Levinson and Balkin 1991; Goodrich 1999; Manderson 2000; Manderson and Caudill 1999; Petersen 1998; Weisbrod 1999). Others have theorized law through theatre, film or performance (Balkin and Levinson 1999; Balkin 2003; Mc Namee 2004, 2009a, 2009b; Pratt and Johnston 2007; Peters 2008; Rogers 2008; Leiboff and Nield 2010). Lawyers, however, hardly ever engage with the improvisational qualities of law. This is not to say that lawyers do not theorize improvisation. The issue of whether copyright law sufficiently protects improvised works, for example, occupies many (for example, Donat 1997; Rahmatian 2005; Arewa 2011). Yet, rarely do they use improvisation as a 'model' for theorizing law.

Rare and notable exceptions can be found in the 2010 Special Issue of *Critical Studies in Improvisation*/Études critiques en improvisation entitled '*Lex Non Scripta*, *Ars Non Scripta*: Law, Justice and Improvisation'.[2] In her introduction to the issue, Tina Piper (2010), who co-edited the collection along with Ellen Waterman, divides the 'modes in which the study of law and improvisation can and does take place' (2) into three different categories or approaches: (i) translational/descriptive; (ii) prescriptive; and (iii) formal. Piper notes cautiously that all three approaches may be present in any one study of law and improvisation. However, more often than not one mode of analysis dominates.

Of these methodological approaches, the first one, what Piper calls the 'law *as* improvisation' approach, employs improvisation 'as a metaphor for understanding, describing, and characterizing aspects of law that are challenging to comprehend' (2). Improvisation is translational in that concepts more at home in improvisational studies are applied to 'describe law in external terms, rather than in words purely internal to its discourses' (2). The reverse is also possible: 'Scholars could use the tools of legal theory (norm generation or legal subjectivity, for example) to understand how and why groups and individuals improvise' (3). Other normative legal concerns such as justice, democracy, resistance and ethics similarly provide translational tools for understanding the structure and power of improvisation.

The 'prescriptive' approach differs from the translational format in that it 'envisions using (or avoiding) law or improvisation *instrumentally* to achieve objectives such as justice, understanding (through dialogue) and peace (by resolving conflict)' (3, emphasis added). Piper refers to this type of argument as '"Law!" or "Improvisation!"' in that '"law" or "improvisation" could be used to improve the functioning of the other' (3). Tracey Nicholls's work (2010, 2012) typifies this line of inquiry. In her article, 'Speaking Justice, Performing Reconciliation: Twin Challenges for a Postcolonial Ethics' (2010), Nicholls suggests applying the 'behaviour and practices that constitute an "ethos of improvisation"' (2) in order to overcome the inadequacies or injustices of truth and reconciliation commissions. Improvisation, for Nicholls, works instrumentally to:

> ... provide tools to enhance justice and resolve conflict by training participants in the habits of improvisation: dialogue, sustained listening, widening of community, absence of judgment, and acceptance of a loss of control, providing insights into the conditions that should be present for improvisation to succeed.
>
> (Piper 2010: 3)

In its sociability and responsiveness to context, in other words, improvisation offers law the possibility of justice (Manderson 2010: 7).

The final mode of entry into the study of law and improvisation, according to Piper (2010), is the 'formal' approach. This inquiry, also referred to as 'improvisation *and* the law' or the 'law *of* improvisation' (3), 'investigates state-based or written acts of law-making and their effect on improvisation' (3). The impact of copyright law on improvisation would constitute one such study. Others may include the impact of city by-laws that 'restrict types of performances to specific types of venues' on the 'creation of improvised works' (3–4).

Regardless of the approach taken, all are united in their placement of law 'next to' improvisation, a common occurrence, says Manderson (2000), in scholarship focused on law and the arts, such as 'law and literature' or 'law and music'. Law, in other words, is theorized therein as an entity persistently separate and distinct from that which it is being compared, be it literature, music or otherwise (31). Each sphere may have 'certain aspects in common' with the other, and be able to teach the other 'certain things', but their separation 'treats them as fit subjects for comparison but not interaction' (31).[3]

Some limited legal scholarship exists, such as that of Manderson (2000), which perceives aesthetics not as a subject or object, but as a 'way of seeing'. In contrast to 'law and ... ' scholarship, which 'juxtaposes two nouns' (31), the 'aesthetic dimensions of law explore the behaviour of two *verbs*' (31, emphasis added). Such an approach assumes that 'a relationship of *inevitable interaction* is already present' (31, emphasis added). Aesthetics, in other words, 'is already in the law' (31). Thus, to Piper's typology of approaches offered above we must add one more, that of 'law *with* improvisation'. Placing law 'with' improvisation creates a relational association, which recognizes 'some subsisting relation and thence some commonality' (Fitzpatrick 2001b: 59) between the two concepts or disciplines.

Ben Authers's 'Truth in the Telling: Procedure, Testimony, and the Work of Improvisation in Legal Narrative' (2010) exemplifies the 'law with improvisation' approach, exposing how improvisation is already in the law, acting as a truth discourse or claim of truth. Writing about the legal trial as a 'privileged space for the public determination of legal truth' (1), Authers explains how 'improvised, contingent production of testimony' is valorised as 'essential to the construction of legal truth' (4). He writes:

> If, according to the common law tradition ... , responsibility is best determined in 'a fair and public hearing by an independent and impartial tribunal,' and the privileged form of evidence in this forum is contingent, conversationally produced testimony, then the space of the trial would seem to be one in which improvised forms of narrative carry with them significant institutional weight. Moreover, even in the face of legal realities that overtly discount improvised practice – witnesses do not always first meet and discuss their stories with the lawyers examining them in the courtroom,[4] and defence lawyers have access to certain prosecution evidence (and often vice versa) in advance of the trial that allows them to prepare for testimony – the *appearance* of improvisation through testimony and the recollection of memory remains and has force. These procedural appearances constitute the substance of the law. ... In a way, it doesn't matter if the production of testimony is 'really' performing improvisation in the courtroom. What is important is that judicial structures characterise the presentation of persuasive testimonial evidence as contingent and conversational, as collaboratively improvised testimonies that are sufficiently legally persuasive to form the basis of a judicial decision, and so legal truth.
>
> (Authers 2010: 4, emphasis in original)

It is with this 'law with ... ' category that *Justice as Improvisation* sits most comfortably. Not purely translational, it refuses applications of improvisation as *metaphor*[5] to better understand complex areas of law. It also does not prescribe that law *should* be more improvisational, as does the prescriptive approach. Nor is its aim to demonstrate the formal impact of the law on improvisation. Instead, what follows re-imagines law and justice as fundamentally improvisational in nature. It does so, particularly in this chapter, through the formal structure of the most basic of legal mechanisms, judicial decision-making.

While the trope of structured or 'organized freedom' (Fischlin and Heble 2004: 32), as the complex mediation that takes place in an improvised performance between the individual choices made 'in the moment' by improvising soloist and the 'variegated contexts that feed into that moment' (30), is readily employed in critical improvisation studies, lawyers and legal theorists rarely apply such to descriptions of law. Ideally, law should be free from freedom. All decisions and actions, in other words, should be structured in accordance with pre-determined rules and procedures (precedent), which rein in or control any unpredictability (discretion).[6] This seemingly straightforward account of precedent and discretion nonetheless belies the rather complex relationship of law to improvisation. For every lawyer or legal theorist who condemns discretion in action and judgment (see, for example, the discussion below on judicial activism), there are others, such as legal realists (Frank 1949) or critical legal theorists, who applaud any inventive techniques in law. Margulies (1997), Beyer (2000), Bucholtz (2003) and Silbey and Ewick (2003), for example, apply jazz as metaphor in relation to law and legal theory to highlight the possibility of invention and transformation in our current legal culture, as a means of making it more responsive and hospitable to the 'other' of legal discourse. Law and literature proponents similarly celebrate the relationship between invention and law. Eberle and Grossfeld (2006), for instance, emphasize the parallels between poetic invention and law and the 'mutual influence' (401) poetry and law exert on one another. Aristodemou, in turn, conceives law as a form of literary invention and her book *Law and Literature: Journeys from Her to Eternity* (2000) 'examines the law-making qualities of fiction to explore the fictionality of law' (back cover).

The lack of consensus between lawyers, judges and legal theorists as to the role improvisation or creative invention plays in law actually flows from the very nature of law. Illuminated by the discussion below, precedent and discretion will be shown to be neither purely structured nor perfectly free, rendering applicable the structure–freedom paradox – most commonly associated with improvisation in CSI – to law and legal theory.[7]

The freedom of precedent

As reasoned and rule-bound, the common-law tradition is often viewed as antithetical to improvisation (Soules 2004: 270). One structural device relied upon to effect this so-called determinacy is that of legal precedent or *stare decisis*.[8] Precedent is defined as an 'adjudged case or decision of a court, considered as furnishing an example or authority for an identical or similar case afterwards arising from a similar question of law' (Black 1990: 1176). In its reliance on past legal decisions, precedent assures that 'like cases will be treated alike, and that similarly situated individuals are subject to the same legal consequences' (Rehnquist 1986: 347). In instances where a dispute is fundamentally distinct from all previous cases, judges have the authority and duty to make new law. This is called *primae impressionis*, a 'case of a new kind, to which no established principle of law or precedent directly applies, and which must be decided entirely by *reason* as distinguished from authority' (Black 1990: 1189, emphasis added). Thus, even novel cases should follow a structure of reason or general legal principles (see, for example, Dworkin 1986).

The rationale behind the doctrine of precedent is quite straightforward, namely judges should not have 'unconstrained discretion to enforce whatever rules they please' (Nelson 2001: 4). It encourages the view that judges should not spontaneously invent law and any judicial activism[9] should be strictly controlled or reined in. Nitta explains:

> One of the most important values in our political system is that all people should be subject to 'rules of law and not merely the opinions of a small group of men who temporarily occupy high office'. The doctrines of precedent and *stare decisis* support this value by: (1) fostering impartiality by providing a neutral source of authority by which judges must justify their decisions and (2) limiting the actual impact that a single person has on shaping the law. Therefore, by offering a framework in which judges must decide a case, precedent minimizes the influence of personal bias or beliefs on judicial decisions and consequently promotes the public's faith in our system of justice.
>
> (Nitta 2001: 798–99, citations omitted)

Precedent thereby limits the scope of judicial power. It restricts the role of a judge to determine the law in each case, 'not according to his [or her] own judgment, but according to the known laws' (809). Nitta argues that '[j]udicial power, therefore, does not allow a judge to invent laws, but to determine only what the law is in accordance with laws previously pronounced' (809–10). Moreover, precedent is often viewed as integral to justice; it 'encourages the public to have faith that justice will be done and consequently allows the public to trust their affairs to the adjudication of the courts' (798).

Precedent also buttresses the separation between legislative and judicial power. Once again relying on Nitta (2001): 'The Framers [of the Constitution] intended that, unlike legislators who are empowered to make law, judges are limited to pronouncing the law after interpretation and application of the law to the facts of the particular case' (810). Judges, in other words, must judge or 'exercise 'judgment' in determining what the law is rather than 'will' what the law should be' (810). Failure to heed such precedent is denounced as 'akin to inventi[on]' (Mandell 2001: 1290).

The conceptual distinction between judge-made and judge-found law reinforces the union of law and certainty or predictability. Remaining strong, this distinction structures much of contemporary legal and political thought (Anderson 1987: 131). The debate over judge-made and judge-found law is of relevance to this present chapter as it supports an understanding of law as that which opposes improvisation and works to 'locate law, invest it with legitimacy, and so lend it stability' (Ball 1989: 2280).

The 'view of most laymen and the anthem of the legal conservative' (Dworkin 1986: 114) in contemporary society positions law in opposition to any invented or improvised elements. Law, it is argued, should simply be 'found' or 'discovered' by judges and 'invention' in and of law is nothing short of 'stagecraft or tyranny' (5). According to this view, '[t]he law is the law' (114) and judges ought only to apply it and not change it to 'fit their own ethics or politics' (114). Whereas most lawyers and legal theorists admit that, at times, there may be no law to be enforced, in these instances, judges must decide novel cases in a manner that 'engages his [or her] own political or moral convictions as little as possible and gives as much deference as possible to institutions conventionally authorized to make law' (119). Thus, any law 'made' by judges in these cases should be what she or he believes 'the actual legislature then in power would choose' (119) or, failing that, what best represents the 'will of the people as a whole' (119).

At the heart of the debate over judge-made and judge-found law is the alleged threat of 'judicial activism' in relation to democracy and justice.[10] Activist courts, it is argued, 'announce principles and reach decisions not plausibly derived from the Constitution' (Bork 2003: 19); instead, they 'tend to enact the values of the dominant social class' (19). According to Bork, the present dominant class is 'the intelligentsia, and its values are frequently opposed to the moral assumptions of much of the rest of the electorate' (19). The consequences of this judicial invention in law are far-reaching:

> The Constitution is the most revered document in our society. When the Supreme Court, rightly or wrongly, enunciates a principle as constitutional law, people assume that the principle is in fact of constitutional stature, that it is, therefore, basic to our freedoms. In that way, the morality of the cultural 'elites' are [sic] spread to the rest of society.
>
> (Bork 2003: 20)

In relation to the United States Supreme Court, Bork argues that:

> ... [it] is not supposed to invent law but to apply it, and there is no law that underlies those decisions; they are merely expressions of the judges' will, judicial invasions of territory that belongs to the moral choice of the American people and their elected representative.
>
> (Ibid.)

Such invention of law 'from whole cloth' (Baker 2002: 140) is seen to 'rightfully undermine our confidence in courts' (140); it would give judges licence 'to do what they please' (Kaufman 1980: 81) and would facilitate a perception of law as that which 'contained no set and enduring truth' (Fitzpatrick 2001b: 87).

Precedent, as outlined above, seemingly provides the common law with the structure and/or form necessary to strictly manage and control any unpredictable elements. A curious quality of precedent as a source of law, though, deserves note:

> So far as it expresses the opinion of wise or learned men, or so far as it expresses the opinion of the community, it may be a source of law; but its peculiar force as a judicial precedent lies, not in its accordance with philosophy or common sense; not in the fact that it is right, not that it ought to have been made, but that it *has* been made. Of course the decision of a court may unite the character of a judicial precedent with the character of an expression of wise thought or of popular sentiment, but often these characters are separated.
>
> (Gray 1895: 27–28, emphasis in original)

Accordingly, it matters little whether the precedent is 'good' or 'just' only that it 'is', that is, exists *as* decision or judgment.[11]

The question as to why courts should unquestionably respect or follow 'unfortunate, unwise, and unjust' precedent was the focal point of David Lyon's article 'Formal Justice and Judicial Precedent' (1985), wherein he writes:

> ... treating like cases alike is often regarded as a requirement, indeed perhaps the central or most fundamental requirement, of *justice*. When so viewed, the practice of precedent is placed on a moral footing. It implies that the failure to follow precedent is not merely unwise but positively wrong.
>
> (Lyons 1985: 497, emphasis added)

The doctrine of *stare decisis*, for Lyons, 'implies moral grounds for respecting flawed precedents' (498) and intimates that 'there might be moral grounds for respecting morally deficient aspects of a legal system' (498). This is what he terms the 'formal justice argument' and he finds support for this argument in the jurisprudential literature of, for example, Neil MacCormick and others (498).

Notwithstanding this argument, freedom embeds itself into the very structure of precedent through the 'problematic notion of a "like" or "similar" case' (499). Lyons explains:

> The basic problem is simple. Take any case that is to be decided and any other case that has already been decided. However similar they may be,

> in respects that may seem important, they will also be very different in some respects, and vice versa. Some general facts about one case will be general facts about the other, and some general facts about one case will not be general facts about the other. So objective grounds exist both for *and* against regarding *any* past case as 'similar' to one that has been decided.
>
> (Lyons 1985: 499, emphasis in original)

What follows is the 'structure–freedom paradox' (Fischlin and Heble 2004: 33) at work in common law:

> … a principle prescribing that decisions follow those that have already been made in 'similar cases' can seem literally impossible to follow. If all factual aspects of cases were relevant, and any similarity and any difference between cases were sufficient to make them similar and different, respectively, then each past case would both be and not be a precedent for any case to be decided. On that interpretation, the principle would be impossible to follow because it would be, strictly speaking, incoherent.
>
> (Lyons 1985: 499)

Accordingly, the logic of the formal justice argument matters little to the actual practice of law: 'Courts might speak of "following prior decisions in similar cases," and the like, but any actual use of precedents would be either confused or arbitrary' (499).

Lyons's article proceeds to detail ways in which the judges' freedom to apply precedent arbitrarily can be restricted or limited through what he calls 'grounding aspects', that is, factual aspects as grounds for certain legal consequences, which would count as precedent in latter case with similar factual circumstances (500). Similarly, interpretational precedents as to the specific wording of a legal text, its origins and applications, etc. should be followed in future encounters with the same legal text. In the words of Lyons, '[t]o follow an interpretational precedent amounts to following a court's judgment as to the legal difference such factors make to the reading of a text' (500–1).[12]

Even where clear 'grounding aspects' exist, which is not always the case, freedom once again surfaces in instances of conflicting precedent, or 'past decisions that provide, in effect, incompatible guidance for a judicial decision' (501). In situations where different decisions exist as to similar cases, precedent cannot completely structure the judicial decision-making process: 'while it may be possible to follow each precedent, it will be impossible to follow all precedents' (501).

Many legal theorists, in addition to Lyons, recognize the inherent flexibility of even the most unshakeable precedent. For example, James Dennis writes in his article, 'Interpretation and Application of the Civil Code and the Evaluation of Judicial Precedent' (1993):

> The common-law theory of precedent allows the court in the controversy before it to exercise a great deal of flexibility in deciding which previous case is sufficiently similar to be chosen as a precedent and in formulating a rule based upon the material facts of the precedent case.
>
> (Dennis 1993: 4)

Citing Julius Stone's 'classical analysis' (1964) of the 1932 case of *Donoghue v. Stevenson*,[13] Dennis notes that 'the material facts of a case usually may be stated at various levels of generality, each of which is correct for that case' (4). Precedent, in this sense, can be a very fluid doctrine: 'Insofar as the rule or *ratio decidendi* of the precedent case is determined by each material fact, a number of *rationes* may be extracted depending on how the material facts are selected and generalized by the subsequent courts' (4). Accordingly, any, what Dennis calls, 'honest description' of the use of precedent in common law 'must admit the following':

> First, there is no single correct method for determining the rule for which the case stands. Consequently, there usually can be more than one acceptable formulation of the rule to be extracted from a precedent, and any rule extracted from a case is subject to two types of creative judicial activity: narrowing of the rule by admitting some exception not before considered and widening of the rule by discarding a restriction in the rule as formulated from the earlier case, on the ground that it has not been required previously by any rule of statute or precedent.
>
> (Dennis 1993: 5)

In light of the above, it is obvious that precedent is not as structured and inflexible as is typically imagined. Judges are in fact free to 'expand, contract, and manipulate the *ratio decidendi* of a previously decided case' (5).

It follows, then, that law can neither dispense with, nor be completely determined by, the device of precedent (Deutscher 2005: 98). In the words of Rogers (2008), '[w]hile norms and legal precedents may be applied they must be re-read, re-created or re-constructed for each new set of circumstances' (431). The legal decision thus always contains the possibility of being 'otherwise' (Fitzpatrick 2001b: 89). Novelty and creativity, however, must be subordinated to the structure of tradition and precedent in order for law to remain legitimate and commanding in contemporary society. Law, in other words, cannot be seen to be produced 'on the spur of the moment'. To be just, it must apply fairly and equally and be known by all in advance (Pue 2000: 17).

The structure of discretion

Integral to the legal concept of judicial precedent is that of discretion, for 'the primary purpose of *stare decisis* is to protect the rule of law by avoiding an endless series of changes in judicial decisions' (Nelson 2001: 4). Its purpose, in other words, is to 'increase the predictability' (Lyons 1985: 496) of judicial decision-making and eliminate or constrain the freedom (discretion) of the judge to decide a matter in an unpredictable fashion. The consequence of this curtailment of freedom is increased security, minimizing of risk and general avoidance of 'frustrating expectations' (496). Discretion not only concerns the decisions of judges and legislators, that is, the *creation* of case law, legislation, and procedural rules and regulations. It also applies to the *application* of written law by those in charge of administering them, such as police officers and legal bureaucrats, as well as judges.[14] The presence or absence of freedom in the administration of written law, that is, its deployment or utilization in a manner which officials see fit, is what distinguishes 'law on the books' from 'law in action' (although, judicial precedent, as both object of law and activity that produces law, reveals that this distinction is not always so clear).

Common-law jurisdictions embrace the doctrine of *stare decisis* in order to 'restrain the discretion that legal indeterminacy would otherwise give judges', as Nelson's study of precedent in Antebellum America chronicles (Nelson 2001: 8). Rules or protocols, such as those established by precedent, are presumably antithetical to discretion (Epstein 2006: 19). The antipathy of judicial discretion to rules has both negative and positive consequences. Asks Pardo (2009): 'Is the mere existence of discretion the first stop on the road to judicial tyranny? Or is it an indispensible element in the pursuit of justice?' (430). Evidencing the dual nature of discretion is, on the one hand, the maxim engraved on the United States Department of Justice which reads, 'Where law ends tyranny begins' (quoted 430). This self-same discretion, seen as tyrannous to rule, has conversely inspired others to praise it as the handmaiden of justice and fairness (see, for example, Tyler et al. 2007: 459–60; Ramirez 2009: 594; Carson 2011: 15).

The complex and contradictory nature of judicial discretion has preoccupied many a legal scholar and jurisprude. Almost every law-school alumnus will recall, perhaps begrudgingly, the 'Hart–Dworkin debate' as to, *inter alia*, the existence of judicial discretion.[15] I do not wish to resurrect or comment upon such matters here. Instead, this account will concentrate on a form of discretion deemed all the more pressing in contemporary (post-September 11) society, namely the broader political and legal discretion given to government leaders in cases of emergency, especially instances of so-called terrorism.

What follows is not an exposition on the so-called 'war on terror'; and the description of the issues relates only to the question of the compatibility of legal rules with improvisation. Specifically, this section examines one particular instantiation of legal improvisation, that of the 'deference thesis' in the United States, or the idea that 'during emergencies the legislature and judiciary should defer to the executive' (Posner 2012: 214). This doctrine effectively provides the leader of a country, such as the President of the United States (who controls the executive), with unfettered discretion to act as he or she wishes in such circumstances. The aim here is not to examine or criticize in detail the 'deference thesis', or explain divergent approaches in other jurisdictions. Instead, I will look to the doctrine to examine the relationship between structure and freedom, rules and improvisation, as it relates to the issue of discretion in contemporary law.

This discussion of the 'deference thesis' and the war on terror may, on the surface, seem to fit uncomfortably with the preceding discussion of judicial precedent. However, when applied to the structure–freedom paradox in law, its placement becomes clear. Terrorism is construed in the West as an improvised threat to law and legality, one which demands equally improvised responses 'that can neither be described nor be controlled by rules' (306–7). Terrorism *as* improvisation is therefore positioned in opposition to, and outside of, law, rules and structure. Precedent is deemed ineffectual in the face of wholly unprecedented threats (307). Thus, government leaders must have complete freedom from law when responding to incidences, either imagined or real, of terrorism. What follows will complicate this positioning of discretion as unqualified freedom as against a purely unresponsive and inflexible law.

This examination of discretion and legal improvisation will centre around two articles on the 'deference thesis', namely Eric Posner's 'Deference to the Executive in the United States after September 11: Congress, the Courts, and the Office of Legal Counsel' (2012) and Stephen Holmes's 'In Case of Emergency: Misunderstanding Tradeoffs in the War on Terror' (2009). Posner's article explicitly responds to many of the points made by Holmes on the relationship between rules and improvisation. Accordingly, I will first summarize the relevant portions of Holmes's article and then move onto Posner's critique of such. I will then add my own thoughts as to why neither argument stands up to scrutiny when it comes to theorizing legal improvisation.

Holmes's position on the 'deference thesis' is as follows:

> Far from being a carefully calibrated response to the terrorist threat, the executive–discretion agenda exaggerates the upsides and discounts the downsides of unregulated executive discretion. The 'game' of counter-terrorism cannot be successfully conducted by ad hoc decisions made in defiance of all rules and outside of all institutionalized decision-making procedures, practices, and institutions.
>
> (Holmes 2009: 354)

Throughout his article, Holmes attempts to prove that '[r]ule-governed counterterrorism is both feasible and desirable' (354). He cites the emergency room in which discretion is minimized and doctors and nurses strictly adhere to rules and protocols in the face of 'disorienting crisis' (302) as an example of the benefits incurred by following rules in times of emergency. His discussion of emergency-room procedures is meant to demonstrate that successful responses in situations of emergency require 'not improvisation on the fly but coordinated adherence to pre-established procedures rendered quasi-instinctive by practice and repetition' (302).

Applying emergency-room techniques to the issue of 'effective management of national-security emergencies' (303), Holmes criticizes those who denounce rules in favour of flexibility when confronting the terrorist threat. As their argument goes:

> ... anyone who favors adhering to inherited legal rules, such as habeas corpus or the Geneva convention, must be frivolously underestimating the danger we face. In confronting the terrorist threat, effectiveness requires flexibility, and flexibility presupposes the shedding of rules.
>
> (Holmes 2009: 303)

Holmes admits that some rules, slavishly followed, 'would impede apt responses to danger and disaster' (303). However, he holds steadfast to the idea that 'rules may play an emphatically positive role during crises and calamities' (303), as is evidenced by the emergency-room example.

Holmes's analysis is not necessarily incompatible with the vision of improvisation offered by critical improvisational scholars (see, for example, Chapter 5 of this book). He recognizes, although on this he sometimes waivers, that general rules and situation-specific improvisations are not mutually exclusive. For example, he writes:

> There is no reason why mechanically following protocols designed to protect harried nurses from negligently administering the wrong blood type should preclude the same nurses from improvising unique solutions to the unique problems of a particular trauma patient. Drilled-in emergency protocols provide a psychologically stabilizing floor, shared by co-workers, on the basis of which untried solutions can then be improvised. In other words, there is no reason to assert, at least not as a matter of general validity, that the importance of flexibility excludes reliance on rules during emergencies, including national-security emergencies.
>
> (Holmes 2009: 309)

It is here that Holmes best seems to understand the paradox that is the law of the extempore:

> The extreme urgency of a threat requires rather than excludes adherence to pre-existing rules, if only to permit emergency workers, with no time to think, to coordinate their responses swiftly and effectively. Second, when crafted over time by emergency responders who have learned from their mistakes, non-negotiable rules can sometimes prove more effective, pragmatic and adaptive than unregulated and unmonitored discretion. And, third, rules to be applied in case of emergency can significantly increase the flexibility of operational personnel in a crisis situation by freeing them from their own psychological compulsions and behavioural rigidities.
>
> (Holmes 2009: 310–11)

In the end, Holmes's article does shed some light on the structure–freedom paradox in law. Yet, there remains much more to be said on the subject.

Posner's more recent article allows us to delve slightly deeper into the relationship between law and improvisation, at least as it relates to discretion and the 'deference thesis'. Posner reads Holmes as saying 'rules dominate standards at moments of crisis' and '[a]n executive that is unconstrained, that is, not bound by rules, will make worse policy choices than an executive that is bound by rules' (Posner 2012: 213). While I do not necessarily agree with Posner's interpretation of Holmes's argument,[16] he does make some valid and interesting points.

Posner takes from Holmes the idea that 'when the stakes are high and time is of the essence, agents should follow rules rather than improvise' (218). What this means for him is that, if 'the benefits of lack of constraint are zero, then the deference thesis is clearly wrong. Constraints both prevent executive abuses such as violations of civil liberties and ensure that counter-terrorism policy is most effective' (218). Posner does not accept this. He frames his objection as follows:

> The arresting medical protocol example helps clarify the tradeoffs involved, but it remains merely an illustration of the familiar rules versus standards tradeoff that has been a staple of legal literature since time immemorial. A rule is a norm that directs the decisionmaker to ignore some relevant policy considerations when deciding on a course of action; a standard is a norm that directs the decisionmaker to take into account all relevant policy considerations when deciding on a course of action.
>
> (Posner 2012: 218)

This distinction prescribes that '[r]ules should be used to govern recurrent behavior, and standards to govern unusual behavior' (219). He therefore advocates a more woolly and overlapping model of the rules versus standards distinction.

Posner demonstrates how many rules and protocols, such as those governing the emergency room, are in fact 'presumptions, which may be overcome by the press of events' (221). No rule, he argues, is unalterable. Even Holmes's example of the first-order rule to 'always wash your hands before inserting a stent' (Holmes 2009: 310). What if, Posner suggests, the water in the hospital is tainted? What if it is discovered in the midst of an emergency that 'the patient has a rare allergy to the only soap in the emergency room; or, for that matter, the emergency room runs out of soap' (Posner 2012: 220–21). In such instances, common sense dictates that doctors and nurses deviate from protocols; otherwise, the patient's life wound be endangered to an even greater extent (and they risk being sued) (221). As Posner rightly points out, '[t]his is why medical professionals are so highly trained; if one could really treat patients by following algorithms, one would not need doctors who have *vast training and experiences that supplies them with the judgment and the ability to improvise*' (221, emphasis added).

As an alternative to strict adherence to rules that may 'unavoidably produce wrong results if they are not applied sensitively' (221), Posner suggests that, in 'times of high stress' or when the 'stakes are high', rules often turn out to be *presumptions*, which are themselves subject to principles or standards (223). These presumptions can be freely violated if 'circumstances suggest that the presumption is based on factual assumptions that turn out not to be true in the particular setting in which the decisionmaker finds himself' (221). This is quite a tricky suggestion, and Posner offers no further insight into the issue or how it might apply to the legal realm.

Perhaps it would be more productive to proceed to Posner's distinction between 'rule-development' and 'rule-application' (221) as they apply to freedom and structure in law. In emergencies described above the rule-development stage takes place usually, but not always, *before* a response is required and the rule applied. In contrast, the rule-application stage takes place *during* emergencies.[17] What follows from Holmes's argument, writes Posner, is that 'rule application should be controlled by protocol, so the executive does not need (much) discretion while pre-emergency, rule development does not need to be rushed and secret, so the executive can collaborate with Congress' (222). Posner finds this argument problematic for the reason that officials can follow protocols in emergencies *only if* 'the emergency is the same as earlier emergencies' (222). September 11, for him, was unprecedented and thus no rules could have anticipated or been developed in advance of the emergency (cf. Holmes 2009: 307). He explains:

> Protocols were worthless because nothing like the attack had ever happened before. … The government could not follow rules; it had to improvise subject to a vague standard – protect the public while maintaining civil liberties to the extent possible. Improvise it did – instituting

> detentions, sweeps, profiling, surveillance, and many other policies on an unprecedented (in peacetime, if that was what it was) scale.
>
> (Posner 2012: 224)

The discussion above highlights the complexity of legal improvisation in relation to discretion. Although both Holmes and Posner focus on situations of emergency, specifically terrorist attacks in the West, their analyses are applicable to the structure–freedom paradox in the common law. Holmes advocates adherence to rules as opposed to discretion whenever possible, and views the truly unprecedented as a rare and exceptional occurrence. Posner, on the other hand, holds that rules are only valuable where the emergency is the same as an earlier emergency and where precedent exists to guide the action; this seldom occurs, to his mind, and thus extensive and frequent discretion is a necessity.

The main issue of contention between the two theorists appears to be what constitutes the truly new and unprecedented. For Posner, rules constantly frustrate 'because there always seems to be some new, unanticipated case where the application of rules leads to an injustice' (Posner 2012: 219), whilst Holmes argues that even events such as September 11, however novel, are not unprecedented (Holmes 2009: 307). This divergence goes to the very heart of the structure–freedom paradox and not only influences how discretion is conceptualized in the common law, but precedent too. Is each individual case truly unique and unprecedented, or is newness rare in the legal system? How one answers this question determines the role and amount of legal improvisation permitted in the law. Yet, if we re-imagine improvisation, as CSI scholars and Derrida have, as neither strict adherence to nor complete disregard for rules, protocols, principles or laws. Then, the question is not about the novelty of each individual case, but instead about the very nature of judging. How do we determine where discretion and precedent begin and end? Do judges themselves even know?

The NYC 'police cards' revisited

To assist with the above questions, I return to the case study. To recap briefly, the NYC cabaret licensing laws first came into effect on 1 January 1927, in response to the 'too much running "wild"' supposedly taking place in NYC nightclubs (Chevigny 1991: 55–56). Mayor Walker re-drafted these laws in early 1931, giving the NYPD Division of Licenses control of the cabaret licensing from the NYC Licensing Bureau. Then, on 20 June 1940, the Police Commissioner created the NYPD Cabaret Rules and Regulations, which regulated the employees of cabarets and nightclubs through the Cabaret Employee's Identification Card (the 'police card') (Cohen 1993: 18). This system of legal regulation gave the NYPD the power to fingerprint and photograph employees of licensed venues and to issue identification cards to persons of 'good character' (Chevigny 1991: 58). No person convicted of a felony or certain misdemeanours and offences could be employed in a cabaret, 'except in the discretion of the police commissioner' (*Friedman v. Valentine* 1941: 439).

The NYC 'police cards' were criticized on several levels. Lawyers, such as Maxwell Cohen, claimed in court on behalf of the owners, operators and employees of cabarets that the creation of the Cabaret Employee's Identification Card system of rules and regulations exceeded the rule making power of the police commissioner and were thereby illegal. In the alternative, they maintained that, if legal in their creation, the laws were, as developed, unconstitutional (*Friedman v. Valentine* 1941: 439; *Simone v. Kennedy* 1961: 840; see also Cohen 1993: 24). Outside the courtroom, musicians and concerned citizens argued that the NYPD applied the rules in a manner that was corrupt (Gelb 1960a: 1, 23; Gelb 1960b: 1, 33; Gelb 1960c: 1, 44; Nicholson 1995: 167), discriminatory (Peretti 1997: 138) and racist (Gourse 1997: 91). The 'police cards' were therefore criticized at both the stage of rule development and rule application, as per Posner's distinction above. I will focus on the first set of objections here, or those made and responded to in a court of law as to constitutionality or legality of the NYC 'police cards'.

The case of the NYC 'police cards' offers many examples of legal improvisation and quite clearly evidences the common law's desire to absorb singularity as the unprecedented into the general only to re-create itself as the singular. To better understand the paradox of structure and freedom as it relates to judicial precedent and discretion, I wish to focus here on the leading judgment on the issue of the NYC 'police cards', namely that of *Friedman v. Valentine*. Justice Pecora presided over this case in the New York County Supreme Court on 10 November 1941; the decision was later upheld by the Appellate Division on 2 July 1943. The petitioners in this action were Samuel Friedman, president of the joint council of labour unions whose members worked in NYC cabarets, and an unnamed cook and waiter. The respondent, Lewis J. Valentine, was the police commissioner of NYC at the time.

The case of *Friedman v. Valentine* illustrates the legal improvisation inherent in the doctrines of judicial precedent and discretion. It also documents the difficulty of conceptually separating these doctrines into their rule-development and rule-application stages. Turning first to the relationship between discretion and legal improvisation, in *Friedman v. Valentine* (1941) the petitioners asked the court to restrain the NYPD police commissioner from 'enforcing rules promulgated by him for the regulation of cabarets' (439) on the grounds that the commissioner did not have the (rule-making) power to issue the regulations (440). As this was the first time this issue had been before a judge, there was no precedent to guide the court's reasoning. Instead, Justice Pecora used his discretion to rule on the discretion of the police commissioner to create the NYPD Cabaret Rules and Regulations. Where no previous precedent exists on an issue, the court must simultaneously develop and apply a new rule in the case at hand. Thus, any comment on the legality of the development of the cabaret-card laws is, quite curiously, also a comment on the judge's own discretionary power.

To decide the matter, Pecora J. looked to the legislation governing the wider powers of the police commissioner and the NYPD. Section 436 of the New York City Charter provides that:

> [t]he commissioner shall in his discretion issue, revoke and suspend licenses for … cabarets, … and make such rules and regulations for the supervision and operation of such … cabarets … as are not inconsistent with any other provision of law.
>
> (*New Honeymoon Danceland v. Valentine* 1945: 638)[18]

Section 436–1.0 of the Administrative Code of the City of New York further provides for the regulation of cabarets and the licensing thereof. Nothing in the section 'exclude[s] the right to promulgate rules to regulate cabarets' (440). 'In fact', writes Pecora J, interpreting the section broadly, '[it] recognizes by its terms the power of the police commissioner to exercise supervision over cabarets through the issuance of regulations' (440). Forgoing a narrow or literal reading of the legislation, Pecora J proceeds as follows:

> Section 436–1.0 does not constitute a complete regulatory provision governing the conduct of the cabaret business. It is merely a framework, leaving to the discretion of the police commissioner the devising of necessary details related to supervision … The power of the Legislature to confer authority upon an official to promulgate regulations to effectuate a policy expressed in a statute is too well settled to merit further discussion.
>
> (*Friedman v. Valentine* 1941: 440)

Of note, Section 436–1.0 does not explicitly confer power on the police commissioner to regulate the employment of cabaret employees. Instead, it grants the police commissioner discretion to promulgate regulations, but does not say how exactly this discretion is to be exercised. This section accordingly endeavours to capture under its authority unprecedented situations previously not contemplated or covered by the law. According to Pecora J., where a regulation is within the scope of legally delegated authority, the presumption is that there exist facts justifying the regulation (430). If not rebutted, the regulation is justified. In the case of *Friedman v. Valentine*, Pecora J. found that the petitioners could not show that the regulations were not justified 'by the conditions existing in the cabaret industry' (441). Accordingly, the NYPD Cabaret Rules and Regulations were held to be 'neither arbitrary not capricious' (441); the police commissioner was within his discretionary power to make such regulations and they, in turn, were legal.

As an exercise in (masking) legal improvisation, the reasoning is of intrigue. The power to make a rule becomes a justification for the rule itself. This is not unlike the unfettered discretion given to the executive branch of government (or the President) in situations of emergency, as discussed above. In such cases, the unprecedented justifies the discretion, which, in turn, perpetuates the unprecedented. Improvisation supports law while law propagates improvisation.

This paradoxical and self-sustaining bond between law and improvisation, structure and freedom, is further unpacked in relation to judicial precedent. In *Friedman v. Valentine*, Justice Pecora ruled on the question of whether the NYPD Cabaret Rules and Regulations were unconstitutional, that is, violated the due process clause of the Constitution by 'interfering with the right to pursue employment without interference by the police commissioner' (441). The right to employment was held to be conditional and therefore '[a]ny occupation may be reasonably regulated if others may be exposed to danger or misfortune by such calling' (441). More pointedly, he argued that '[t]he test of constitutionality is whether an evil exists and whether there is a logical relation between the eradication of the evil and the enactment of regulations intended to cure the condition' (441). The judge found that such a 'logical relation' did exist in the circumstances of the case 'as a result of certain evils which flourished in and followed the prohibition era' (439). Fingerprinting employees was thus found to be 'a lawful and proper exercise of power' (441) because 'establishing the identities of all persons connected with the cabaret business ... will result not only in purging the business of unfit elements, but will also aid effectively in the solution of crimes or offenses peculiarly connected with the operation of cabarets' (440).

In relation to the question of legal improvisation, as with the example of terrorism offered above by Holmes and Posner, 'evil' exists here only as an unprecedented potentiality. Pecora J. cites no particular instantiations of 'evil' existing in the clubs. Instead, he points to the *possibilities* on offer by unsupervised cabarets, such as:

> ... the ownership or control of cabarets by criminals and racketeers in the names of 'dummies' or 'fronts'; the employment of criminals and other undesirables in cabarets who come in contact with patrons under conditions conducive to criminality; and the growing use of cabarets as bases of operation by criminals who were acting in collusion with employees and concessionaires therein.
>
> (*Friedman v. Valentine* 1941: 439–40)

Justice Pecora thus applies the label of 'evil' as a mechanism for absorbing the unprecedented into the doctrine of legal precedent. Over-generalized categories, such as 'evil' (or 'reason'), which have no fixed or determinate meaning, produce a bond between the unprecedented and the legal such that singularity is absorbed into (il)legality, which, in turn, creates a new and (un)precedent-ed law.

As one final comment on precedent, the discussion above explains how initial judgments on an issue simultaneously develop and apply rules thereby folding the unprecedented into the newly formed precedent. Here, perhaps more surprisingly, applications of previously developed precedent also show themselves to be instances of legal improvisation. Chapter 2 makes note of the fact that the 1941 decision of *Friedman v. Valentine* would 'haunt almost every attempt to fight the Card system' (Cohen 1993: 22). This is demonstrated by *Simone v. Kennedy* (1961). In the latter case, Justice Fine of the New York County Supreme Court dismissed the plaintiffs' claim in a few short sentences:

> The claim that the regulations requiring fingerprinting and identification cards are unconstitutional and illegal has already been held to be without merit in *Matter of Friedman v. Valentine*. ... This court is bound by the determination of the Appellate Division that the regulations are valid. ... The court, accordingly, holds that the regulations herein attacked are constitutional and valid.
>
> (*Simone v. Kennedy* 1961: 840–41)

The judge frames his decision as an *inevitability*. He is 'bound' to make this judgment, he writes. However, as was noted above, precedent is not as structured and inflexible as often characterized. Judges are in fact free to decide otherwise; and to decide in favour of a particular precedent *is* improvising the law.

As the cases of *Friedman v. Valentine* (1941) and *Simone v. Kennedy* (1961) clearly evidence, it is impossible to escape the necessity of improvisation in judging. Yet, at the same time, to improvise completely, to fully escape the 'known and familiar' (Landgraf 2011: 93), this too is impossible. Thus, while there is much more to say on the subject and many more examples of the structure–freedom paradox, both in relation to the NYC cabaret laws and the common law more generally, recognition of this paradox only takes us so far. Instead, in order to creatively work through this paradox as one of impossible necessity, we must return to Derrida and to the La Villette Jazz Festival to ask the question critical improvisation scholars know all too well: 'Why, exactly, does improvisation matter?' (Heble 2005: 1).

Chapter 7

Justice *as* improvisation

Derrida's interest in justice is long-standing:

> It goes without saying that discourses on double affirmation, the gift beyond exchange and distribution, the undecidable, the incommensurable or the incalculable, on singularity, difference and heterogeneity are also, through and through, at least oblique discourses on justice.
>
> (Derrida 2002b: 235)

That said, by his own admission, '[he] began using the name or the word "justice" very late in [his] process' (Derrida 1999: 72). Derrida's 1989 lecture at the Cardozo Law School conference on 'Deconstruction and the Possibility of Justice' 'signposted a change in direction in deconstruction' (Douzinas 2005: 171), as Douzinas elaborates:

> … 'Force of Law' signified a clear turn towards political and ethical engagement, symbolized by the discussion of law and justice. After that talk, deconstruction became obsessed with questions of ethical responsibility, the meaning of friendship and the complex relationship with the other.[1]
>
> (Douzinas 2005: 171; cf. Hägglund 2008)[2]

Peter Goodrich concurs:

> There were other events and other headings, of course, but the dramaturgical setting of the law school and the question of justice raised by lawyers signaled an all-important shift in his work towards the political, towards the justice that, as he pointed out, precedes and exceeds mere law.
>
> (Goodrich 2008: 231)

As does Adam Thurschwell, who attended the Cardozo conference:

> I do not mean to overstate the break represented by 'Force of Law', because its themes are unquestionably foreshadowed in several earlier

> pieces (as Derrida himself pointed out), nor do I want to oversimplify the audience's reaction to it. But it nevertheless seems clear that 'Force of Law' not only firmly established the general question of law and politics within the field of deconstruction, it determined or brought to the foreground many of the themes (the undecidability of the decision, hyperbolic responsibility for the Other, the 'spectral', the singularity and *à venir* of justice) that became increasingly significant in Derrida's 'post-Force of Law' work.
>
> (Thurschwell 2008: 153)

Derrida, a philosopher concerned with 'ethical and political responsibility' (154; de Ville 2011: 8),[3] was also a huge jazz fan (O'Reilly 1999; Stein 2002; Gallope 2011: 4), whose interest in musical improvisation is quite apparent from his probing interview with Ornette Coleman in *Les Inrockupitibles* (1997)[4] – including his concern with the relationship between improvisation and social or political action[5] (Coleman and Derrida 2004: 323). Derrida refused to write on the subject of music, though, and he never addressed the politics and ethics of improvisation directly in his texts.[6] Instead, his 'loftiest aim' was to give his texts 'the condition of musicality' (quoted in O'Reilly 1999; see also Roberts 1991), which, for Coleman at least, means a 'much more democratic relationship to information' (Coleman and Derrida 2004: 319).

Uniting 'the "post-Force of Law" Derrida' (Thurschwell 2008: 154) with the 'jazz philosopher', as we may now perhaps call him, and beckoning CSI theorists back on stage, this chapter asks 'why, exactly, does improvisation matter' (Heble 2005: 1) to deconstruction and, by extension, to law?

Unpacking the creative potential of deconstructive legal improvisation requires, first, a deconstructive understanding of 'creation', which, not unlike law and improvisation discussed in Chapter 3, also exhibits the same tension as between the singular and the general. Attridge (2004) links creation to singularity and alterity. 'The creation of the other', as he calls it (22), is both an activity and a passivity: 'To be truly creative is to wrest from the realm of the familiar the hitherto unthought, to bring into existence by skilful and imaginative intellectual labor an entity that is irreducibly different to what is already in being' (22). Yet, it also has 'an element of passivity, of attempting to heighten responsiveness to hints of relationships, to incipient arguments, to images swimming on the edges of consciousness, an element of "letting them come" as much as seeking them out' (22–23). The new and original, in other words, is never simply produced by the 'active shaping of existing, conscious, mental materials' (23); there is always an element of mystery to the process and product.[7] Thus, for Attridge, 'the creation of the other' simultaneously refers to the act *of* creating and that which is created *by* the other (23). Attridge explains:

> ... the act of breaking down the familiar is also the act of welcoming the other; the event of the familiar breaking down is also the event of the

> irruption of the other. … If one is able to break down the old in a creative and not just a negative manner (and at the time it is not possible to be sure which of these one is doing), the new comes into being; at the same time, the breakdown of the old is produced by the pressure of its internal contradictions – which, since its contradictions are a function of what it excludes, is the same as saying that it breaks down under the pressure of the other.
>
> (Attridge 2004: 26–27)

Accordingly, 'creation', 'creative' and 'creativity' signify here the notion that 'novelty is achieved by means *both* of the refashioning of the old *and* of the unanticipated advent of the new; or, more accurately if more paradoxically, that the advent of the new *is* a particular kind of refashioning of the old' (24, emphasis in original). In the words of Attridge: 'Thinking creatively about creation means thinking of these as two sides of the same coin' (25).

With this conception of creation in mind, revisiting the Coleman–Derrida collaborative engagement described in Chapter 3, I ask: if jazz music, even that as 'radically improvisational' (Soules 2004: 270) as Ornette Coleman's, can never be truly inventive or properly escape the 'clammy grasp of law' (Haldar 2004: 7), what so moved Derrida to join Coleman on stage at the 1997 La Villette Jazz Festival? Expressed more generally, wherein lies the creative potential of deconstructive legal improvisation? And how might this creative influence set in motion more democratic, ethical and resistant means of legal engagement with society?

The necessity of improvisation's impossibility[8]

The negativity associated with Derrida's approach to improvisation (Gallope 2011: 18), addressed briefly in the introduction to this book, lies, I believe, in his insistence on 'maintaining the notion of a true alterity' (Landgraf 2011: 31), or his presentation of the other as 'always wholly other' (Miller 2007: 258). For Landgraf (2011), this insistence essentializes the difference (31) between the possible and the impossible such that Derrida's work becomes a '*celebration* of improvisation's impossibility' (29; emphasis added). This, for Landgraf, is nothing to celebrate:

> The inventiveness of Derrida's own discourse, then, is the paradox that completes his argument – by keeping it open, unresolved, unsolvable. Only by insisting on the impossibility of invention as the condition of its possibility, Derrida can account for singularity without negating iterability and yet without having to affirm some preexisting order that would reiterate invention within a rationalist cosmology. It is in this context that Derrida's specific statement regarding the impossibility of

> improvisation must be viewed: 'I believe in improvisation, and I fight for improvisation, but with the belief that it is impossible.'
>
> (Landgraf 2011: 29)

Landgraf's critique is not simply a rebranding of the tired 'deconstruction is nihilism'[9] argument. He accepts that Derridean iterability ties alterity, singularity and originality to repetition and wholeheartedly embraces the idea that improvisation must rely, to a certain extent, on 'experience and repetition' (16). For instance, he writes:

> Far from being the expression of unbridled freedom, improvisation marks a process that acquires a degree of consistency by connecting to – repeating and altering – what has come before. In art this is maybe more obvious than in other circumstances. In jazz, for example, improvisation not only requires extensive practice but is often described as a 'doing' that looks back as it moves forward creatively, responding to, rephrasing, changing and rejecting what has been played before.[10]
>
> (Landgraf 2011: 16–17)

Despite this, Landgraf seemingly laments the fact that improvisation in the 'traditional or pure sense' (33) (as the entirely original and new) is 'highly elusive' (33) because, 'from the perspective of iterability, every concept will reveal itself as tied to repetition, to non-singularity, as affected by a basic generality, as belated, differed, and always already doubled' (33). Again, he expounds:

> If Derrida is led to claim the impossibility of improvisation, it is because he presupposes an 'absoluteness' (in terms of freedom, originality, authenticity, and singularity) of improvisation that is incompatible with the structure of iterability. Improvisation defined in such stringent terms cannot exist because it could not be communicated, shared, and hence neither recognized nor otherwise experienced. Gary Peters argues as much, pointing out that Derrida's hesitations about improvisation – and those of its possibility – are based on unrealistic assumptions about it. The challenge is to think of innovation and subsequently improvisation not as *an Other of*, but as *deriving from* repetition and structure. Is it possible, in other words, to conceive of processes that can 'calculate' the production of the incalculable?
>
> (Landgraf 2011: 33–34, emphasis in original)

In the passages reproduced above, Landgraf appears to (mis)read Derrida as advocating iterability as the enemy of creativity and improvisation. This, as we shall see below, is just not the case.

The creative power of improvisatory expression is frequently said to lie in its originality, and creativity is most often conceived as a trumping of the 'underlying aesthetic of creative potential', an overcoming of 'the compulsion to repeat' (Fischlin 2010: 6). In the words of Daniel Fischlin, '[i]ts form is continuously revealing itself as an unfolding of potential that arises anew out of shifting contexts that compose the here and now' (6). However, this unique event of creative expression must paradoxically repeat itself in its uniqueness (6). Creativity, in other words, must itself be iterable, repeatable. Otherwise, we could not know it as creative and original. Creation involves both 'situatedness and datedness' (Attridge 2004: 110), but also difference: it must be different 'on every occasion' (111). It thereby 'possesses the paradoxical quality of a singularity that is confirmed only in repetitions, and in repetitions that are different every time' (111). It is the necessary iterability of the event of creativity, which gives iterability its creativity and permits the creation of the unique and new. Again, quoting Fischlin (2010): 'Improvisation would be incomplete without repetition. Repetition would be incomplete without improvisation. The two are inseparable conceptually' (6).

Only the most superficial readers of Derrida (de Ville 2011: 2) would interpret his 'legal texts' so negatively, as to call for the end of justice, ethics and politics. Instead, legal scholars often find themselves energised by Derrida's claims regarding the 'impossibility' of justice (see, for example, Douzinas (2005), Goodrich (2008) and Thurschwell (2008) above). Following 'Force of Law', these theorists read the impossibility of justice's possibility not pessimistically, but creatively, as an aporia or 'passion of thought' (Zlomislic 2007: 27). Through this recognition of its aporetic qualities, a more optimistic and hopeful vision of justice emerges.

On the importance of aporia, as creative paradox, to issues of justice, ethics and politics, Derrida himself writes in 'Hospitality, Justice and Responsibility: A Dialogue with Jacques Derrida':

> Decision, an ethical or political responsibility, is absolutely heterogeneous to knowledge. Nevertheless, we have to know as much as possible in order to ground our decision. But even if it is grounded in knowledge, the moment I take a decision it is a leap. I enter a heterogeneous space and that is the condition of responsibility.
>
> This is not only a problem but the aporia we face constantly. For me, however, the aporia is not simply paralysis, but the aporia or the non-way is the condition of walking: if there was no aporia we wouldn't walk, we wouldn't find our way; oath-breaking implies aporia. This impossibility to find one's way is the condition of ethics.
>
> (Derrida 1999: 73)

In *The Other Heading: Reflections on Today's Europe*, Derrida adds:

> I will even venture to say that ethics, politics, and responsibility, *if there are any*, will only ever begun with the experience and experiment of the

> aporia. When the path is clear and given, when a certain knowledge opens up the way in advance, the decision is already made, it might as well be said that there is none to make: irresponsibly, and in good conscience, one simply applies or implements a program. Perhaps, and this would be the objection, one never escapes the program.
>
> (Derrida 1992d: 41, emphasis in original)

The impossibility of justice – 'Justice is the experience of the impossible', writes Derrida in 'Force of Law' (2002b: 244) – is therefore interpreted through *différance,* through 'formal play of differences' (Derrida 2002e: 26), 'of traces' (26), which 'forbid at any moment, or in any sense, that a simple element be *present* in and of itself, referring only to itself' (26, emphasis in original). The 'impossible possible' thus becomes 'the possible *as* impossible, of an impossible-possible that can no longer be determined by the metaphysical interpretation of possibility or virtuality' (Derrida 2002d: 54, emphasis in original).

Applying this 'logic' (and the optimism of legal scholars) to the 'impossibility' of improvisation, we find that improvisation 'of some inaugurality' (Derrida 1998: 66) may be 'the impossible itself' (66), but the aporia or *différance* of improvisation ensures that its impossibility is 'not the *opposite* of the possible' (Beardsworth 1996: 26, emphasis in original). Instead, it 'supports' (Derrida 2005a: 91) and '*releases* the possible' (Beardsworth 1996: 26, emphasis in original). It follows then that Derrida is 'not against the impossible' (Caputo 1997: 20), not against improvisation. Quite the opposite. 'I believe in improvisation and I fight for improvisation. But always with the belief that it's impossible' (Derrida 2004c).

Improvisation, applying Derrida's 'logic' in relation to deconstruction, 'loses nothing from admitting that it is impossible' (Derrida 1989: 36). It is instead 'possibility', which hinders and constrains – for possibility contains 'the danger of becoming an available set of rule-governed procedures, methods, accessible approaches' (36). It contains the danger, if you will, of becoming fully determined law. It is thus the *impossibility* of improvisation, which gives it 'hope and possibility' (Fischlin and Heble 2004: 11). If improvisation were truly possible, in the sense of being wholly improvised or original, there would be no call for creativity and invention or, by analogy, for jazz. It is therefore 'the attempt at such an improvisation, necessarily failing' (Bennington 2000), which 'leaves a trace or a mark that can be seen as a *promise* of such an inaugurality' (Bennington 2000, emphasis in original). In its failure, improvisation survives. '*Affirmez la survie.*'[11]

Improvisation thus matters to Derrida because '[d]econstruction is inventive or it is nothing at all' (Derrida 1989: 42) and deconstruction is 'not just inventive, it is called by the other' (Bernasconi 1993: 118). The '"inventive" side to Derrida's philosophy', argues Beardsworth (1996: xiv) aims to 'reinvent invention' in order to 'make a space for an inventiveness open to the wholly other' (Attridge 1992b: 310). This openness of invention towards the other, 'towards the unknown' (quoted in Bailey 1992: 54), sustains improvisation as a creative art form.

Similarly, the responsively open dimension of improvisation matters to law for, without such, 'we might not associate a legal decision with justice, even if it were fully in conformity with the law' (Deutscher 2005: 98). The openness, which accompanies any legal improvisation, borrowing from Drucilla Cornell (1992), 'protects the possibility of radical transformation within an existing legal system' (167) and enables us to 'resist or rise up against an iniquitous law' (Bennington 1993: 194). It ensures, in other words, that 'law cannot *inevitably* shut out its challengers and prevent transformation' (Cornell 1992: 165, emphasis in original). As Bennington (1993) writes, '[i]n this opening of the other (toward the other, called by the other), without which the same would not be, there is a chance of something happening' (14–15). This openness to the other thus becomes 'openness to transformation' (Cornell 1992: 166) within law, within society. And this matters not simply to lawyers, but also to critical improvisation scholars. This openness in improvisation nurtures the possibility of 'improvised musiking'[12] (Fischlin and Heble 2004: 26; see also Fischlin 2003: 10), as that which links improvisation to democracy (Beyer 2000: 552), ethics (Heble 2000: 200) and resistance (Fischlin and Heble 2003; Fischlin and Heble 2004: 2, 4; Siddall 2005: 10).[13]

Ensemble improvisations: democracy and community

As a community of others, jazz musicians in the 1940s found solace in the after-hours jam session, a space unregulated by the NYC cabaret laws.[14] Ralph Ellison has described the jam session as 'the jazzman's true academy' (Ellison 1953: 208). It was in these sessions that a musician 'learn[ed] tradition, group techniques and style' (208). Free from the 'constraints that commercial engagements place on repertory [and] length of performance' (Berliner 1994: 42), jam sessions gave the musician the 'freedom to take artistic risks' (42) and thus assisted the musician in finding his or her 'own unique voice' (Ellison 1953: 209) and achieving, in short, his or her 'self-determined identity' (209).

Many have argued that the balance struck within the (creative) jam session between the 'individual desires of the soloist' (Beyer 2000: 552) and the 'necessity of playing with a group' (552) provides 'a perfect metaphor for democracy' (552; see also Sancton 1990). And the relationship 'between the soloist and the accompaniment in jazz' (Beyer 2000: 552) has been compared to 'the symbiosis between individual rights and social responsibilities in democratic society' (552). Jazz is accordingly labelled 'a democratic music' (Townsend 2000: 1), as Lewis Gordon explains:

> Total strangers can meet, choose a tune, and strike up a performance that seems almost magic. A form of *virtue-based democracy* emerges. ... The

> community, the musical moment, the people assembled, all understand that the music is to be played, and played well. A good jazz performance is a moment of and for communal celebration.
>
> (Quoted in Neal 2004: 201–2, emphasis added)

The jam session as a democratic space, or 'jamming' as a democratic practice, counters the myths of improvisational creativity as 'a burst of inspiration from a lone genius; that a person working alone is always more creative than a group; and that social conventions and expectations always interfere with creativity' (Sawyer 2006: 259; see also Borgo 2005: 183–91).[15]

As evidence of jazz's democratic conceptualization, on 18 September 1998, in conjunction with the Millennium Evenings lecture series, the then President of the United States, Bill Clinton, formally recognised jazz as a 'metaphor for American democracy' (Beyer 2000: 551).[16] Wynton Marsalis, one of the attendees, 'advocated a thesis of jazz and American political philosophy broader than a concept of individual freedom' (552). In both jazz and democracy, he argued, the central concern is how to reconcile the individual with the collective. Marsalis views the 'ideal American society' (552) as 'parallel[ing]' (552) the 'proper jazz performance' (552). When jazz is played 'properly', Marsalis recounts in a 1990 *Time Magazine* interview, 'it shows you how the individual can negotiate the greatest amount of personal freedom and put it humbly at the service of a group conception' (quoted in Sancton 1990). Mirvis (1998) calls this 'collective individuality' (589). Thus, democracy, like jazz, is not simply about protecting 'individual freedoms' (Beyer 2000: 552); it is also about the demands of the collective or community. Accordingly, Marsalis's freedom-with-others stance does not simply work to deconstruct 'repressive laws' (553) or dominant conceptions of jazz or democracy; it simultaneously 'reconstruct[s]' (552) a model of 'community' (552), which takes into account the relation between the individual and the collective, the singular and the general.

Derrida offers valuable insight into the construction of 'community' as it pertains to democracy and improvisation. Derrida, it must be noted, was very apprehensive about the concept, or, as Jean-Luc Nancy comments, 'any kind of communitarian theme; he did not like the word *community*' (Nancy and Fabbri 2007: 433, emphasis in original). For Nancy, Derrida's apprehension was 'excessive and probably had an affective origin (the word *community* suggested to him the religious Jewish community, from which he wanted to keep his distance, just as he did from the Christian community)' (433, emphasis in original). That said, Derrida's refusal to engage with 'community' had a 'precise political logic' (433). As Morin (2006) explains, he 'recognise[d] the necessity of putting community under erasure', which, based on the logic of the dual affirmative, meant *affirming* the concept as both inaccurate *and* necessary.

Marie-Eve Morin, in her essay 'Putting Community Under Erasure: Derrida and Nancy on the Plurality of Singularities' (2006), interprets Jean-Luc Nancy as similarly putting community under erasure. However, she finds that, where Derrida focuses more on the *inaccuracy* of the traditional concept through his critique of the classical model of 'fraternity' (discussed below), Nancy is more likely to emphasize the *necessity* of community (Morin 2006). Derrida, in other words, 'admits never having been able to write the word "community" in his own name' (Morin 2006; see also Derrida 1997a: 304–5). In contrast, Nancy finds using the concept community to be unavoidable: 'Community is given to us with being and as being, well in advance of our projects, desires, and undertakings. At bottom, it is impossible for us to lose community' (Nancy 1991: 35).

In his essay 'Liberty, Equality, Fraternity, or, How Not to Speak in Mottos' (2005b), Derrida poses the 'question of determining and naming community, the common, the sharing of the incommensurable freedom or equality of each and every one' (56) and criticizes Nancy's naming of this community as 'fraternity' (56). For Derrida, fraternity, or 'the figure of the brother' (58), has enjoyed a 'privileging' (58) in 'ethics, law, and politics, and particularly in a certain democratic model' (58). *The Politics of Friendship* (1997d) represents Derrida's attempt to think through a politics (along with ethics and democracy) 'beyond the principle of fraternity' (viii). Of central concern to Derrida is the 'dynamic between inclusion and exclusion in the creation or construction of community: who belongs to the *we* of any given community, and from what standpoint inside or outside of that *we* can the answer be determined?' (Perpich 2005: 447, emphasis in original). For Derrida, fraternity is a 'mechanism of identification that determines who belongs to the community and who does not' (Morin 2006). Morin explains:

> This process of identification, this fraternisation, consists in two movements: making the other my brother, that is, identifying him (or her) as somehow like me, and excluding the false brothers, the others who are not really like me. By the way they function, fraternal communities exert a double violence on individuals: an internal and an external violence.
>
> (Morin 2006)

Community as fraternity tends toward the neutralization of differences, 'treating all members as brothers, that is, as the same'. This fraternal community presents itself as homogeneous and thus as universal (Morin 2006).

The danger this fraternal gathering poses to 'the respect for the singularity and alterity of the other' leads Derrida to insist on separation and secrecy. In his interview with Antoine Spire, entitled 'Others Are Secret Because They

Are Other' (2005d), Derrida states, '[a] singularity is of its nature in secret' (162) and '[w]hat is absolutely secret is the alterity of the other, its singularity' (Morin 2006). Unconditional 'fidelity to the other' (Derrida 2005d: 155) is thereby 'marked in death' (155), the secret of which we will never know. In this fidelity to the other, this 'fidelity in friendship' (155), Derrida deconstructs:

> ... the models and figures of friendship that are dominant in the West: *fraternal* friendship – a familial and genealogical figure, even if it is spiritual – between two men; no friendship between a man and a woman; the exclusion of the sister; presence; proximity; a whole conception of justice and politics; and so on.
>
> (Derrida 2005d: 155, emphasis in original)

Derrida deconstructs fraternity (and thus community[17]) in the name of democracy[18] in a 1997 lecture at the University of Sussex:[19]

> Democracy means, minimally, equality. ... There is no democracy except as equality among everyone. ... On the other hand, you have to reconcile this demand for equality with the demand for singularity, with respect for the Other as singular, and that is an aporia. How can we, at the same time, take into account the equality of everyone, justice and equity, and nevertheless take into account and respect the heterogeneous singularity of everyone?
>
> (Derrida 1997c)

This deconstruction centres around what Derrida calls 'democracy "to-come"'.[20] By this, he does not mean 'a future democracy, a new regime, a new organisation of nation-states (although this may be hoped for)' (Derrida 1997c). Instead, by this 'to-come' he means 'the promise of an authentic democracy which is never embodied in what we call democracy. ... Democracy is a promise' (Derrida 1997c). This 'to-come' must be 'rigorously distinguish[ed] from the future', as Derrida explains in 'Force of Law':

> The future loses the openness, the coming of the other (who comes), without which there is no justice; and the future can always reproduce the present, announce itself or present itself as a future present in the modified form of the present. Justice remains *to come*, it remains *by coming*, it *has* to come [,] it *is* to come, the to-come, it deploys the very dimension of events irreducibly to come. It will always have it, this à-venir, and will always have had it.
>
> (Derrida 2002b: 256, emphasis in original)

Simon Critchley helps clarify what Derrida means by democracy 'to come':

> *La démocratie à venir* is an extremely difficult notion to get hold of because it has an essentially contradictory structure: that is, it has both the structure of a promise, of something futural 'to come', and it is something that takes place, that happens right *now*.
>
> (Critchley 2003: 111, emphasis in original)

Derrida's conception is further explained by Jean-Luc Nancy in an interview following Derrida's death:

> In Derrida the to come, the *à venir*, is always strictly opposed to the future, to *l'avenir*, that is, to the present-future that is projected, represented, given in advance as an aim and a possible occurrence. The to come that he loved to speak of designates the proper nature of what is essentially and always in the coming, of what has never come or come about, come down and made itself available. If democracy is given, if it is there, made, confected [*faite*], established, then one will no longer be able to say that democracy is to be improved; but if one says that it has not been perfected [*parfaite*], then it must be understood that its essence perhaps eludes all representable, anticipatable, and realizable perfection – not because it would be a utopia but because its essence is the very tension of an exigency that is not related to a realization.
>
> (Nancy and Fabbri 2007: 431)

The 'to-come' in Derridean theory 'turns upon two notions of the future: the future as programmed and planned; and radical openness of the future as the wholly unexpected, what cannot be anticipated' (Barnett and Low 2004: 15); its promise lies in 'the relationship between these two temporal registers' (15; see also Derrida 1997a: 306). The Derridean democracy to-come therefore does not signify 'a specific political regime, although it is not opposed to it either' (Beardsworth 1996: 146). Instead, as Beardsworth explains:

> It is with regard to an absolute future that informs all political organizations, but which is heard most, despite their legal form, within democratic organizations of power. This absolute future is the promise that the 'we' of the community (family, nation, world, even, as Derrida says in [*Specters of Marx* (1994)], humanity) – *qua* the 'we''s radical lack of identity – will have returned from the beginning to haunt any determination of the community.
>
> (Beardsworth 1996: 146)

This 'we' is articulated in terms of aporia: 'The only community of "we" that is possible is the impossibility of "we" and this possibility makes possible. This is the "promise of democracy"' (ibid.).

Applied to jazz, the promise of democracy, as discussed by Marsalis above, is both literally and conceptually *fraternal*, threatening the singularity and alterity of the other. Gender subsumes the very language of jazz, 'both the musical conventions within which it operates and the discourses that are produced about it' (Heble and Siddall 2000: 142). Despite its 'boasted egalitarianism and freedom' (Davies 1987: 29), jazz has often discouraged female participation (29). States one anonymous male jazz player, 'Jazz is a male language. It's a matter of speaking that language and women just can't do it' (quoted 163). Heble and Siddall further detail:

> Jazz, from its very inception, has been a world that is difficult for women to inhabit. Women were seen as rivals to male band leaders, and life as a jazz performer meant being on the road, away from one's family, playing in rough bars and dance halls. The public space and, concomitantly, the discourse of jazz very quickly emerged as masculine.
>
> (Heble and Siddall 2000: 151)

The 'jazz community' thus often translates into one of 'exclusion and marginalization' (Tucker 2004: 244) for female musicians.[21]

If Derrida's democracy 'to come' involves a constant negotiation between the closure of community as universal and an openness to the singularity of its membership, then needed are 'intuitive strategies of listening' (Heble and Siddall 2000: 157), which unsettle 'conventional distinctions' as to what constitutes community. Improviser and composer Pauline Oliveros,[22] in her abandonment of 'received notions of musical intelligibility in favour of what she calls *intuitive and receptive* models of composition and performance, … has done much to reclaim styles of musical practice that have been dismissed and undervalued as "feminine"' (157, emphasis added). In her performances,[23] Oliveros explores 'the possibilities of sound that can be produced in a given context and a given moment' (158). Heble and Siddall provide an example:

> At a solo accordion recital during the 1997 Guelph Jazz Festival [in Canada], … a violent thunderstorm began at the very moment that she sat down to play her instrument. This gothic atmosphere was enhanced by the venue, which was an old stone church sanctuary with stained glass windows. Despite the crashing thunder, bursts of light, and pelting rain, Oliveros proceeded with slow, meandering, and quiet chords that explored subtle changes in sound. While some artists might have been annoyed at having to compete with the noise of the storm, and others might have succumbed to the temptation to imitate its frenzy, power, and intensity, Oliveros explored a notion of receptivity that varied from the obvious response that the storm seemed to call for.
>
> (Heble and Siddall 2000: 158)

Despite the individual nature of her solo recital, Oliveros's performance says much about democracy and community in improvisation. Her 'aesthetic of receptivity' 'rehabilitates a model of creative practice that, because of its reliance on intuition, has been traditionally devalued as "feminine"' (158–59).[24] In so doing, it signals a more deconstructive reading of improvisation as community or democracy 'to come', as a coming gathering that is never fully constituted or perfected, but one that is instead receptive to the singularity of the given context and moment.

The ethical force of improvisation

If jazz improvisation is, by its very nature, democratic and community-oriented (Fischlin and Nandorfy 2012: 257), it is also an 'exemplary ethical music' (Heble 2000: 200). The extemporary nature of improvisation links invention to singularity and alterity such that '[t]he other, the unprecedented, hitherto unimaginable disposition of cultural materials that comes into being in the event of invention, is always singular' (Attridge 2004: 63). The ethics of improvisation arises from its relation to the other: immediacy and proximity emerge as 'ethically charged features of social interaction' (Gilroy 1995: 24). This relation to otherness 'arouses ... a sense of *responsibility*' (Attridge 2004: 123, emphasis in original), involving both a responsibility *to* the other – 'the other calls me to account, I answer to it as best I can' (123–24) – and a responsibility *for* the other: 'Being responsible for the other involves assuming the other's needs (if only the need to exist), affirming it, sustaining it, being prepared to give up my own wants and satisfactions for the sake of the other' (124). Responsibility 'is an ethical term' (126), one that 'implies an "ought"' (126). Being responsible for the other, 'as it comes into being (and thus bring it into being)' (126), asserts Attridge, 'is to be under an obligation to it' (126). It is this 'ethical responsibility for the other' (128), which lies 'at the heart of creativity' (128).

Borrowing again from Attridge, improvisation (jazz or otherwise) 'is directed toward an undoing of closed structures in order to make possible the coming of the other' (Attridge 1992b: 311). Surrounded by laws, 'improvisation dares to defy codes while it simultaneously runs the risk of becoming fully codified' (Corbett 1995: 223). It involves 'the permanent play of threshold and transgression' (224) and an attempt to 'risk the unknown' (225).

If improvisation never explored 'unknown territory', it chances stagnation and the threat of non-existence (223). Stresses Williams: 'If it was all thought out before it was done, there would be no need to do it, you know?' (quoted in Berliner 1994: 268). In order to *be*, improvisation must always be directed at the unknown other: 'the other in so far as it is unknown, the unknown in so far as it is radically other' (Hill 1997: 195–96). Improvisation thus 'links repetition to alterity, in the context of the ethical obligation to the other and a call for justice' (Ziarek 1997: 131). Moreover, it is the very persistence of alterity as 'a certain beyond or excess' (132) that enables the 'very possibility of ethics' (132). As Derrida (2002b) explains, 'iterability inscribes the promise as guard in the most irruptive instant of foundation. … [I]t inscribes the possibility of repetition at the heart of the originary' (272). Promise and possibility are thereby unleashed in every instance of the impossible and this unleashing frees the improviser 'to express and communicate complex ideas, values and attitudes', ones that may have been 'previously repressed' (Comte 2001).

Derridean notions of responsibility and ethics are 'closely tied to that of singularity' (Edkins 2005: 378). As Derrida writes in *The Gift of Death* (1995c), 'responsibility demands irreplaceable singularity. Yet only death or rather the apprehension of death can give this irreplaceability, and it is only on the basis of it that one can speak of the responsible subject' (51). He elaborates:

> What gives me my singularity, namely death and finitude, is what makes me unequal to the infinite goodness of the gift that is also the first appeal to responsibility. … One is never responsible enough because one is finite but also because responsibility requires two contradictory movements. It requires one to respond as oneself and as irreplaceable singularity, to answer for what one does, says, gives; but it also requires that … one forget or efface the origin of what one gives.
>
> (Derrida 1995c: 51)

Responsibility thus needs singularity, needs 'always being alone, entrenched in one's own singularity at the moment of decision' (60). Yet, writes Derrida, 'as soon as one speaks, as soon as one enters the medium of language, one loses that very singularity. … Once I speak I am never and no longer myself, alone and unique' (60). Responsibility then 'cannot be expressed in a general code of ethics' (Edkins 2005: 378). Instead, 'the generality of ethics incites to irresponsibility. It impels me to speak, to reply, to account for something, and thus to dissolve my singularity in the medium of the concept' (Derrida 1995c: 61).

The aporia of responsibility 'arises from the impossibility of our responding to another as singularity without the inevitable sacrifice of our response to all the other absolute singularities to whom we are similarly bound' (Edkins 2005: 381). Again, Derrida is of assistance:

> … what binds me thus in my singularity to the absolute singularity of the other, immediately propels me into the space or risk of absolute sacrifice. There are also others, an infinite number of them, the innumerable generality of others to whom I should be bound by the same responsibility. … I cannot respond to the call, the request, the obligation, or even the love of another without sacrificing the other other,

> the other others. ... As a result the concepts of responsibility, of decision, or of duty, are condemned a priori to paradox, scandal, and aporia. Paradox, scandal, and aporia are themselves nothing other than sacrifice, the revelation of conceptual thinking at its limit, at its death and finitude.
>
> (Derrida 1995c: 68)

Accordingly, for Derrida, the only ethical response is a response that sacrifices ethics, that is, sacrifices 'whatever obliges me to respond, in the same way, in the same instant, to all the others' (68).

The responsibility or ethics of deconstruction become here the ethics of 'deconstruction as the invention of the other in music' (Cobussen 2002e: par. 5). Throughout history, music has been connected to the 'logic of alterity' (quoted par. 4), to the 'other of language, of conceptual thought and of conscious self-possession' (par. 4). Music as 'subordinate', 'secondary', 'subversive', supplementary' and 'marginal' (Cobussen 2002g: par. 1). Recall Plato's flute-girl who, in 'The Symposium', was 'told to go away' (Plato 1999: 703) so that the men could 'have conversation instead' (703).[25] As Cobussen (2002g) argues, it is this '[m]usic as the other' (par. 1), with its potential to 'bring us in contact with the other other' (par. 1), which brings us into the realm of the ethical (par. 1). Music becomes an 'ethical space ... that cannot *not* solicit a response' (Cobussen and Finn 2002: s. 6, emphasis in original). A 'positive response to an alterity which necessarily calls or motivates it' (s. 6). 'Creativity *as* ethics' (s. 6, emphasis added), insist Cobussen and Finn. Encountering the other 'in all its various forms'; 'open to the other as *other*' (Sellers 1991: 144, emphasis in original), loving the other *as* other. It is a desire for a love that 'lets the other live, that does not incorporate, but lets the other be other' (Conley 1990: xiii).

Ethics, explains Cobussen (2002g) in relation to Derrida's work, 'coincides with the experience of hospitality' (par. 5) and this experience coincides with a certain level of *risk*:

> The unconditional, hospitable host does not ask for the name or intentions of the other. As such he takes a big risk. This is a highly risky strategy and perhaps not recommendable. There is always a chance of meeting the hostile trespasser that destroys everything. At the same time, it is perhaps this pure, unqualified hospitality we dream about, also because it is unattainable.
>
> (Derrida, quoted in Alterhaug 2004: 113)

So too, in its pushing 'beyond the concept ... without any guarantee or certainty' (Cobussen and Finn 2002: s. 12), improvisation 'both traces and involves risks – where things do not go according to a preconceived plan' (s. 12). Ethics chances failure. Attridge tackles this issue when he asks,

> What is the ethical ground for attention to and affirmation of otherness, when the result of this effort may be without any humanly recognizable merit, or indeed – since the other that is brought into being may … turn out to be a monstrosity – may serve quite inhuman ends?
>
> (Attridge 2004 126)

He gives the example of the flourishing of Nazism and suggests that certain outcomes, i.e. the Final Solution, 'would be likely to lead to the retrospective reinterpretation of the event as uninventive, since it would not give rise to further invention, but rather to a closing down of possibilities' (160, n. 4). As Fischlin and Heble (2004) note, 'the battle over how to think improvisation is neither inconsequential nor unrelated to larger issues' (16). Accordingly, the risks associated with the ethics of improvisation are not insignificant and, true to its etymology, improvisation, with its origins in the Latin word *improvisus*, calls forth the 'unforeseen' (Alterhaug 2004: 98). That said, in its respect for both the law to which it is tied *and* the other-than-law that has no name, in its working (and re-working) both inside and outside codes in order to 'risk the unknown' (Corbett 1995: 225), improvisation opens up an ethical space and calls forth the other, beckoning 'this other invention of which we dream' (Derrida 1989: 55).

Improvisation as resistant critique

'How do you protest a system that co-opts and marginalizes almost every unique and original thought that confronts it? And how do you stay silent?' So asks jazz trumpeter-composer Dave Douglas in the liner notes of his 2001 album *Witness*. In addition to being both democratic and ethical, improvisation is often heralded as 'a site for locating resistant critiques' (Fischlin and Heble 2004: 4) and an 'important locus of resistance to orthodoxies of the imagination (knowing), of relations with others (community), and of relations to the materials of the world around us (instruments)' (11). Many critical improvisation theorists (see, for example, Monson 1996; Heble 2000; Fischlin and Heble 2003; Fischlin and Heble 2004) advance jazz improvisation as a 'profound form of resistance' (Siddall 2005: 10). Improvised music is frequently associated 'with social resistance' (10) and aligned with critiques of injustice and oppression (Fischlin and Heble 2004: 8). Gillian Siddall (2005), for instance, has written extensively on the 'socially liberatory possibilities' (10) of improvised jazz music. She argues that improvising jazz musicians 'challenge their listeners to engage with unfamiliar musical codes that have the potential effect of facilitating new social codes' (17); and 'resistant and recuperative possibilities' (16) are 'offered by … discordant sounds' (16).

The bebop movement 'brought this theme of resistance to international attention' (Lewis 2004b: 134), posing 'both implicit and explicit challenges to Western notions of structure, form and expression' (134):

> Bop improvisers ... used 'heads,' or precomposed melodic material, as starting points for a piece. Bop heads, however, as Gridley points out, 'resembled little or nothing that the average listener had heard before'. ... In a further abstraction, bebop improvisers felt no obligation to use the melodic material of the 'head' as material for improvisational transformation. Instead, the underlying harmonic sequence, usually subjected to extensive reworking by the improvisers, became the basis for improvisation. Often this harmonic material was appropriated from the popular show tunes of the day, linking this with earlier jazz styles. The musicians often 'signified on' the tunes, replacing the melodic line with another, then naming the new piece in an ironic signifying riff on Tin Pan Alley as well as upon the dominant culture that produced it.
>
> (Lewis 2004b: 134)

Bebop's challenge to the dominant culture was not limited to the musical (135) and, as detailed in Chapter 5, the revolutionary qualities of bop musicians had much to do with their 'assertion of self-determination' (135) in relation to 'their role as musical artists' (135). Perhaps more so, their 'radical redefinition' (135) of 'African-American improvisative musicality' (135) was viewed as 'a direct challenge, by extension, to the entire social order as it applied to blacks in 1940s apartheid America' (135).

Fischlin and Heble (2004) consider the resistant or liberatory power of jazz in their critique of Tzvetan Todorov's highly acclaimed book *The Conquest of America* (1999). In this book, the 'initial contact between Mexican (Aztec) and European (Spanish) cultures was defined by the collision between "ritual discourse" associated with indigenous populations, and improvisatory discourse, associated with Europeans' (14). The relevant passage in Todorov is reproduced below:

> Now, the Spanish invasion creates a radically new, entirely unprecedented situation, in which the art of improvisation matters more than that of ritual. *It is quite remarkable, in this context, to see Cortés not only constantly practicing the art of adaptation and improvisation, but also being aware of it and claiming it as the very principle of his conduct.*
>
> (Todorov 1999: 87, quoted in Fischlin and Heble 2004: 14, emphasis added by Fischlin and Heble)

Fischlin and Heble criticize the conception of improvisation advanced by Todorov in that it 'appropriates the resistant, improvisatory practices that will emerge out of colonization as the very instrument by which colonization takes place' (15). In their view, 'Todorov gets it wrong' (15):

> ... improvisation ... depends on that dissonant relation to hegemony: Cortés's action, from within his own cultural context and in relation to

> what Cortés understood to be hegemonic power (located in Spain), are never improvisatory so much as they are predictably manipulative and adaptive, dictated by the self-interested goals of the imperial ideology he sought to enforce.
>
> (Fischlin and Heble 2004: 15)

For Fischlin and Heble, 'Todorov's use of "improvisation"' (15) 'appropriates to itself modes of resistant discourse that one might associate with improvisation in the contemporary historical context' (15). He does this to reinforce 'the ways in which colonial discourse operates by abjecting and disempowering difference' (15). Again, quoting Fischlin and Heble:

> To have been truly improvisatory in the relation to otherness that Cortés initiates, would have required his turning away from the predictable acts of imperial greed and destruction to initiate something quite different – like a peaceful and productive alliance with indigenous cultures in the name of forming a transcultural community based on dialogue and 'true' improvisation rather than on the monological deployment of European power.[26]
>
> (Fischlin and Heble 2004: 15)

The 'primary otherness' of improvisation, borrowing again from Attridge (2004) in relation to literature, thereby 'lies in its resistance to immediate assimilation and interpretation, its refusal to yield wholly to the codes and strategies' (112), which we, as listeners, for example, are trained to bring to bear on music. Improvisation, though, exists '*only* by virtue of those codes and strategies' (112, emphasis added). It cannot, in other words, signify resistance 'in and of itself', as Siddall explains:

> While one might argue that any improvised sound is resistant because it eschews the stasis of a pre-written composition, and, in the case of much avant-garde jazz, appears to flout established conventions of music, one might just as easily argue that all improvised music signifies in some way in relation to established musical codes, that one can only interpret it as resistant in the context of musical conventions that we perceive it to be resisting.
>
> (Siddall 2005: 14)

Here she makes an important point. Improvisation can never be *fully* or *essentially* resistant. Derrida's reading of invention is germane here. Improvisation, as with invention, 'presupposes conventions and institutional rules' (Derrida 1989: 59). Only 'by bending these rules with respect for the rules themselves' (59) can improvisation allow 'the other to come or to announce its coming' (59–60). Thus, it is by 'defying and exhibiting the precarious structure of its rules, even while respecting them' (60), that improvisation brings us closer to pure improvisation.

Through this 'mark of respect' (60), this 'respect for the rules themselves' (59), improvisation invents. The resistant potential of jazz improvisation thereby lies not in its revolutionary qualities, which pit it 'against codification' (Corbett 1995: 237); its power lies instead in improvisation's 'diffuse' (237) nature, in its ability to work 'from the inside and the outside of codes' (237), highlighting internal contradictions or 'those laws' differences from themselves' (Attridge 1992b: 311). Improvisation, to quote Derrida in another context, is both 'passivity' (Derrida 1989: 55) and activity; a *waiting* for the other to come and a *call* for just such a coming. It is a 'dream' (55), a dream of the 'other invention' (55), which for Derrida is 'the invention of the entirely other, the one that allows the coming of a still unanticipated alterity and for which no horizon of waiting as yet seems ready, in place, available' (55).

Otherness may always be singular, 'always [be] that which resists or exceeds existing frameworks' (Attridge 2004: 129). However, the singularity of otherness is 'not an inviolable identity outside codes and conventions but is produced through them' (129). Newness and transformation relies on the 'relation of alterity to the field which it transforms' (136). Otherness enters a culture not as 'a pre-existing entity somewhere outside of, and unrelated to, what is known' (136). Instead:

> … it manifests itself as an event of reshaping, ranging from the major to the minuscule, brought about by an individual's or group's exploitation of a culture's contradictions, overdeterminations, marginalization, gaps, and tensions. In coming to be acknowledged – which means in the process of shifting frameworks so that it can be acknowledged – the other exposes a reality or truth of which the culture and its subjects were unaware, and unaware for reasons that are far from arbitrary. This uncovered reality may be pleasant; it may equally be unpalatable or even dangerous. Its occlusion is likely to be in the interest of those in power, and, as the history of censorship shows, it may be politically unacceptable to state authorities.
>
> (Attridge 2004: 136–37, footnotes omitted)

Returning to the Derridean dual affirmation mentioned in Chapter 3, improvisation both affirms the law as it is and as it can be otherwise. The glance towards infinite possibility impedes closure and enables change and transformation within a given system. Novelty enters through repetition, which is simultaneously same and other, as Derrida explains:

> … there is no incompatibility between repetition and the novelty of what is different. In a tangential and elliptical way, a difference always causes repetition to deviate. I call that *iterability*, the other

> ([Sanskrit] *itara*) appearing in reiteration. The singular always inaugurates, it even 'comes about' unforeseeably, like the new arrival, via repetition.
>
> (Derrida 2005d: 136, emphasis in original)

Applied to the legal realm, the openness of singularity to alterity 'protects the possibility of radical transformation within an existing legal system' (Cornell 1992: 167) and enables us to 'resist or rise up against an iniquitous law' (Bennington 1993: 194). That is to say, it ensures that 'law cannot *inevitably* shut out its challengers and prevent transformation' (Cornell 1992: 165, emphasis in original). As Bennington (1993) writes: 'In this opening of the other (toward the other, called by the other), without which the same would not be, there is a chance of *something happening*' (14–15, emphasis added). This openness to the other thus becomes an 'openness to transformation' (Cornell 1992: 166) within law, within society.

Any deconstructive reading of law and improvisation, which is concerned with issues of justice, democracy, ethics and resistance, must thus, borrowing from Elisabeth Grosz in another context, be committed to *both* an affirmation of the already existent *and* an affirmation of overcoming this sameness (Grosz 2003: 239). Whereas many social activists and theorists would prefer to 'simply and resoundingly' (239) say no to the violence that imbues the present, 'deconstruction teaches us to own up to our complicity in the suffering we cannot help but produce' (Fleming 1998: 420). The 'inherited nature of ... discourse' (Grosz 2003: 239) means that we are constitutively immersed 'in the very systems from which we seek to distance, and against which we seek to position, ourselves' (239). Our only choice is that of 'the lesser violence within an *economy of violence*' (Derrida 2001c: 400, n. 21, emphasis in original).

The Derridean double affirmative alerts us to 'the danger of repeating and being unable to recognize the very implications it believes it has repudiated' (Grosz 2003: 239). Both critical improvisation and legal studies need deconstruction, need Derrida, in order to challenge their (necessary) complicity with the very forces viewed to be outside discourse (240). Only by acknowledging this complicity can we direct our critique against it (Derrida 2001a: 355). 'The task', then, to quote Shildrick (2002), 'is not to destroy the foundations of the logos so much as to open them up to take account of all that has hitherto been excluded or disavowed' (121). The task, in other words, is to help prepare us to welcome 'the monstrous to-come' (Bennington 1993: 316), which is a coming that never arrives, but which promises nevertheless 'gradual and necessary transformation' (Derrida 2002c: 241). At once an impossibility and a coming, the monstrous improvisation promises the possibility of a legal system that judges 'according to the "lesser violence"' (Beardsworth 1996: xiv). It is in this less violent judgment that the promise of law lies.

Improvisioning

'Improvisioning', an expression crafted by Daniel Fischlin (2010), acts as both an opening to understanding the practice and benefits of improvisation in relation to the most basic of legal mechanisms, judicial decision-making, *and* an ending to this book. Improvisioning signifies the unification of diverse improvisatory practices with that which those practices express, namely the envisioning or 'calling forth of the unexpected' (1), or the making present of a more creative vision of justice and social change. Rzewski (2002) is one of many who note the proximity of improvisation to change and possibility: 'Improvisation tells us: *Anything is possible – anything can be changed – now*' (385, emphasis in original). Ajay Heble (2005) observes that, 'especially for aggrieved peoples', improvised musical practices offer a 'particularly powerful place' of hope in our culture (2):

> An ability to cultivate resources for hope out of seemingly hopeless situations, to foster new structures of understanding, after all, resounds in the history of improvisational creative practices. Such examples attest to the creative and innovative ways in which aggrieved peoples have responded to oppression. Particularly compelling is music's ability through forms of different, and more hopeful, ways of doing things. Improvisation, in short, can play a signally important role in cultivating resources for hope. It speaks directly to the risks we need to take in order to create opportunities for change, in order to envision a more hopeful, more just, world in the face of the degradations and injustices that beset us.
>
> (Heble 2005: 2)

How, then, might the concept of improvisioning apply to precedent-sensitive judicial reasoning? As Derrida (2004a: 332) has noted, it is necessary to improvise. It is also necessary to judge. But, to improvise *well*, to judge *well*, that requires a more thorough knowledge of improvisational practices. Studies of improvisatory techniques or strategies take on particular urgency in an era when diverse peoples and communities struggle to have their interests recognized and adjudicated. The issue, though, is not simply one of judging better or making more just decisions (if we knew what such meant) on the *spur of the moment*. It is about opening up a space for more *creative* decision-making, in which novelty arrives via a 'particular kind of refashioning of the old' (Attridge 2004: 24).

Taking its cue from Fischlin's expression, this concluding section glances outwards towards an *application* of improvisational strategies to judicial decision-making. What follows is admittedly brief. It seeks guidance from CSI-informed organizational theory[27] with the view to envisioning what critically improvisational judgment might look like. A conception of judging anchored in improvisational strategies not only makes possible more creative, spontaneous and courageous decisions, but also envisions new ways of 'doing' law. Improvisation for the spirit (of the law),[28] one might even say.

Mary Crossan (1998: 594) links improvisation to the practice of management by focusing on key characteristics that support *good* improvisation (595). The first of these characteristics is '*interpreting the environment*' (593, emphasis added). Improvisation is most closely associated with 'spontaneity of action' and this applies not only to musical or theatrical improvisation, but also to organizational management. An 'extraordinary amount of managerial activity' is, she notes, 'spontaneous' (595). Moreover, 'as the cycle time for innovation is shortening, time-based competition has become an important consideration for management' (595).

This applies equally to the legal realm where increased pressure is being placed on judges to not only decide *well*, but also decide *faster*.[29] The improvisational principle of 'interpreting the environment' assists in this regard, as Crossan explains:

> A principle of improvisation is the environment will teach you if you let it, rather than trying to control it. Learning from the environment often requires that individuals break out of their traditional frames of reference to see the environment in its full richness and complexity. Doing so requires the application of intuition.
>
> (Crossan 1998: 595)

The inability to 'break out of traditional mindsets' (595), Crossan notes, can have tragic consequences and 'interpreting the environment, seeing it in its full richness and complexity, is one of the critical challenges facing organizations' (595). 'Interpreting the environment' is thus vital to the creation of more just judicial solutions.

Being able to interpret the opportunities and threats to the environment is only valuable, again relying on Crossan, 'if that new understanding is reflected in the pattern of actions of the organization: its strategy' (595). Thus, the second characteristic of good improvisation is '*crafting strategy*' (593, emphasis added). Crossan calls for a less controlled or planned strategy, preferring one that is 'emergent', that is, 'intuitive, action-oriented, spontaneous … and ongoing' (595–96). This applies equally to precedent-sensitive judicial reasoning. As much as one party almost always feels wronged or persecuted, generally speaking, judges and judicial decisions cannot appear unjust, authoritarian or repressive. What's more, the 'story' or image of law must be 'plausible, cohesive and anticipate customer or audience needs' (596); it must 'build on what others have offered, and … offer something in return' (596). One of the key challenges of good improvisation is knowing when a story is losing effect and when (and how) to redirect it (596). So too must the common law, and the judges who apply it, be able to recognize the ineffectiveness of certain legal strategies and admit when reform or change is needed.

'Cultivating leadership', a third characteristic of good improvisation addressed by Crossan in relation to organizational theory, implies that 'individuals take different leads at different times' (596). In the legal arena, especially the courtroom, this characteristic may be difficult to achieve as lawyers, judges and clients appear to have very defined and established roles. However, according to Crossan, '[i]mprovisation highlights the need for individuals to expand their set of competencies in order to take on a variety of roles' (596). Justice demands an understanding of the singularity of the individual case in relation to the more general rules and laws. To understand better the participants of the legal system – victims, witnesses, defendants, clients, etc. – judges need to be able to empathize with their situations and stories. This requires giving up control at times and taking on different leadership roles at different times (596).

'*Yes-anding*', the fourth characteristic of good improvisation (596), means building upon material offered to an improviser to foster teamwork (593). Crossan notes that this 'is a simple concept, but challenging to implement' (597). The idea of fostering teamwork may be particularly challenging to implement in a legal system founded on hierarchy and authority. Then again, most, if not all, participants of the system share the common goal of wanting justice achieved. One concern specific to the legal arena is that 'yes-anding' to *all* material offered to a judge in a case is practically impossible in relation to precedent-sensitive judicial decision-making. Judges *must* decide, must make a choice to accept one party's version of the event(s) over the other. She cannot 'yes-and' to one, without 'no-buting' to the other. This is the very nature of the adversary system.[30] It is not, I think, impossible to 'yes-and' the law, but to do so would take great ingenuity and creativity on the part of the judge.

All the characteristics of improvisation offered above are almost impossible to achieve without the attitude and skills necessary to improvise effectively. Chapter 5 detailed these skills extensively in relation to jazz improvisation. Applied to the common law, this requires '*risking the four Cs*: the desire to be consistent, comfortable, confident and competent' (597). Crossan, once again, provides further explanation:

> Not being in control makes many individuals quite uncomfortable. Some situations require individuals to stretch their competency base and take on new behaviours. And individuals must rely on, and support others …
>
> The spontaneous nature of improvisation taxes more fully the fundamental skills of listening and communication. It demands that

> individuals give their full concentration and attention to the moment, rather than being preoccupied by what happened, or what could happen.
>
> (Crossan 1998: 597)

Developing the necessary skills of improvisation is not something that is completely beyond the scope of judicial or legal training, even if, at present, they are not incorporated into the law school or legal-practice curriculum. In fact, the *Sunday Times* (5 February 2012) published a story about a leading girls' school that is teaching students about risk and how to learn from failure to emerge stronger (Grimston 2012: 15). Wimbledon High School in south London ran a 'Failure Week' in early 2012 to teach students 'the need to confront failure head-on so it held fewer fears' (15) and show them the benefits of improvisation, especially when events do not unfold as expected or desired. Crossan (1998) lists various workshop techniques as a 'very practical means to introduce and experience improvisation' (598). Regrettably, an extended discussion of such practices is not possible here.

The final characteristic of good improvisation upon which Crossan focuses is '*assessing organizational culture*' (597). The environment of an organization (including that of the legal system) needs to be able to 'tolerate mishaps for improvisation to work' (597). Crossan lists certain environments less tolerant of error, which may not be conducive to improvisation, such as a jetliner on take-off (598). However, as this book has sought to demonstrate, improvisation occurs even in the most seemingly structured environments, such as the legal system. Moreover, all contexts require the skills of improvisation in times of crisis (598). Therefore, trusting that failure can be overcome and working on techniques to produce better improvisers and more just improvisation, not only in times of crisis, but in every context, this is the goal of critical improvisation studies.

As one final point, Bergart's 'Innovation Boot Camp',[31] an 'experiment in learning to be spontaneous' (Bergart 2010: 2), is a perfect example of what can be achieved when given the 'structure and time to practice innovation-generating techniques' (2). One lesson learned from the those practices utilized by Bergart, which may be applicable to the realm of judicial decision-making, is the notion that '*thinking outside the box*', often seen to be the 'goal of creativity', does not necessarily entail 'far-out and unusual ideas' (quoted 3). Quoting Patricia Ryan Madson (2005), '[a] true understanding of this phrase ["thinking outside the box"] means seeing what is really obvious, but up until then, unseen' (quoted 3). Clever and original ideas, in other words, 'only gain value when they give meaning and worth to other people' (3). Applied to judicial decision-making, advocating a justice that is improvised is not an invitation to revolution. The heretofore unthought arrives in court (or chambers) not as the purely new, but as a particular kind of re-fashioning of the old, to borrow again from Attridge. That said, as society changes, so too must law. And recognizing the creativity and innovation at the heart of legal reasoning, while, at the same time, teaching techniques aimed at demystifying both improvisation and justice, can only benefit law in the long term as it seeks to remain legitimate and forceful in society.

In conclusion, through the twining of Derridean and CSI theory, this book has offered a vision of legal improvisation as the complex negotiation of singularity and generality, the extempore and law. The creative 'processes' that energize both improvisation and Derridean iterability – 'creative in the sense of a productive activity, not a creation *ex nihilo*' (Cormack 2007: 8) – are invaluable for law and justice. Ever emergent and never fully realized (otherwise there would be no need for reform), a justice rooted in improvisation offers the following:

> ... an adaptive (non)organizing principle of human agency that is both provisional and potential, both contingently mediated and startlingly experimental, both an evocation of the possible and the doable, and an articulation of the unthought and the unexpected. As an expression of multiple adaptive forms that have these qualities, improvisation has much to tell us about the way in which communities based on such forms are politically and materially pertinent to envisioning alternative ways of knowing and being in the world.
>
> (Fischlin and Heble 2004: 34)

As lawyers and legal theorists, we have much to learn from Derrida. Likewise, we have much to learn from the critical study of improvisation and from improvisation itself, 'from performance practices that accent conversational energy and inventive flexibility, from art forms that disrupt orthodox standards of coherence, judgment, and value with a spirit of exploration and restless innovation' (Fischlin and Heble 2004: 35). Deconstructive legal improvisation is not simply concerned with improvising or judging well on the spur of the moment, or 'preparing to be spontaneous', to borrow from Barrett (1998: 606). It is about being more *creative* in our legal decision-making. Strong links exist between improvisation and innovation (Bergart 2010: 1) and boundless potential resides in the 'rhetoric of excess' (Fischlin and Heble 2004: 34) often used to describe improvisation, especially its excess of creativity and possibility.[32] Giving Fischlin and Heble the near to last word on the subject:

> What we can learn from the relationships articulated and envisioned through these acts of [improvisation] is precisely that we mustn't allow our thinking to settle into orthodoxy, that in the ongoing search for new categories of momentum and new forms of community resides the hope

> that will sustain and empower us in our efforts to edge toward another possible future, a more just place, on the other side of nowhere.
>
> (Fischlin and Heble 2004: 36)

The other side of nowhere, from where justice *as* improvisation calls. Improvisioning a more creative legal future. One in which improvisation and law are united, not opposed, in the endless quest for 'a way out of no way' (Neal 2004: 195).

Notes

1 Introduction: the law of the extempore

1 In the words of Phil Daquila (2009b), who reproduces this story on his website: 'Disasters do not follow prescribed plans, so preparing for that inevitability was being valued.'

2 For Phil Daquila's application of this principle, see his documentary 'Preparing for the Unpredictable' (2009c), which examines how emergency management has turned to the principles of improvisation to prepare firefighters for decision-making during disasters in North Carolina. The use of improvisation by US Navy SEALs is not limited to fire-fighting, as Abrahamson (2006) notes: 'Navy SEALs rely on improvisation rather than orders to achieve the sort of mission robustness that can keep them out of enemy hands during dangerous infiltrations, leaving them read to adapt to unpredictable, complex, and fast-changing situations' (99).

3 Cobussen explains the importance of the 'other' to deconstructive theory:

> Especially in his later works, Derrida often speaks of 'l'invention de l'autre', where 'l'autre' ('the other') may be regarded as that which remains unthought, that which escapes the grip of our concepts. The other is whatever resists, escapes definition whenever definition is put in place. Recognition of the other opens the ethical dimension of deconstruction which consists in opening, uncloseting, destabilizing foreclusionary structures so as to allow passage toward the other. No culturally based directive, but the other appealing to me very concretely. No laws of tolerance, hospitality or acceptance but my singular relationship to a singular other. Deconstruction can be thought of as a reading and writing strategy that takes notice of traces of the other, of the unthought, the invisible, the unheard without absorbing, assimilating or reducing it to the same (to the cognitive power of the knowing subject or self-consciousness).
>
> (Cobussen 2002e: par. 3)

4 Derek Bailey (1992) has written that '[i]mprovisation enjoys the curious distinction of being both the most widely practiced of all musical activities and the least acknowledged and understood' (ix). He is not alone in documenting the prevalence of improvisation in society (Snow 2004: 49; Cobussen 2008b: 14), or lamenting the difficulties its conceptualization poses (Landgraf 2011: 1).

5 Michael Jarrett makes a similar argument:

> The entire history of jazz can be heard as one colossal improvisation defining what improvisation can be: jazz is one answer to the question, What is improvisation?

> Getting this definition into words, however, or between the covers of a book requires either trickery or violence. When we write about improvisation, what are we really writing about?
>
> (Jarrett 2004: 321)

6 Helping define the field of study called critical improvisation studies or critical studies in improvisation (CSI) are, for example, Heble (2000); Fischlin and Heble (2003, 2004); Fischlin et al. (forthcoming); Heble and Wallace (forthcoming); Siddall and Waterman (forthcoming); and Lewis and Piekut (forthcoming).

7 This is the definition adopted by the 'Improvisation, Community and Social Practice' (ICASP) project, a seven-year, $4 million international community/university research scheme, funded through the Social Sciences and Humanities Research Council of Canada's (SSHRC) Major Collaborative Research Initiatives (MCRI) programme. It brings together a dynamic international research team from eighteen universities, including the University of Guelph, McGill University, University of British Columbia, University of Cambridge, University of Western Sydney, Columbia University, University of California, New York University and Harvard University, among others. The project provides information-sharing opportunities through its online journal, colloquia, website and publications, and fosters innovative partnerships with several community-based organizations. For more information, see the ICASP website (available HTTP: www.improvcommunity.ca (accessed 8 June 2012)) and University of Guelph (2007).

8 One of the most important CSI innovators is Dr Ajay Heble, a Professor at the School of English and Theatre Studies at the University of Guelph, Canada. Heble is the Project Leader for the ICASP project, founding editor of the journal *Critical Studies in Improvisation*/Études critiques en improvisation, and founder and artistic director of the Guelph Jazz Festival, which was the 2010 winner in the arts organization category of the Ontario Premier's Award for Excellence in the Arts and three-time recipient of the Lieutenant Governor's Award of the Arts (1997, 2000 and 2001). Ajay is also a pianist.

9 For other research being pursued in the area of law and improvisational studies, see Chapter 6. On the use of improvisation as the object of study in other areas of the humanities and social sciences, see, for example, Hallam and Ingold (2007) (Anthropology); Esterhammer (2004) (English); Peters (2009) (Philosophy); Landgraf (2011) (Art, German); Weick (1998), Crossan (1998), Hatch and Weick (1998), Barrett (1998) (Organization Science). See Borgo (2005) for a study of improvisation and contemporary science.

10 According to the ICASP website:

> This project investigates the ways in which improvised music plays a role in shaping notions of community and 'new forms' of social organization, with the goal of developing a new field of interdisciplinary scholarly endeavour, one that promises to place the civic function of improvised artistic practices firmly at the centre of both broad public debate and informed policy decisions about the role of arts in society.
>
> (Available HTTP: www.improvcommunity.ca/about/research (accessed 8 June 2012)

11 This statement borrows from Nachmanovitch (1990): 'all art is improvisation' (6). See also Landgraf (2011). Bradin Cormack's *A Power To Do Justice* (2007) is a fascinating study of sixteenth-century jurisdictional crisis. The book opens with the provocative claim that '*law is fundamentally improvisational*, unfolding into doctrine only as and through practice' (1, emphasis added).

12 'Minimum structures' are required for improvisation, as Barrett and Peplowski (1998: 559) detail. The Derridean notion of 'iterability' has likewise been described by Kronick (1999) as 'the minimal structure that makes history comprehensible' (56).

13 In her poetic study of the practice of improvisation, entitled 'One Time Alone: Improvisation Takes Place' (2008), Geraldine Finn 'explores the relationship between the place of improvisation and improvisation of place' (203) through Derrida, Paul Celan, the Rwandan genocide and Ornette Coleman, amongst others (203).

14 Gioia thoughtfully considers the free jazz movement in his book *The History of Jazz*:

> It is impossible to comprehend the free jazz movement of these same years [1960s] without understanding how it fed on this powerful cultural shift in American society. Its practitioners advocated much more than freedom from harmonic structures or compositional forms – although that too was an essential part of their vision of jazz. Many of them saw their music as inherently political. They saw that they could, indeed must, choose between participating in the existing structures – in society, in the entertainment industry, in the jazz world – or rebelling against them. The aesthetic could no longer be isolated from these cultural currents.
>
> (Gioia 1997: 338)

Also of note:

> From a purely musical point of view, freedom/atonality in jazz music had appeared many years before Ornette Coleman and Cecil Taylor raised it into a decisive issue. Lennie Tristano had experimented with free techniques in a series of pieces – 'Intuition,' 'Digression,' 'Descent into the Maelstrom' – some of them dating back to the late 1940s. Bob Graettinger's writings for the Stan Kenton band, most notably his 1948 magnum opus *City of Glass*, were uncompromising works that defied the conventions of existing jazz harmonic and melodic techniques, as was Jimmy Giuffre's 1953 recording of 'Fugue'. Contemporary classical composers were also attempting to use jazz instrumentation to explore avant-garde techniques, as in Stravinsky's *Ebony Concerto* (1946) or Milton Babbitt's *All Set* (1957) …
>
> But each of these precursors of free jazz was *white*, and each was, to a greater or lesser extent, representative of the established order of things. The proponents of free jazz who came to prominence at the close of the 1950s were, in contrast, almost all outsiders: as African Americans they were outsiders from mainstream society; as musical renegades they were outsiders from mainstream jazz.
>
> (Gioia 1997: 339, emphasis added)

15 The music *was* important, though. Notes Berliner (1994): the bebop era represents a period of 'great empowerment in jazz history' (7), one in which 'a concentration of virtuosos forged and refined many practices that have remained conventions of the language of jazz' (7).

16 I will be using the term 'aporia' throughout this book. Aporia comes from the Greek *aporos*, meaning 'without passage' or 'without issue' (Beardsworth 1996: 32). According to Beardsworth, '[a]n aporia is something which is impracticable. A route which is impracticable is one that cannot be traversed, it is an uncrossable path. Without passage, not treadable' (32). For an extended discussion of aporia in Derrida's writings, see Zlomislic (2007).

17 Compare with Henry Louis Gates's concept of 'Signifyin(g)' as a model of improvisation that is '"nothing more" than repetition and revision' (Gates 1988: 63–64). Although his approach differs significantly from Derrida's, there are potential parallels between Gates's theory and Derrida's understanding of improvisation as 'iterability' (Derrida 1989: 51).

18 McCormick (2001) describes 'deconstruction' as 'the literary theory wing of post-structuralism, a roughly described antifoundational intellectual movement originating in France in the 1960s' (419, n. 3). In contrast, Derrida (1999) said of deconstruction: 'Deconstruction is not a philosophy or a method, it is not a phase, a period or a moment.

It is something that is constantly at work and was at work before what we call "deconstruction" started, so I cannot periodize' (65).

19 The caution is now customary when positing a theoretical or methodological orientation that is deconstructive in nature. Not only was Derrida extremely suspicious of the title 'deconstruction' (Critchley 2005: 27), to call it a 'framework', 'method', 'theory' or even a 'reading' shamefully belittles the complexities of deconstructive thought (Beardsworth 1996: xv). Borrowing from Jacqueline Rose, 'it would be a grave error to describe [deconstruction] as system or school of thought because it has seized schools and systems by their very nerve endings, leaving nothing as it was before' (Cixous and Derrida 2004). Derrida's reluctance to label deconstruction a method or theory is explained by Beardsworth as follows:

> Derrida is careful to avoid this term ['method'] because it carries connotations of a procedural form of judgment. A thinker with a method has already decided *how* to proceed, is unable to give him or herself up to the matter of thought at hand, is a functionary of the criteria which structure his or her conceptual gestures. For Derrida, ... this is irresponsibility itself. Thus to talk of a method in relation to deconstruction, ... would appear to go directly against the current of Derrida's philosophical adventure.
>
> (Beardsworth 1996: 4, emphasis in original)

One may be obliged to employ such words as theory or method when describing deconstruction, but the spectre of this warning necessarily haunts each use.

20 Modern jurisprudence 'constructs theories that portray the law as a coherent body of rules and principles, or of intentions and expressions of a sovereign will' (Douzinas et al. 1991: ix). These theories may necessarily diverge or conflict, but they are united in their consensus as to the object 'law' (Fitzpatrick 1992: 2). As Peter Fitzpatrick explains, '[j]urisprudence is littered with isolated and opposed notions about law but the field retains a unity of engagement with law' (2–3).

21 For more on the role of melody in jazz improvisation, see Chapter 5.

22 Postema leaves aside questions of the *foundations* of normativity, both generally speaking and legal normativity in particular (Postema 2004: 206). Instead, his starting point is the seemingly uncontroversial notion that the essence of law is its distinctively normative character or its ability to 'guide human action normatively' (219). On this, he writes: 'In the history of jurisprudence, no serious theory of law of which I am aware denies this proposition' (219).

23 'Extempore' literally means 'out of the time' (OERD 1996: 494). On the Derridean 'to come', see Chapter 7.

24 Landgraf (2011) uses the term 'doing' deliberately to invoke Judith Butler's linking of 'the "doing" of gender specifically to improvisation' (15). Quoting Butler's *Undoing Gender* (2004): 'If gender is a kind of a doing, an incessant activity performed, in part, without one's knowing and without one's willing, it is not for that reason automatic or mechanical. On the contrary, it is the practice of improvisation within a scene of constraint' (1; quoted in Landgraf 2011: 15).

25 On the regulation of rock music see Holt (1990) and Soocher (1998). On rap, see Kahan (1993), Wolfe (1993), Glassner (2003) and Martinez (2004). For an article on the content regulation of recorded music, see Fernandez (2002). I greatly appreciate the comments of my PhD examiner, Professor Roger Cotterrell, in this regard.

26 In 'Play – The First Name' (2004a), Derrida comments: 'It is indeed necessary to improvise. It is necessary to improvise *well* ... This chance frightens me, I have no idea what's going to happen' (332, emphasis in original).

27 Gallope (2011) focuses his critique of Derrida solely on his reading of 'Play' (2004a).

28 I found myself at the receiving end of this accusation in Michael David Székely's analysis of my article 'Deconstructin(g) Jazz Improvisation: Derrida and the Law of the Singular Event' (2006):

> In one sense, then, it seems that Ramshaw's Derridean view of jazz improvisation culminates in a negative critique, which is to say that it demonstrates what jazz improvisation *cannot* do, what it *cannot* be, and how its claim to singularity is 'impossible'.
>
> (Székely 2008: 40, emphasis in original)

Fortunately, Székely is quick to identify the promise that attaches itself to the aporia of the extempore in both improvisation and law:

> In another sense, however – and the more important sense, I believe – there is, as Ramshaw attests, a much deeper and more nuanced notion of 'the impossible', in which it can, by virtue of its impossibility, actually 'release' and 'support' possibility.
>
> (Székely 2008: 40)

For a concise account of Derrida's (negative) reception in American legal academia, see Goodrich et al. (2008). See also de Ville (2011: 3).

29 To haunt, to be spectral, Rottenberg (2002) explains in relation to Derrida's work, 'is to be neither present nor absent; it is neither to be nor not to be' (5). Spectrality 'exceeds all ontological oppositions between absence and presence, visible and invisible, living and dead' (5). See also Derrida (2007).

30 Petra Gehring (2008) dismisses insinuations of Derrida's importance to law: 'lawyers would have no problem affirming the "aporias" of the legal sphere which Derrida ... worked out and presented as contradictions. These paradoxes are not new for legal discourse' (68). Yet, as de Ville (2011) aptly notes, the paradoxes detected by critical legal scholars 'do not become aporias in the sense that they do in Derrida' (11). This will be explained further in Chapters 3 and 7.

31 For more on this event, see Chapter 3.

32 According to Martin (2002), 'whatever the particular mixture of musical elements in a jazz performance, it is in the *practice* of improvisation – not rhythm, nor melody, nor harmony – that jazz differs most from established procedures in the tradition of western art music' (133–4, emphasis in original). Of note, though, distinctions between jazz and the Western canon are not so simple or uncomplicated. Desmond Manderson (2010) writes: 'We think of classical music as the very opposite of improvisation, as the creature of calculated perfectionism of creation and reproduction' (1). Yet, '[t]here is an enormous tradition of improvisation in classical music, as there is in all musical traditions' (1).

33 Variations on this response have also been attributed to 'Fats' Waller and Duke Ellington (Townsend 2000: 162).

34 See Chapter 5.

35 Before the music got the name 'bebop', it was simply called 'playing modern' (Ward and Burns 2001: 292) or '"New York" jazz' (Gitler 1985: 6). In fact, according to one of its originators, Kenny 'Klook' Clarke, '"Bebop" was a label that certain journalists later gave it, but we never labeled the music. It was just modern music, we would call it. We wouldn't call it anything, really, just music' (quoted in Gillespie 1996: 563).

36 According to Muyumba (2009), bebop '[d]eveloped in a range of locations from Kansas City dance halls to jam session parlors' (36). The focus here will be on NYC. For further discussion of the birth of bebop at Minton's and Monroe's, see Baraka (1963: 197–8), Ellison (1996: 545), Muyumba (2009: 26), Neal (2004: 201), and Peretti (1997: 100–3).

37 The contemporary presentation of jazz music as a string of improvised solos nestled within opening and closing sequences that outline the theme or melody of the piece of music

(Berliner 1994: 63; Hall 1999: 1599) was a formula from which bebop musicians rarely departed (Gioia 1997: 203). Berliner (1994) writes that bebop was a great period of 'empowerment in jazz history', in which 'concentration of virtuosos forged and refined many practices that have remained conventions of the language of jazz' (7).

I am aware that both the jam session and the improvising solo pre-date the emergence of bebop (Kofsky 1998a: 106). Still, I will not be discussing either phenomenon outside the context of bebop here.

2 The rise and reform of the New York City cabaret laws

1 According to Sidney Bechet, '[j]azz could mean any damn thing: high times, screwing, ballroom. It used to be spelled jass, which was screwing' (quoted in Green 1966: 43).

2 For more on Mayor Walker, see Northrop and Northrop (1932), Fowler (1949), Walsh (1974), Mitgang (2003) and Peretti (2007).

3 Peretti writes that although it may have seemed paradoxical that Walker led this crusade, it was actually 'in accordance with the wider moralistic campaign he led against traditionally objectionable forms of popular and mass culture in the city' (Peretti 2007: 56). For more on the paradoxes of Walker's governance, see Ramshaw (forthcoming).

4 Many of the *New York Times* articles, collected from the *NYT* online archive, are without page numbers. Copies of the original articles are on file with the author.

5 Applications for these special permits are to be made to the Commissioner of Licenses and a fee of $5 must be paid for each such permit granted (Local Law 12 1926: s. 5; see also *NYT*, 17 December 1926).

6 Also proposed was that hotels of 300 rooms or more, instead of 50 rooms as in the 1926 law, would be exempt from licensing (*NYT*, 6 February 1931; *NYT*, 16 May 1931).

7 On 30 December 1937, Local Law 12 and its amendment was incorporated in its entirety into the NYC Charter and later became Administrative Code, s. 436–1.0 (Cohen 1961: 3). The source of this information was attorney Maxwell Cohen's affidavit in the 1961 case of *Simone v Kennedy*, which is contained in the 'Cabaret Card' Clipping File, Institute for Jazz Studies, Rutgers University.

8 According to the *New York Times* (12 February 1933: 27), upon the completion of this inquiry, two magistrates, Jean H. Norris and Jesse Silbermann, had been removed from office; three had resigned under fire, i.e. Francis X. McQuade, Henry M.R. Goodman and George W. Simpson; a sixth, Abraham Rosenbluth, had gone into exile.

9 See Northrop and Northrop (1932: viii) and *NYT* (7 May 1958: 35) for more detail.

10 Ramshaw (forthcoming) provides further information on the Seabury Commission.

11 For more information on Seabury's investigation into this framing ring and the 'police trials' that followed, see the *New York Times* articles between 25 November 1930 and 23 March 1931 in the Bibliography.

12 Opening in Philadelphia on 4 February 1932, 'Face the Music', a musical comedy revue by Irving Berlin and Moss Hart, 'ridiculed, burlesqued and "exposed"' the NYPD in light of the findings of the Seabury investigation as that which 'uncovered big fortunes among active members of that city's boasted "finest"' (*NYT*, 4 February 1932: 25; see also Atkinson 1932: 24).

13 According to the *New York Times* (25 September 1940), fingerprinting of cabaret employees began on 1 October 1940. The deadline for registering fingerprints was 31 December 1940 (*NYT*, 1 December 1940), at which time over 15,000 employees were registered (*NYT*, 29 December 1940).

14 Applicants were charged a $2 'service charge' (s. 6(l)), which was then deposited into the Police Pension Fund (s. 6(l)); cards were renewable every two years (s. 6(k); see also Chevigny 1991: 58; Cohen 1993: 1).

15 Freeman (1960b) writes in the *NYT* that 'the regulations gave the police discretionary right to deny police identity cards to ex-convicts, narcotics addicts, racket suspects and

homosexuals' (30). That the 'police cards' were used to target and investigate gay employees of cabaret clubs deserves thorough investigation. Unfortunately, I do not have the archival material at my disposal to give the issue proper attention here.

16 It is important to note that the burden of proving necessity and justification is not on the plaintiffs, but instead lies with the police department (Cohen 1993: 21).

17 Of note, Justice Pecora, in reserving judgment, declared in court on 20 December 1940 that 'some regulations were necessary for "so-called cabarets where large numbers of people gather indiscriminately," but added that "there is a rather serious question as to whether some of the regulations contravene fundamental rights"' (*NYT*, 21 December 1940). He was particularly concerned that '[t]he provision that no person whose record is unsatisfactory to the Police Department may be employed is too broad'. Assistant Corporation Counsel Weinstein assured the judge of the following amendments: 'record' meant 'criminal record' and that it must be satisfactory to the Police Commissioner, not the Police Department.

18 Some speculation exists over the actual date. Cohen writes in *The Police Card Discord* that the Cabaret Employee Identification Card rules and regulations 'were not applied to musicians until about two years later [that is, 1942]' (Cohen 1993: 19).

19 The vulnerability of musicians to the cabaret card system of regulation was heightened by the fact that, for jazz musicians, 'the nightclub would continue to be one of the main sources of sustenance, regardless of how inhospitable that environment might be for a sophisticated music such as bebop' (Kofsky 1998a: 114).

20 Pianist Billy Taylor and drummer Shelly Manne argue that the jazz musician is more 'accessible' to the drug pushers because 'many of the nightclubs, many of the places in which jazz musicians work, are easily accessible to the people who want to push narcotics' (Adderley et al. 1960).

Dexter Gordon reveals the following in an interview with Ira Gitler:

> People always talk about why so many jazz musicians were strung out in the post-war period. Some believe it was because of the frustration of trying to play a music that people weren't accepting, or the pressure of being different. Others cite the influences of the music environment – the people, the whole night-life underground, tracing it back to Storyville in New Orleans and working for the gangsters in Chicago.
>
> (Quoted in Gitler 1985: 283–4)

21 Clarke (1994) argues that California, one of the first states to enact anti-marijuana legislation in 1915, did so in a 'subliminally racist attempt to keep its Spanish-speaking population under control' (204).

22 According to Gillespie (1979), many, if not most, beboppers used and abused drugs and alcohol. 'They used to tell jokes about it. One bebopper walked up to another and said, "Are you going to flat your fifths tonight?" The other one answered, "No, I'm going to drink mine." That's a typical joke about beboppers' (283).

23 On the financial benefits of converting to Islam (Farrell and Johnson 71), see Langston Hughes's poem 'Jam Session'.

24 Holiday's genius, argues Angela Davis (1998), came from her profound ability to 'musically [convey] her own state of mind' (194). She 'never performed the same piece at the same tempo twice' (Berliner 1994: 309) and 'constantly varied its mood to suit her own' (309). According to Erenberg (1998), 'Holiday's improvisations, inflections, and phrasings were very advanced for audiences' (171).

25 It is uncertain whether Levy was actually influential enough to get the police to ignore this blatant contravention of a NYC police regulation or whether the detectives allowed Holiday to work in Club Ebony in order to monitor her drug use. Chilton (1975) asserts,

'[c]ertainly the police not only attended the club, but also kept Billie under close observation even though her parole had ended' (124).

26 For more on Holiday's 1949 arrest and trial for narcotics possession, see Ramshaw (2004).

27 According to Gioia:

> Accounts of how he earned this sobriquet ['Yardbird', often shortened to 'Bird'] differ – it may have initially referred to nothing more than a fondness for poultry – but eventually it took on a larger significance, representing to his fans the unprecedented free-flying creativity of his alto sax lines.
>
> (Gioia 1997: 207)

28 For a more detailed account of Parker's musical progression and career, see Gioia (1997: 205–9).

29 Like Parker, pianist and composer, Thelonious Monk, also lost his card in 1951 when arrested in an automobile with bebop pianist Bud Powell. It is alleged that heroin was found at Monk's feet and, while it remains a mystery whether it belonged to him, Monk '"took the weight," as jazz musicians said' (Gourse 1997: 87) and lost his cabaret card in the process (Chevigny 1991: 61), along with 'his right to work in New York' (Gourse 1997: 87). Monk eventually got his card back in 1957, 'with the help of influential friends' (Neidlinger, quoted in Chevigny 1991: 61). However, for Monk, 'the relief came too late' (Gourse 1997: 92). The financial hardship provoked by the loss of his cabaret card, along with the necessity of having to tour outside NYC, meant that Monk was forced to venture outside his structured family environment and this had a negative impact on his already fragile psychological state.

30 Committee members included, among others, Harold Humes, Norman Mailer, Art D'Lugoff, James Baldwin, Frank O'Hara, Nat Hentoff, Nina Simone, Theodor Bikel, George Hoefer and Gene Lees. The legal advisor was Maxwell T. Cohen.

31 Frank Sinatra, for example, had boycotted NYC cabarets since 1957 in a protest against fingerprinting (Lissner 1966: 1, 24) and famously admitted to working in NYC clubs in the 1950s, such as the Copacabana, without a cabaret card. He is quoted as saying: 'I will not seek a cabaret card in New York because of the indignity of being fingerprinted, mugged [photographed] and quizzed about my past' (quoted in Chevigny 1991: 63).

32 In 1986, Chevigny successfully challenged the constitutionality of the incidental music exception to the NYC cabaret law, which excluded wind, brass and percussionist instruments and limited the number of players to three. *Chiasson v NYC* (1986) declared unconstitutional those provisions that limited the types of musical instruments that could provide incidental music (par. 33). *Chiasson v NYC* (1988) held that the portion of the incidental music exception, limiting the number of musicians to three, was similarly unconstitutional (par. 13). Chevigny's book, *Gigs: Jazz and the Cabaret Laws in New York City* (1991) charts this legal battle.

33 This lawsuit was brought under the free expression provisions of the New York State Constitution and not the Federal First Amendment. This is because, '[a]lthough the First Amendment does not explicitly protect the right to dance socially, "free expression" has traditionally been defined more broadly in New York because this city is an artistic center' (O'Rourke 2006; see also Romano 2002, 2005, 2006, 2007).

3 Deconstructive legal improvisation

1 The term 'deconstructive legal improvisation' is a play on 'deconstructive inventiveness', which Derrida describes in 'Psyche: Inventions of the Other' (1989): 'deconstructive inventiveness can consist only in opening, in uncloseting, destabilizing foreclusionary structures so as to allow for the passage toward the other' (60).

2 Coleman's music generated '[t]he same kinds of comment and misguided protest' as that of Parker, Gillespie and Monk in the 1940s (Baraka 1963: 234–35).

3 Many studies of Derrida and improvisation make mention this event. See, for example, Székely (2008: 38); Chemillier (2009: 10–11), Adleman (2010), Gallope (2011: 2–5) Landgraf (2011: 19–29).

4 As a young man, Coleman was distressed about having to make his living playing in gaming houses and brothels (Nettelbeck 2004: 199). His mother's comment – 'Do you want to be paid for your soul?' – allegedly liberated him from the 'world of commerce and corruption' (199) and led him to 'make music with and for his soul' (199). This anecdote, recounted by Coleman before the concert, was, among many, inspirations for Derrida's text (200; see also Derrida 2004a).

The entire text, 'Joue – le prénom' ['Play – The First Name'], prepared in advance of the performance, along with the interview that preceded the session, 'La Langue de l'autre' ['The Other's Language'], were originally published in *Les Inrockuptibles* (20 August–2 September 1997: 37–43) and later translated into English in *Genre: Forms of Discourse and Culture* (2004a). See also 'Le musicien, le philosophe et les fanatiques', *Jazz Magazine* 473 (1997): 26–28. For an extended analysis of 'Joue – le prénom' ['Play – The First Name'], see Wills (2006: 36–45).

5 Bruce King (2004) admits to being 'a member of that audience booing Derrida to shut up'. He defends his actions by stating: 'Derrida was not listed on the programme, he was not announced, and I paid my money to hear Coleman'. David Wills (2006) provides further details regarding the event: 'At the concert, he remained on stage for only about fifteen minutes (thanks to Peggy Kamuf we can remember it now), and so read about half, perhaps a little more, of his written text ["Play – the First Name"], interlaced with some playing by Coleman' (28, 30).

6 Derrida recalls: 'His [Coleman's] fans were so unhappy they started booing. It was a very unhappy event. It was a very painful experience' (quoted in Stein 2002; see also Wills 2006: 40).

7 Harmolodics: 'Harmony, Motion and Melody'. According to Steve Lake, writer for *Wire* magazine:

> … harmolodics in practice means this: You solo all the time and you stay out of the other guy's way. The source for this improvisation is of Ornette's notating but the charts are only there as raw source material. You don't necessarily play the note that's written on your sheet music, Dewey Redman once said, you just have to hold in your mind the way in which Ornette might play it.
>
> Once the head of the melody is negotiated, and that too may be placed quite approximately, the musician is free to play on any of the melody's centres. A certain note sequence might set up its own momentum when explored more thoroughly. Or, more vaguely still, the player might choose to focus on what he considers the *feeling* of the melody.
>
> (Lake 1985, emphasis in original)

8 According to Gioia (1997), 'harmolodics', as a theoretical approach, 'came to represent more a metaphysical doctrine than a musicological tool' (346).

9 For a critique of the division between the melodic and harmonic forms, see Chapter Three of Derrida's *Of Grammatology* (1976).

10 By 'background', Coleman is referring to the 'general framework of jazz improvisation which had established itself soon after the birth of jazz as a more or less incontestable norm' (Jost 1994: 17). This 'framework', Jost claims, 'consisted of a code of agreements which made up … the "musically universal" in jazz, and remained constant throughout the years of jazz evolution, while the "musically particular" changed' (17).

11 The rigid dichotomy constructed as between Derrida and Coleman, while productive for this enquiry, is actually somewhat misleading. It is not Coleman, but those 'on the outside' (Coleman and Derrida 2004: 320), who view free jazz as music without law. In an interview with Derrida on 23 June 1997, Coleman explains:

> OC: … when I was doing free jazz, most people thought that I just picked up my saxophone and played whatever was going through my head, without following any rule, but that wasn't true.
> JD: You constantly protest against that accusation.
> OC: Yes. People on the outside think that it's a form of extraordinary freedom, but I think that it's a limitation.
> …
> What's really shocking in improvised music is that despite its name, most musicians use a 'framework [*trame*]' as a basis for improvising. … [I]t's totally improvised, but at the same time it follows the laws and rules of European structure. And yet, when you hear it, it has a completely improvised feel [*air*].
>
> (Coleman and Derrida 2004: 320–21)

12 Piyel Haldar (2004) is referring here to the doctrine of *L'Amor Fou* [mad love], adopted most famously by the twentieth-century surrealists and poetic-terrorists, which thinks a 'moment of pure passion as a literary experience that properly escapes the clammy grasp of law' (7). In other words, '[i]n being abandoned by any form of sovereignty … mad love marks a point at which the subject falls away from the law. In that moment of abandon, the subject falls out of love for the law' (7). While the subject and the relationship between the surrealist technique of 'automatic writing' and the law. In this paper, he considers the case of *Cummings v. Bond* [1927] 1 Ch. 167, which was a dispute over the ownership of copyright of a manuscript produced through a séance held by medium Dorothy Cummings.

13 Michael Gallope writes of the Q&A session, attended by Derrida, which followed the NYC's Film Forum screening of *Derrida* in October 2002:

> … I raised my hand from the audience and asked Derrida quite directly: 'What kind of music do you listen to and why do you listen to it?' His answer, to say the least, initially seemed un-illuminating, if not a little nasty:
> I usually don't answer such questions. What would such mean? Um, I love jazz, and Bach, and Mozart … and … you shouldn't ask such a question! [Audience laughs.] I love music, and I'm not competent … I'm not, I have no real musical culture … I mean, in a professional sense. But I love music, and I listen to music all the time … And, well, free jazz, uh, or Bach or Mozart.
>
> (Gallope 2011: 2)

14 In his interview with *Jazz Magazine*, Derrida confesses that he will not authorize himself to write on jazz: 'I enjoy listening to jazz a lot, I would never have agreed to do this [that is, perform with Coleman] if I didn't like jazz, but it is a foreign world to me, I would never permit myself to write on jazz' (quoted in Wills 2006: 42). Instead, Derrida (1989) restricts his discussion of 'invention' in 'Psyche' to what he views as the 'only two major types of *authorized* examples for invention': invention of '*stories* (fictional or fabulous)' and invention of '*machines*, technical devices or mechanisms, in the broadest sense of the word' (32, emphasis in original).

15 The best estimate I can give is sometime between 1982, the year Scritti Politti released the song 'Jacques Derrida', and early 1988 when Gartside mentions in a 5 March 1988

interview in *Melody Maker* that he had 'met Derrida' (Reynolds 1988). No mention is made of this meeting in any interviews I have read prior to this date.

16 For a view, which opposes Cobussen, see Jacques Attali's *Noise*:

> To my mind, the origin of music should not be sought in linguistic communication. Of course, the drum and song have long been carriers of linguistic meaning. But there is no convincing theory of music as language. The attempts that have been made in that direction are no more than camouflages for the lamest kind of naturalism or the most mundane kind of pedantry. The musical message has no meaning, even if one artificially assigns a (necessarily rudimentary) signification to certain sounds, a move that is almost always associated with a hierarchical discourse.
>
> (Attali 1985: 25)

17 As Derrida writes in *Of Hospitality*, 'Reticence, as you know, is the figure of a deliberate keeping-quiet so that more than eloquence can be heard in it' (Derrida and Dufourmantelle 2000: 95; see also Cobussen 2002b: par. 2).

18 See, for example, 'Declarations of Independence' (1986), 'The Laws of Reflection: Nelson Mandela, In Admiration' (1987), 'Before the Law' (1992a), 'The Law of Genre' (1992b) and 'Force of Law: The "Mystical Foundation of Authority"' (2002b).

'Force of Law', Derrida's most significant 'legal' text, comprises two smaller, albeit still lengthy, essays, 'Of the Right to Justice/From Law to Justice' and 'First Name of Benjamin'. Zacharias charts the history of this text:

> The former essay was first presented as a keynote address at a conference at the Cardozo Law School [in 1989]; the latter was distributed as a companion to that keynote, handed out to participants but not read aloud. Both essays concern the questions of law and justice; in fact, the second may be considered something of a demonstration of the first. ... One year later, at a University of California – Los Angeles conference entitled 'Nazism and the "Final Solution": Probing the Limits of Representation', Derrida returned to this second essay, adding a 'prolegomena' and a 'post-scriptum', and reading the extended essay aloud as a second keynote address.
>
> (Zacharias 2007: 103–4)

All references to 'Force of Law' will be from the *Acts of Religion* (2002) version, which revised the 1989 translation, published originally in the *Cardozo Law Review* (1989–90) and Cornell et al.'s *Deconstruction and the Possibility of Justice* (1992), in order to 'include the changes made in the latest French edition of the text, published in 1994' (Anidjar 2002: 229).

19 See 'Psyche: Inventions of the Other' (1989).

20 According to the *Oxford English Reference Dictionary*, to 'improvise' is to 'compose or perform (music, verse, etc.) *extempore*' (OERD 1996: 710, emphasis added).

21 Invention is defined as the 'creation of something which did not exist before' (Black 1990: 824).

22 Although a philosopher, not a lawyer, many have noted the 'juridical context and significance' of Derrida's writings (Goodrich 2005: 15). See, for example, Goodrich et al. (2008) and Davies (2001).

23 This phrase was first coined by Sun Ra, 'jazz innovator and Astro-Black philosopher', in the 1980 documentary *Sun Ra: A Joyful Noise* (Fischlin and Heble 2004: 1). Fischlin and Heble have appropriated it as the title of their edited collection on the topic of jazz improvisation and dialogic communities. Explaining the meaning of this phrase, Fischlin and Heble write:

> The other side of nowhere ... tropes a mysterious horizon beyond which the potential for thinking alternatives – whether musical, social, communitarian, theoretical, and so forth – is activated as a generative principle of seeking out contrarian knowledges,

> dissonant social practices, and transgressive uncertainties, all in opposition to orthodoxies that limit or circumscribe the limits of human potentiality. The other side is unknowable but there nonetheless; no one can be fully sure what lies on the other side and yet it references a somewhere crucial to the dynamics of improvisatory practice.
>
> (Fischlin and Heble 2004: 10)

24 The division between invention as 'unveiling discovery' or 'productive discovery' (Derrida 1989: 49), as finding what already exists or actually producing the new, will be familiar to lawyers. For this self-same distinction animates the debate between judge-found and judge-made law, as outlined in Chapter 6.
25 For more on the notion of the origin as fiction, see Birmingham (1997).
26 Contrary to popular belief, the signing of the Declaration of Independence, which signalled American independence from Great Britain, did not occur on the Fourth of July, 1776 (Finkelman 1981: 1141). Instead, '[i]t was only passed in rough form by Congress on that day. The signing did not occur until August 2, and some members who were absent that day signed later' (1141 fn1).
27 Explains Landgraf:

> This self-referential quality, where performance points towards itself as performance, is central to performed improvisations. They must be clearly marked, be it by the event announcing its own doings as improvised or more structurally, as in bebop, where the standard repetition of the theme at the beginning is reliably followed by the improvisational sections until one returns to the theme, signaling the conclusion of the piece.
>
> (Landgraf 2011: 144)

28 Pope (2005) remarks similarly regarding Derrida's 'Psyche: Inventions of the Other' (1989):

> ... it is precisely the act of 'inventing', poised between the old and new senses of the word, to which Derrida draws attention in this paper and the performance that occasioned it. Indeed it is the tension between the written paper and the actual lecture – to be even more precise, between what was scripted in advance, what was improvised in the event, and what was subsequently redrafted for publication – that is the mainspring of this piece.
>
> (Pope 2005: 64)

29 Iterability invites both negativity and promise and there is 'a certain affinity between hospitality and mourning' (Derrida 2007: 453). Singularity, in other words, only takes place through repetition. Yet, with the repetition 'the erasure of the first occurrence is already underway – whence loss, mourning, and the posthumous, sealing the first moment of the event, as originary' (453).
30 For more on the violence of law in relation to Benjamin's distinction between 'founding' and 'preserving' violence, see Derrida (2002b).

4 The 'wildness' of jazz improvisation

1 See also Hermann Hesse's novel *Steppenwolf* (1929: 37). For an analysis of Hesse and jazz, see Jones (1991: 47–49).
2 *New York Times* (30 January 1922) reported: 'Jazz goes back to the African jungle and is one of the crying evils of today. ... It is a savage crash and bang' (16). This chapter will

not engage with the question of the African origins of jazz. See instead Newton (1959: 16); Kaufman and Guckin (1979); and Appelrouth (2003: 119).

3 Not only did white Americans hold derogatory views of jazz music. As noted by Ralph Ellison in *Shadow and Act*:

> ... jazz was regarded by most of the respectable Negroes of the town as a backward, low-class form of expression, and there was a marked difference between those who accepted and lived close to their folk experience and those whose status strivings led them to reject and deny it.
>
> (Ellison 1953: 238)

Jazz 'was a music made for the poor', derided as 'not respectable by the vast majority of the black middle classes' (Hore 1993). In the words of Calmore, '[j]azz has too often hung like a skeleton of middle-class black America, locked away in a psychic closet, a sign of running away from our cultural heritage' (Calmore 1992: 2158–9).

4 The mythology surrounding jazz as wild and immoral finds its origins in the association with prostitution and the brothel, 'usually the Negro brothel' (Leonard 1962: 36; see also Holiday 1992 [1956]: 11).

5 The Cotton Club, at 142nd and Lenox Avenue, opened in 1922 by owner Bernard Levy (Ostransky 1978: 201). It remained in Harlem until 16 February 1936, at which time it moved downtown to Broadway and 48th Street (200 West 48th Street). The jungle decor remained. The Cotton Club closed down for good on 10 June 1940 (Haskins 1977: 113–14, 156).

6 The Cotton Club had a policy, which was 'opposed to mixed parties' (Van Vechten, quoted in Haskins 1977: 36). Only the lightest-complexioned blacks gained entrance, and even they were carefully screened. As Haskin explains:

> The club's management was aware that most white downtowners wanted to *observe* Harlem blacks, not mix with them; or, as Jimmy Durante put it, 'it isn't necessary to mix with colored people if you don't feel like it. You have your own party and keep to yourself. But it's worth seeing. How they step!'
>
> (Haskins 1977: 37, emphasis in original)

Thus, at the Cotton Club, the audience was primarily white, while the performers were black. But there were further restrictions on the performers, or at least the female ones: 'The chorus girls had to be uniformly "high-yaller" ['nothing darker than a light olive tint' (Haskins 1977: 75)], at least 5'6', dancers, and able to carry a tune. And they could not be over twenty-one' (33). This ensured that all female employees were 'light-skinned women who could appeal to white concepts of beauty, but had the touch of darker exoticism and hence animality' (Erenberg 1981: 257).

7 For more on jazz's abandon, see Appelrouth (2003: 123, 129).

8 Remarks Robert Orr: 'It was the atomic age of music. We were dropping bombs on Japan and Max Roach was dropping musical bombs. It was a crazy era because everyone was sort of wild at the time' (quoted in Szwed 2002: 33).

9 The origin of the name 'bebop' or 'bop' is unknown. Musician Budd Johnson attributes the label to Dizzy Gillespie, who used to 'hum everything to everybody to get them to see what he was still talkin' about' (quoted in Gitler 1985: 119). Says Johnson in an interview with Ira Gitler:

> So he would sing [imitates Gillespie], and actually, that's how I think it got its name, bebop. Because he would be humming this music, and he'd say, 'Ooop bop ta oop a la doo bop doo ba.' So people said, 'Play some more of that bebop' because he would be saying, 'Bebop.' And the cats would say, 'Sing some more of that bebop,'

> and actually, I think that's how it got its name, because that's the way he would have to sing it to make you get the feeling that he wanted you to play with.
>
> (quoted in Gitler 1985: 119)

Langston Hughes offers another possibility:

> '*You* must not know where Bop comes from,' said Simple, astonished at my ignorance.
>
> 'I do not know,' I said. 'Where?'
>
> 'From the police,' said Simple.
>
> 'What do you mean, from the police?'
>
> 'From the police beating Negroes' heads,' said Simple. 'Every time a cop hits a Negro with his billy club, that old club says, "BOP! BOP! ... BE-BOP! ... MOP! ... BOP!"'
>
> ...
>
> ' ... That's where Be-Bop came from, beaten right out of some Negro's head into those horns and saxophones and the piano keys that plays it ... '
>
> ...
>
> ' ... If they do not hit me, they have already hurt my soul. A dark man shall see dark days. Bop comes out of them dark days. That's why real Bop is mad, wild, frantic, crazy – and not to be dug unless you've seen dark days, too. Folks who ain't suffered much cannot play Bop, neither appreciate it. They think Bop is nonsense – like you. They think it's just crazy crazy. They do not know Bop is also MAD crazy, SAD crazy, FRANTIC WILD CRAZY – beat out of somebody's head! That's what Bop is. Them young colored kids who started it, they know what Bop is.
>
> (Hughes 1961: 118–19)

10 For more on the relationship between bebop and the European aesthetic, see Laver (2009: 4–7).

11 'Corporate liberalism' is described by Belgrad as the following:

> ... a social and economic arrangement that has predominated in the United States since the 1920s, replete with a value system that has been called 'the culture of abundance' ... Corporate liberals instituted an 'American Way of Life' defined by a complementary combination of scientifically managed work with mass leisure and consumption. High wages, vacation time, and installment buying maintained a consistently high demand for industrial products, reversing the economic slump that had followed the end of the First World War. The federal government actively facilitated this arrangement by devoting its resources to projects that would benefit the business community as a whole, and big business in particular. It provided highways and electric power, developed industry standards, collected data, funded research, and cultivated domestic and foreign markets.
>
> (Belgrad 1998: 3)

Although the Great Depression of the 1930s 'threw corporate liberalism into crisis' (3), the war years 'ushered in a new era of corporate-liberal predominance' (3).

12 Disillusioned with the 'avant-garde dream of social change through art', and rejecting 'bohemian counterculture in favor of black nationalism and Black Power militancy', LeRoi Jones moved to Harlem in the early 1960s and renamed himself Imamu Ameer Baraka or Amiri Baraka (Belgrad 1998: 260).

13 The 'riff' is 'a catchy, strongly rhythmic fragment of melody or harmony that is repeated' (Kernfeld 1995: 91). Writes Kernfeld (1995): 'This sort of rhythmic motive is widespread in African-American music, and it is often impossible to determine whether a riff has been newly coined or borrowed' (91).

14 Gioia concurs:

> Frequently bebop composers simply grafted an exotic name and a new (and usually more complex) melody onto chords of earlier popular standards. ... The instrumentation of modern jazz also stayed true to prewar models. True, the beboppers preferred the small combo format to the prevalent big band sound, but the underlying rhythm section of piano, string bass, drums, and occasionally guitar remained unchanged, as did the use of saxophones, trumpets, and trombones as typical front-line instruments.
>
> (Gioia 1997: 202–3)

See also Muyumba:

> Emulating its mother tongue, the blues, bebop is a matrix in which all musical styles (for instance, New Orleans syncopation, Ellingtonia, southwestern swing, rags, gospel, Broadway show tunes, popular songs, and contemporary classical music) are fodder for melodic quotation or technical integration into the language of bebop composition and improvisation.
>
> (Muyumba 2009: 26)

15 On this point, Kofsky notes Williams's disappointment in being 'brought up short by the realization that a "typical" Parker phrase turns out to be much the same phrase one had heard years before from, say, Ben Webster' (quoted in Kofsky 1998a: 106–7). His disappointment, however, emanates from an impoverished view of improvisation as creating the wholly new. Chapter 4 complicates this conceptualization.

16 Kofsky (1998a) contends that 'the decisive additional ingredient that detonated the revolution was the *anger* with which young blacks greeted the nation's failure to implement the democratic ideology employed as a psychological weapon in World War II' (110–11, emphasis added).

17 For more on this debate, see Kofsky (1998a: 111; 1998b: 80–83).

18 That bebop was concerned with more than musical innovation appears readily accepted by contemporary theorists on the issue. See, for example, DeVeaux (1997), Gioia (1997), Lewis (2004b), and Muyumba (2009), to name a few.

19 Miles Davis was supposed to play trumpet on the recording of 'KoKo', but, as the story goes, he was unable to master its speed and complexity. Davis's biographer, John Szwed, however, asserts that he did not perform because the arrangement 'was new to him' (49) and he 'wasn't worth three dead flies' (Reig, quoted in Szwed 2002: 49) after all the partying done at the recording session (49). Regardless the reason, Gillespie 'filled in for the opening and closing parts on the trumpet, then moved back to the piano for the rest of the record' (49) and Davis 'missed out on a piece considered to be one of the most important in jazz history' (49).

20 Townsend (2000) writes: 'Improvisation and a regularly stated beat [a "swing beat"] are alien to the tradition of European–American concert music but fundamental to jazz, and historically this has proved to be an unbridgeable divide' (140).

21 Speaking specifically about Charlie Parker's playing, Miles Davis recalls: 'When Bird played like that, it was like hearing music for the first time. I'd never heard anybody play like that. ... Everything he played – when he was on and *really* playing – was terrifying, and I was there every night! ... It was unreal' (quoted in Szwed 2002: 62, emphasis in original).

22 On the issue of bebop's speed, Mary Lou Williams recollects: 'You know, when we first heard it during the forties, it sounded like a musician, like *Dizzy was playing a million notes in one bar*' (quoted in Gillespie 1996: 571, emphasis in original). Miles Davis also reportedly said of Bird, 'Parker was too fast to transcribe' (Szwed 2002: 40).

23 Writes Szwed (2002), 'it was *their* music, a music of black people' (40, emphasis in original).

24 Mary Lou Williams recalls a comment by Thelonious Monk, who tried to organize a big band before he began working at Minton's Playhouse in Harlem: 'We are going to get a big band started. We're going to create something that they can't steal because they can't play it' (quoted in DeVeaux 1997: 351).

See also Ralph Ellison, who writes:

> It was a time of big bands, and the greatest prestige and economic returns were falling outside the Negro community – often to leaders whose popularity grew from the compositions and arrangements of Negroes – to white instrumentalists whose only originality lay in the enterprise with which they rushed to market with some Negro musician's hard-won style. Still there was no policy of racial discrimination at Minton's. Indeed, it was very much like those Negro cabarets of the twenties and thirties in which a megaphone was placed on the piano so that anyone with the urge could sing a blues. Nevertheless, the inside-dopesters will tell you that the 'changes' or chord progressions and the melodic inversions worked out by the creators of bop sprang partially from their desire to create a jazz which could not be so easily imitated and exploited by white musicians to whom the market was more open simply *because* of their whiteness. They wished to receive credit for what they created, and besides, it was easier to 'get rid of the trash' who crowded the bandstand with inept playing and thus make room for the real musicians, whether white or black.
>
> (Ellison 1953: 211–12, emphasis in original)

For more on the issues and problems encountered by black jazz musicians in the United States, see DeVeaux (1997).

25 The 'Uncle Tom' caricature, derived from the main character in Harriet Beecher Stowe's novel *Uncle Tom's Cabin* (1852), has become a 'slur used to disparage a Black person who is humiliatingly subservient or deferential to White people' (Pilgrim 2000).

26 Baraka criticizes this treatment of bebop:

> 'You can't dance to it,' was the constant harassment – which is, no matter the irrelevancy, a lie. My friends and I as youths used to emphasize the pronoun more, saying, '*You* can't dance to it,' and whispered, 'or anything else, for that matter.'
>
> (Baraka 1963: 199–200, emphasis in original)

27 In an interview with Ira Gilter, musician Milt Hinton noted that it was less about race and more about skill. He says, 'So, really it was like isolation, what we were trying to do, to isolate everybody – white and black – who had a horn, who would come up to Minton's and buy a beer and figure they could sit in' (quoted in Gitler 1985: 58).

28 According to Beyer (2000), bop's 'countercultural intentions' soon 'began to merge with popular culture during the postwar period' (542): 'Bebop fused with popular culture and, therefore, failed as a legitimate means of political protest and cultural opposition because it could no longer address the cultural causes of racial inequality in America' (543). Bop musicians, despite their alleged 'explicitly political' (Hore 1993) stance and the 'politicized aesthetics of improvisatory wild musical practices' (Fischlin and Heble 2004: 3) more generally, 'never challenged the subordination of African Americans directly; rather, they distanced themselves from white culture through their unique dress, behavior, and musical performance' (Beyer 2000: 543). Again, in the words of Beyer, '[a]lthough conspicuous by their nonconformity, bebop musicians failed to direct their musical influence toward exposing the fundamental political, economic, and social foundations of racism' (543). In the end, 'popular culture adopted the mores and norms of bebop' (543) and 'the once radical musical community lost its potency for political and cultural opposition' (543).

29 By 1950, the cult of bebop had spread to other locations in the United States outside New York City. In a letter to the Mayor of the City of Milwaukee on 15 November 1950, the Assistant City Attorney reported on the findings of a local committee – comprising representatives of various legal organisations including the Children's Court, the Police Department, the Probation Department and the Juvenile Delinquency Committee of the Youth Commission – devoted to investigating the '"bebop" problem' (CUAP 1950c). Of concern was, amongst other things, '[t]he nature and scope of an alleged group of 400, more or less, beboppers possessing a graduated scale of delinquency achievement, the epitome of which is the lowest moral behaviour' (CUAP 1950c). The committee was particularly anxious about the crossing of the 'color line' (CUAP 1950c) encouraged by bebop and the fact that 'small parties have been held in private homes in which both white girls and colored boys have engaged in drinking, the use of narcotics and sex relations' (CUAP 1949).

Elsewhere, when a group of young women were asked on a Milwaukee radio station about the origin of the 'bebop problem', they answered with the following: 'Why, from the music the beboppers started. This music has a different type of beat from slow going music. It's a lower or different type of jazz, more exciting and you never know what's coming next' (CUAP 1950d). Eventually, the school authorities and parents initiated an out-and-out 'fight against "bebopism"' (CUAP 1950a) in Milwaukee. Beboppers were represented as a lawless clique, engaged in 'a specified number of illegal and immoral acts' (CUAP 1950b). Parents and school authorities were advised to encourage '"the bebop type of youth" to normal activities' (CUAP 1950b).

30 Many other factors contributed to the conception of bebop as 'wild' and rebellious. Of particular note are the 'vagaries of circumstance' (DeVeaux 1997: 7), such as the Second World War, which influenced the social construction of bebop. As DeVeaux writes, 'youthful fans called overseas after Pearl Harbor missed out on the crucial intervening developments (the "gradual incorporation" of "new techniques") and failed to recognize the continuity of the new jazz style on their return' (7). Those who remained in the United States were subject not only to 'wartime restrictions on materials' (Belgrad 1998: 181), but also to a recording ban, which 'effectively blocked the production of new recordings' (DeVeaux 1997: 7) between 1942 and 1945. For more on the recording ban, see Charters and Kunstadt (1962: 319), Hore (1993) and DeVeaux (1997: 296).

31 Minton's Playhouse, located on West 118th Street in Harlem, opened in 1938 by Henry Minton, 'a tenor saxophonist and the first black delegate to Local 802 of the musicians' union' (DeVeaux 1997: 219; Ward and Burns 2001: 291). For more on the history of the club, see DeVeaux (1997).

32 On this topic of racial mixing, Sonny Rollins tells Ira Gitler:

> Jazz has always been a music of integration. In other words, there were definitely lines where blacks would be and where whites would begin to mix a little bit. I mean, jazz was not just a music; it was a social force in this country, and it was talking about freedom and people enjoying things for what they are and not having to worry about whether they were supposed to be white, black, and all this stuff. Jazz has always been the music that had this kind of spirit. Now I believe for that reason, the people that would push jazz have *not* pushed jazz because that's what jazz means. A lot of times, jazz means no barriers. Long before sports broke down its racial walls, jazz was bringing people together on both sides of the bandstand. 52nd Street, for all its shortcomings, was a place in which black and white musicians could interact in a way that led to natural bonds of friendship. The audience, or at least part of it, took a cue from this, leading to an unpretentious flow of social intercourse.
>
> (Quoted in Gitler 1985: 303–4)

33 Musicians of different races may have mixed freely in the jam-session atmosphere, but as Hentoff emphasized at the time:

> … there is less socializing off the stand between most white and Negro jazz musicians than an idealistic jazz listener might imagine. Close interracial friendships and visiting between families do exist, but most white jazzmen tend to hang out with other whites and Negroes with Negroes.
>
> (Hentoff 1959: 74)

See also Cerulli (1984: 54).

34 For more on the relationship between art and mystery, see Irish literary critic Denis Donoghue's 1982 Reith Lectures on the issue of 'how society's rationalisation of art is destroying its mystery' (Donoghue 1982). A Special Issue of *Interface*, an interdisciplinary journal for the creative arts, humanities and social sciences (1983), was dedicated to a Symposium on the 1982 Reith Lectures (see Bolland et al. 1983).

35 The word 'improvisation' is derived from the Latin *improvisus*, which 'refers to the "unforeseen" or that which occurs "on the spur of the moment"' (Alterhaug 2004: 98).

36 Most books I have read on the subject accept that ' … bebop focused on the primacy of solo improvisation during group performance' (Muyumba 2009: 26). See also Lewis (2004b: 134) and Belgrad (1998: 188), to list two other examples.

37 As Gioia (1997) writes, '[i]nstrumental solos were at the heart of each [bebop] performance, sandwiched between an opening and closing statement of the melody. Deviations from this recipe were rare' (203; see also Berliner 1994: 63; Hall 1999: 1599).

38 While jazz musicians do not eschew the written score altogether, it plays a lesser role in jazz performances (Panish 1997: 79).

39 Amiri Baraka (1963) explains the negativity surrounding the notion of bebop as an art form: 'the music by the mid-forties had also begun to get tagged with that famous disparagement *art* (meaning superfluous, rather than something that makes it seem important that you are a human being). It had no "function"' (199, emphasis in original).

40 For more on Kerouac's 'spontaneous prose method', and the misunderstandings that plaque it, see Dardess (1975).

41 For further examples of Kerouac's association of bop improvisation with wildness, see 'Jazz of the Beat Generation' (1949) (Kerouac 1995b: 222–23) and 'The Beginning of Bop' (1959) (Kerouac 1995c: 555).

42 The appropriation of bop techniques by beat poets angered many bebop jazz musicians. As Charles Mingus stated at the 1957 celebration of Kerouac's *On the Road*, '[t]hey're stealing our music anyway and not doing it right. The cats that create this music should be part of the whole picture' (quoted in Santoro 2000: 130).

43 While Christine Battersby (1989) agrees that 'the category of genius had to work by a process of exclusion', she points to a further exclusion, namely that of women from the category of genius (4).

44 I would like to thank Dr Shaun Regan, Queen's University Belfast, School of English, for drawing my attention to this essay (and providing me with a copy of the text). Compare the following proverbs: 'Genius is born, not made' and 'Genius is one percent inspiration and ninety-nine percent perspiration'.

5 Demystifying improvisation

1 Berliner concurs:

> At times remarks by musicians appear to support this argument [i.e. that improvised music must be performed spontaneously and intuitively]. 'I have no idea what I am going to do when I take a solo,' Doc Cheatham says. 'That's the thing that I don't

> understand myself, and I've been asked about it so many times. When I play a solo, I never know any more about what I am going to play than you do.' George Duvivier also does not 'want to go into a solo with anything preconceived'. He finds it 'best to go in with an open mind and let it develop'. Other veterans advised Kenny Washington as a youngster 'not to think about playing – just play'.
>
> (Berliner 1994: 2)

2 I am grateful to Andy Laking for sharing his views on jazz improvisation.

3 See Mirvis (1998: 589).

4 Small is writing about music more generally, but its application is equally relevant to improvised music.

5 The dominant scholarly approach to the nature of creativity in the arts and sciences, at least until recently, has, according to Borgo:

> … proceeded from the assumption that creativity is primarily an individual psychological process, and that the best way to investigate it is through the thoughts, emotions, and motivations of those individuals who are already thought to be gifted or innovative. In the past several decades, however, creativity researchers have begun to focus more on the historical and social factors that shape and define creativity, and its role in everyday activities and learning situations.
>
> (Borgo 2005: 183)

6 Moreover, writes Kodat:

> … freedom in jazz does not exist in pure opposition to pre-existing musical convention (or cultural industry imperatives); on the contrary, freedom in jazz emerges *in conversation with* its formal and commercial limitations: jazz 'is only free insofar as it has reference to the strictness of the original form.'
>
> (Kodat 2003: 20, emphasis in original)

7 Ornette Coleman describes improvised jazz music as a 'conversation with sounds' (Coleman and Derrida 2004: 322).

8 According to Belgrad (1998: 189), '[b]ebop musicians further increased the expressiveness of their solo utterances by developing a larger vocabulary of rhythms, tones, and timbres'.

9 Michael Snow writes:

> Of course, everyone 'improvises'. Conversation is the most common form. All the mental states that one experiences in conversation are *somewhat* applicable to musical improvisation. …
>
> Playing music *isn't* 'conversation' though. So much of what happens that's moving, happens simultaneously, in group improvisation.
>
> (Snow 2004: 49, emphasis in original)

10 Of note here, however, is that the 'musical language' (Neal 2004: 202) created by bebop musicians also contributed to its transgressive and wild conceptualization within Western society for it was a 'musical language closed off from musicians unfamiliar with bebop sensibilities' (202). Small explains:

> … it was as if someone had taken a familiar vocabulary and, by altering the syntax by means of which the relationship between the words were established, had created a new language, tantalizingly similar to the old, but one in which the [the older musicians] were unable to converse.
>
> (Small 1985: 303, quoted in Neal 2004: 202)

11 One of the most celebrated ordeals in the jam session was when drummer Jo Jones 'threw his high-hat cymbal on the floor of the Reno Club in Kansas City to make it clear to a struggling teenaged Charlie Parker that he most emphatically did *not* belong – yet' (DeVeaux 1997: 214, emphasis in original). In response to this humiliation, Parker 'went back home and stayed in the house about three months and learned all the changes and all the things, so when he came back out he knew what he was doing. And that's what you had to do in bebop, was to *know* what you were doing' (McGhee, quoted in DeVeaux 1997: 227, emphasis in original).

12 Writes Gioia (1997): 'A sociology of jazz could glean much from these accounts of jam-session disgraces. Such public embarrassments would stand as a frequent rite of passage for the modern jazz musician' (210).

13 The 'saying something' of jazz improvisation simultaneously *communicates* 'theories about musical performance, the nature of identity, political concerns, and race' (Muyumba 2009: 18). This is achieved by 'improvising sonic interactions, interactively shaping social networks and communities that accompany musical participation, and developing culturally variable meanings and ideologies that inform the interpretation of jazz in American society' (18). For more on the broader social implications of improvisation, see Chapter 7.

14 Musicians frequently meet for the first time on the bandstand or stage (Peplowski 1998: 560).

15 Lassonde (2010: 3) prefers the term 'grounding rule' to designations such as 'law', 'norms' or 'rules' when describing the basic principles of improvisation.

16 Barrett and Peplowski (1998) note that 'musicians do not have to stop and discuss what chords and scales they will play on a given song. This frees musicians to *listen* to one another, anticipate and adjust to one another' (559, emphasis added).

17 Heble and Siddall (2000) describe Oliveros as 'one of the most significant and widely respected women in contemporary music' (157). For more on the philosophy and work of Oliveros, see McMullen (2008 and 2010).

6 The structure–freedom paradox in law

1 See Fischlin and Heble (2004: 33).

2 This Special Issue began as a two-day conference of the same name held in Montréal, Canada on 19–20 June 2009. It was hosted under the auspices of the ICASP project and supported by the Suoni de Popolo Music Festival, the McGill Centre for Intellectual Property Policy and the Faculty of Law at McGill University, Canada.

3 Postema's 'Melody and Law's Mindfulness of Time' (2004) provides one example of this approach. Melody, while an appropriate model of law's characteristic normativity, for Postema, is viewed to be so *only* as metaphor (208):

> Compared with other images frequently deployed in the history of jurisprudence to illuminate law's normativity, melody has one signal advantage: No one will be inclined to take it literally. No one will be tempted to look for music from courtrooms, solicitors' offices, parliament chambers, or police precincts. Still, with melody's model we will be able to shed light on familiar but often overlooked features of practical reasoning structured by law.
>
> (Postema 2004: 208–9)

Postema treats law and music as separate and distinct disciplines, disciplines that may have certain aspects in common and certain things to teach each other (Manderson 2003: 31), but only metaphorically and certainly not as inevitably interactive (31).

4 By this, Authers is referring to the fact that witnesses often rehearse their examination-in-chief with their lawyers, which is then 'presented in court as if improvised'. The

cross-examination of witnesses by opposing lawyers, however, usually happens for the first time in the courtroom and thus is 'more readily understood as improvised' (Authers 2012).

5 The 'problematic implications of metaphoricity' (Stanton 1986: 161) have been noted by Derrida. In 'White Mythology: Metaphor in the Text of Philosophy' (1982b), he writes that literal meaning 'becomes a metaphor when philosophical discourse puts it into circulation. Simultaneously the first meaning and the first displacement are then forgotten. The metaphor is no longer noticed, and is taken for the proper meaning' (211). This unnoticed metaphor is labelled 'white mythology', the very foundation of metaphysics:

> Metaphysics – the white mythology which resembles and reflects the culture of the West; the white man takes his own mythology, Indo-European mythology, his own *logos*, that is the *mythos* of his idiom, for the universal form of that he must still wish to call Reason. …
>
> White mythology – metaphysics has erased within itself the fabulous scene that has produced it, the scene that nevertheless remains active and stirring, inscribed in white ink, an invisible design covered over in the palimpsest.
>
> (Derrida 1982b: 213)

6 As Virginia Lee Strain (2011) argues in her study of English Renaissance law reform and literary forms, improvisation (both orthodox – 'improvisation as wildness' – and critical understandings) enters the legal realm through 'discretion and judgment' (178). Whether this legal improvisation is legitimate or desired is another story. Asks Wendy Adams (2010): 'Does not the significance of the rule of law, the requirement that we be governed by rules and not arbitrary, *ad hoc* discretion, call into question the legitimacy of improvisation in law?' (1).

7 Of note, this discussion of the structure–freedom paradox in law leaves unresolved the more fundamental issue of 'whether law exists for the sake of enlarging or for the sake of restricting the liberty of man' (Allen 1931: 331) – a question to which Cicero answered, 'We are the slaves of the law in order that we may be free' (quoted 331).

8 Precedent is defined as an 'adjudged case or decision of a court, considered as furnishing an example or authority for an identical or similar case afterwards arising from a similar question of law' (Black 1990: 1176).

9 The concept of judicial discretion, as that which precedent seeks to curtail, may often, argues Pardo (2009), 'evoke the image of an activist judge running amok with unbridled power, defying the will of the people and the democratically-elected legislature' (453).

10 The BBC (25 January 2012) reported that UK Prime Minister David Cameron warned 'the concept of human rights was being "distorted" – and even "discredited" – by controversial decisions in Europe' and pointed to the '"credible democratic anxiety" about rulings on immigration and prisoner voting by the European court'.

11 '[T]reating like cases alike', argues Lyons (1985), 'is often regarded as a requirement, indeed perhaps the central or most fundamental requirement, of *justice*. When so viewed, the practice of precedent is placed on a moral footing. It implies that the failure to follow precedent is not merely unwise but positively wrong' (497, emphasis added).

12 For more on 'interpretive discretion' or discretion in statutory interpretation, see Foy (2010).

13 In the words of Lord Buckmaster, '[t]he facts of this case are simple':

> On August 26th, 1928, the Appellant drank a bottle of ginger beer, manufactured by the Respondent, which a friend had bought from a retailer and given to her. The bottle contained the decomposed remains of a snail which were not and could not be detected until the greater part of the contents of the bottle had been consumed. As a

result she alleged and, at this stage her allegations must be accepted as true, that she suffered from shock and severe gastro enteritis. She accordingly instituted the proceedings against the manufacturers which have given rise to this appeal.

> The foundation of her case is that the Respondent, as the manufacturers of an article intended for consumption and contained in a receptacle which prevented inspection owed a duty to her as consumer of the article to take care that there was no noxious element in the goods, that they neglected such duty and are consequently liable for any damage caused by such neglect. After certain amendments which are now immaterial, the case came before the Lord Ordinary who rejected the plea in Law of the Respondent and allowed a proof. His interlocutor was revoked by the second Division of the Court of Session from whose judgment this appeal has been brought.
>
> (*Donoghue v. Stevenson* 1932: 566)

14 In the common-law system, which encourages 'judicial deference to legislation emerging from a popularly elected legislature, it is appropriate for courts to minimize apparent changes in the law they are charged with administering' (Lyons 1985: 512).
15 Compare Dworkin (1963: 624–38) and Hart (1994: Ch. 7). For more on this debate, see Shapiro (2007).
16 I find myself once again – quite unwillingly – amidst the Hart–Dworkin debate and the question of 'whether the law contains principles *as well as* rules' (Shapiro 2007: 2, emphasis in the original). Holmes, as with Hart, focuses his discussion on the concept of 'rules', but this does not necessarily mean, as Posner seems to suggest, that, for him, 'law is simply a model of rules (in Dworkin's sense of "rule")' (3).
17 Posner (2012) notes that the rule-development and rule-application stages of emergency procedure 'can run together', that is, sometimes it is necessary to create new rules 'under the shadow of a threat' (222). However, conceptually, they are distinct.
18 The judgment of *Friedman v. Valentine* did not detail fully section 436 of the New York City Charter.

7 Justice *as* improvisation

1 See McCormick (2001) for more on Derrida being *forced* (by his participation in a conference that forced the association between deconstruction and justice) 'to decide over, to take a stand on, ethical/political matters' (398).
2 In his book *Radical Atheism: Derrida and the Time of Life* (2008), Hägglund refutes the notion that 'there was an ethical or religious "turn" in Derrida's thinking' (1) and asserts that 'radical atheism', that is, a desire for God and immortality, 'informs his writings from beginning to end' (1).
3 As de Ville (2011) reminds us, many of Derrida's earlier texts were also concerned with the themes of justice, ethics and politics (1).
4 For example, in this interview, Derrida questions Coleman about the 'structure' of improvisation:

> JD: I am not an 'Ornette Coleman expert', but if I translate what you are doing into a domain that I know better, that of written language, the unique event that is produced only one time is nevertheless repeated in its very structure. Thus there is repetition, in the work, that is intrinsic to the initial creation – that which compromises or complicates the concept of improvisation. Repetition is already in improvisation: thus when people want to trap you between improvisation and the pre-written, they are wrong.
>
> OC: Repetition is as natural as the fact that the earth rotates.
>
> (Coleman and Derrida 2004: 322–23)

5 Derrida queried, 'Do you think that your music and the way people act can or must change things, for example, on the political level or in the sexual relation?' To which Coleman replied, 'No, I don't believe so … ' (Coleman and Derrida 2004: 323).
6 For more on this refusal, see Chapter 3.
7 As Attridge points out, this 'familiar point' has been 'clearly articulated by Kant in his discussion of genius':

> If an author owes a product to his genius, he himself does not know how he came by the ideas for it; nor is it in his power to devise such products at his pleasure, or by following a plan.
>
> (Kant, quoted in Attridge 2004: 150, n. 9)

8 This subheading emanates from Derrida's essay 'As If It Were Possible, "Within Such Limits"' in which he discusses the 'Necessity of Impossibility' (Derrida 2005a: 87).
9 Zlomislic recaps:

> Condensing all of the criticisms against Derrida's writing into a single point, it can be said that Derrida is seen as a relativist. Numerous articles published in established philosophical journals have argued in favour of the relativist interpretation. A number of books and dissertations have attempted to prove Derrida's philosophy leads to nihilism or that deconstruction is a method for literary critics that has nothing to do with traditional philosophy. Simply put, these interpretations are wrong, faulty, and shallow, showing that Derrida has not been read properly. Negligent interpretations of Derrida's work continue to multiply full speed ahead since his death.
>
> (Zlomislic 2007: 3)

10 Again, Ornette Coleman is of assistance. In his interview with Derrida, he says of jazz improvisation, 'What's exciting is the memory that you bring to the present' (Coleman and Derrida 2004: 322).
11 This imperative, translated into English as 'Affirm the survival', was left by Derrida to be read by his son Pierre at his funeral (Butler 2005: 25).
12 See Chapter 5.
13 The discussion which follows, on complex topics such as democracy, ethics and resistance, is, admittedly, all too brief and simplistic. However, far from being the final word on the subject, this concluding chapter is more of a call for future research and exploration in this area.
14 Participants were not required to carry a Cabaret Employee's Identification Card while playing at these after-hours venues. Musicians came to these sessions voluntarily; they were unpaid and attendance was not a condition of their employment. For more on this, see Chapter 4.
15 Muyumba (2009) reads Charlie Parker's improvised melodies as 'democratic doing and undoing' (31), inspiring 'democratic symbolic actions' (30). As many of Parker's 'masterful compositions are based on the basic chords of American popular standards', his music effectively '"undoes" status quo American musical performance theories by offering new modes for "doing" or improvising American music' (31).
16 See also von Eschen's wonderful study of the global spread of jazz by the United States' government in order to 'win converts to "the American way of life"' (as democratic and free) during the Cold War (2004: 7).
17 Derrida (2002c) speaks not of community, but of the '*spectral*' (241, emphasis in original), of 'a bond between singularities' (240). It is a bond that cannot be contained within the traditional concept of community (240). For a discussion of the spectral in Derrida's work, see Rottenberg (2002).

The notion of spectrality also informs the Derridean conception of 'community as self-destructively autoimmunitary' (Miller 2007: 268). Derrida explains this concept more fully in his article, 'Faith and Knowledge: The Two Sources of "Religion" at the Limits of Reason Alone' (2002a). For a discussion of auto-immunity in relation to the work of Jean-Luc Nancy, see Derrida's *Rogues* (2005f: 42–55).

18 Democracy, for Derrida, is conceived in terms of 'an irreconcilable tension between the singular and the universal, ethics and politics, friendship and equality' (Perpich 2005: 452). For him, community is 'lived on the terrain of this disjunction, in an uncertain or undecidable moment between failure and an opening to the future' (452). See also Derrida (1997b).

19 This lecture was given at the Centre for Modern French Thought, University of Sussex on 1 December 1997.

20 Democracy 'to come' can be described as follows:

> For democracy remains to come; this is its essence in so far as it remains: not only will it remain indefinitely perfectible, hence always insufficient and future, but, belonging to the time of the promise, it will always remain, in each of its future times, to come: even when there is democracy, it never exists, it is never present, it remains the theme of the non-presentable concept.
>
> (Derrida 1997a: 306)

21 Tucker (2004) notes that even if women experience 'great camaraderie' with the male musicians in which they have worked and jammed, they often find themselves rebuffed when it comes to the actual recordings of these same men (244). Also, while all-female bands may provide much-needed inclusion, they frequently yield 'mixed blessings': 'It is tempting to romanticize all-women bands as women's jazz communities, but important to note that for women musicians, these organizations were often exploitative, and represented lack of access to the most valued spheres of the industry' (245).

22 For more on Oliveros, see Chapter 5.

23 Oliveros has also written on the subject of women in improvisation. See Oliveros (2005).

24 For further reading on women and jazz improvisation, see Gourse (1995); Smith (2004); and Tucker (2004). On women's lives as inherently improvisatory, see Bateson (1989), quoted in Weick (1998: 550–51).

25 The relevant passage reads: 'Then, said Eryximachus, … I move, in the next place, that the flute-girl, who has just made her appearance, be told to go away; she may play to herself, or, if she has a mind, to the women who are within. But on this day let us have conversation instead' (Plato 1999: 703).

26 See Crouch (1998: 161–62) for a less critical reading of Todorov's book and the improvisational sensibility inherent in the development of the United States.

27 See the special issue of *Organization Science* (1998) on 'Jazz Improvising and Organizing', which explored the notion of the 'adaptive capabilities of organizations' (Lewin 1998: 539) and the benefits of improvisation on such. This special issue emerged from a symposium in Vancouver, Canada on 'Jazz as a Metaphor for Organizing in the 21st Century' (Meyer et al. 1998: 540). As such, most contributors to this volume applied improvisation as a *metaphor* for organizing (540). That aside, many of the ideas expressed therein are relevant to this discussion. See also Francis Fukuyama (2004) on whether public administration is a science or an art.

28 This phrase is adapted from the title of Kate Goodman's book *Improvisation for the Spirit: Live a More Creative, Spontaneous, and Courageous Life Using the Tools of Improv Comedy* (2008).

29 The issue of delay is of particular importance to the area of child law (both private and public aspects). For example, Article 3(2) of the Children (Northern Ireland) Order 1995 states (emphasis added):

> In any proceedings in which any question with respect to the upbringing of a child arises, the court shall have regard to the *general principle* that any *delay* in determining the question is likely to *prejudice the welfare of the child.*

30 Black (1990) defines the adversary system as '[t]he jurisprudential network of laws, rules and procedures characterized by opposing parties who contend against each other for a result favorable to themselves. In such system, the judge acts as an independent magistrate rather than prosecutor' (53).

31 This twelve-week 'Innovation Boot Camp', which commenced in January 2010 and was attended by approximately 30 University of Guelph Library staff, applied improvisational techniques with the aim of amplifying creativity and innovation in the workplace (Bergart 2010: 1)

32 According to Muyumba (2009), ' ... jazz improvisation makes the "optional" obligatory. "The improviser can't play only what's required," Jarrett writes, because "[he or she is] bound to contribute a certain *excess*"' (quoted 19, emphasis added).

Bibliography

Abrahamson, E. (2006) *A Perfect Mess: The Hidden Benefits of Disorder*, London: Weidenfeld & Nicolson.

Adams, W.A. (2010) '"I Made a Promise to a Lady": Critical Legal Pluralism as Improvised Law in *Buffy the Vampire Slayer*', *Critical Studies in Improvisation*, 6(1) (Special Issue: *Lex Non Scripta*, *Ars Non Scripta*: Law, Justice and Improvisation). Online. Available HTTP: www.criticalimprov.com/article/view/1083/1706 (accessed 2 September 2012).

Adderley, J., Adderley, N., Gillespie, J., Kenton, S., Ellington, D., Taylor, B., Manne, S., Guiffre, J., Hentoff, N., Cohen M. and Winick (1960) 'The Playboy Panel, Narcotics and the Jazz Musician', *Playboy Magazine*, November 1960. Online. Available HTTP: www.cannonball-adderley.com/article/lapin01.htm (accessed 8 June 2012).

Adleman, D. (2010) 'Free Jazz: Deconstricting Derridean Genre Theory'. Online. Available HTTP: www.improvcommunity.ca/research/free-jazz-deconstricting-derridean-genre-theory (accessed 8 June 2012).

Allen, C.K. (1931) 'Legal Duties', *Yale Law Review*, 40: 331–80.

Allsop K. (1961–62) 'Twenty-One Years of Jazz', *Gentleman's Quarterly*, Winter: 28–51.

Alterhaug, B. (2004) 'Improvisation on a Triple Theme: Creativity, Jazz Improvisation and Communication', *Studia Musicologica Norvegica*, 30: 97–118.

Anderson, J. (1981) *This Was Harlem: A Cultural Portrait, 1900–1950*, New York: Farrar Straus Giroux.

Anderson, S.W. (1987) 'Surveying the Realm: Description and Adjudication in Law's Empire', *Iowa Law Review*, 73: 131–57.

Anidjar, G. (2002) 'A Note on "Force of Law"', in J. Derrida, *Acts of Religion*, G. Anidjar (ed.), New York and London: Routledge, 228–29.

Appelrouth, S. (2003) 'Constructing the Meaning of Early Jazz, 1917–30', *Poetics*, 31: 117–31.

Arden, P. (2005) 'Busting a Move: Law Prohibiting Dancing in Unlicensed Bars Challenged', *Metro (New York)*, 24–26 June: 1–2. Online. Available http://www.thehousedanceproject.com/MetroByronSmall.pdf (accessed 8 June 2012).

Arewa, O. (2011) 'Creativity, Improvisation, and Risk: Copyright and Musical Innovation', *Notre Dame Law Review*, 86(5): 1829–46.

Aristodemou, M. (2000) *Law and Literature: Journeys from Her to Eternity*, Oxford: Oxford University Press.

Atkinson, J.B. (1932) 'Satire of Politics, Depression and Show Business in a Beautiful Musical Comedy', *New York Times*, 18 February: 24.

Attali, J. (1985) *Noise: The Political Economy of Music*, trans. B. Massumi, Minneapolis and London: University of Minnesota Press.

Attridge, D. (1992a) 'Editor's Introduction, "Before the Law"', in J. Derrida, *Acts of Literature*, D. Attridge (ed.), New York and London: Routledge, 181–82.

——(1992b) 'Editor's Introduction, "*From* Psyche: Invention of the Other"', in J. Derrida, *Acts of Literature*, D. Attridge (ed.), New York and London: Routledge, 310–11.

——(1992c) 'Editor's Introduction, "Ulysses Gramophone: Hear Say Yes in Joyce"', in J. Derrida, *Acts of Literature*, D. Attridge (ed.), New York and London: Routledge, 253–56.

——(2004) *The Singularity of Literature*, London and New York: Routledge.

Attridge, D. and Baldwin, T. (2004) 'Obituary: Jacques Derrida', *Guardian*, 11 October. Online. Available HTTP: www.guardian.co.uk/obituaries/story/0,3604,1324160,00.html (accessed 8 June 2012).

Authers, B. (2010) 'Truth in the Telling: Procedure, Testimony, and the Work of Improvisation in Legal Narrative', *Critical Studies in Improvisation*, 6(1) (Special Issue: *Lex Non Scripta, Ars Non Scripta*: Law, Justice and Improvisation). Online. Available HTTP: www.criticalimprov.com/article/view/1219/1721 (accessed 2 September 2012).

——(2012) 'CSI Special Issue Query', email, 27 May.

Bailey, D. (1992) *Improvisation: Its Nature and Practice in Music*, 2nd edn, New York: Da Capo Press.

Baker, J.E. (2002) 'Constitutional Dignity and the Criminal Law', *Military Law Review*, 174: 125–42.

Balkin, J.M. (2003) 'Idolatry and Faith: The Jurisprudence of Sanford Levinson', *Tulsa Law Review*, 38: 553–77.

Balkin, J.M. and S. Levinson (1999) 'Law as Performance', in M. Freeman and A. Lewis (eds) *Law and Literature: Current Legal Issues, Volume 2*, Oxford: Oxford University Press, 729–51.

Ball, M.S. (1989) 'Stories of Origin and Constitutional Possibilities', *Michigan Law Review*, 87: 2280–2318.

Baraka, A. [LeRoi Jones] (1963) *Blues People: Negro Music in White America*, New York: HarperCollins.

Barker, D. (1986) *A Life in Jazz*, New York: Oxford University Press.

Barnett, C. and Low, M. (2004) 'Geography and Democracy: An Introduction', in C. Barnett and M. Low (eds) *Spaces of Democracy: Geographical Perspectives on Citizenship, Participation and Representation*, London: SAGE, 1–22.

Barrett, F.J. (1998) 'Creativity and Improvisation in Jazz and Organizations: Implications for Organizational Learning', *Organization Science*, 9(5): 605–22 (Special Issue: Jazz Improvisation and Organizing).

Barrett, F.J. and Peplowski, K. (1998) 'Minimal Structures Within a Song: An Analysis of "All of Me"', *Organization Science*, 9(5): 558–60 (Special Issue: Jazz Improvisation and Organizing).

Bateson, M.C. (1989) *Composing a Life*, New York: Atlantic Monthly. [Also published (2001) *Composing a Life*, New York: Grove Press.]

Battersby, C. (1989) *Gender and Genius: Towards a Feminist Aesthetics*, London: The Women's Press Ltd.

Beardsworth, R. (1996) *Derrida and the Political*, London and New York: Routledge.

Belay, B. (1996) 'Justice: The Law of the Law', in J. Brannigan, R. Robbins and J. Wolfreys (eds) *Applying: To Derrida*, Basingstoke: Macmillan, 124–35.

Belgrad, D. (1998) *The Culture of Spontaneity: Improvisation and the Arts in Postwar America*, Chicago: University of Chicago Press.

Benjamin, W. (1986) 'Critique of Violence', trans. E. Jephcott, in W. Benjamin, *Reflections: Essays, Aphorisms, Autobiographical Writings*, P. Demetz (ed.), New York: Schocken, 277–300.

Bennett, C.G. (1967a) 'Councilmen Face Legislative Jam', *New York Times*, 4 September: 16.

——(1967b) 'Cabaret-Card Use Ended by Council', *New York Times*, 13 September: 31.

Bennington, G. (1993) 'Derridabase', in G. Bennington and J. Derrida, *Jacques Derrida*, Chicago: University of Chicago Press, 1–316.

——(2000) 'Double Tounging: Derrida's Monolingualism', in D. Kujundzic (ed.) *Khoraographies for Jacques Derrida, on July 15, 2000*. Online. Available HTTP: www.usc.edu/dept/comp-lit/tympanum/4/bennington.html (accessed 8 June 2012).

Bennington, G. and Derrida, J. (1993) *Jacques Derrida*, trans. G. Bennington, Chicago: University of Chicago Press.

Bergart, R. (2010) 'Improvising Innovation: A Case Study in the University of Guelph Library'. Online. Available HTTP: www.improvcommunity.ca/research/improvising-innovation-case-study-university-guelph-library (accessed 8 June 2012).

Berliner, P. (1994) *Thinking in Jazz: The Infinite Art of Improvisation*, Chicago: University of Chicago Press.

Bernasconi, R. (1993) 'Politics Beyond Humanism: Mandela and the Struggle Against Apartheid', in G.B. Madison (ed.) *Working Through Derrida*, Evanston, IL: Northwestern University Press, 94–119.

Beyer, J.A. (2000) 'The Second Line: Reconstructing The Jazz Metaphor in Critical Race Theory', *Georgetown Law Journal*, 88: 537–63.

Birmingham, P. (1997) 'Towards an Ethic of Desire: Derrida, Fiction, and the Law of the Feminine', in N. Holland (ed.) *Feminist Interpretations of Jacques Derrida*, Pennsylvania: Pennsylvania State University Press, 127–46.

Black, H.C. (1990) *Black's Law Dictionary*, 6th edn, St. Paul, MN: West Publishing Co.

Blackburn, J. (2005) *With Billie*, London: Jonathan Cape.

Blanchot, M. (1999) 'The Song of the Sirens: Encountering the Imaginary', trans. L. Davis, in M. Blanchot, *The Station Hill Blanchot Reader: Fiction and Literary Essays*, G. Quasha (ed.), trans. L. Davis, P. Auster and R. Lamberton, Barrytown, NY: Station Hill Press/Barrytown Inc., 443–50.

Bolland, J., Brown, I. and Singleton, M. (1983) 'The 1982 Reith Lectures – Mystery or Mystification? A Symposium on the Arts in Society', *Interface*, 1: 1–115.

Borgo, D. (2005) *Sync or Swarm: Improvising Music in a Complex Age*, New York and London: Continuum.

Bork, R.H. (2003) 'The Judges Role in Law and Culture', *Ave Maria Law Review*, 1: 19–29.

Brody, R. (2011) 'A Thing the Existence of Which: Jacques Derrida Interviews Ornette Coleman', *New Yorker*, 27 January. Online. Available HTTP: www.newyorker.com/online/blogs/movies/2011/01/jacques-derrida-interviews-ornette-coleman.html (accessed 8 June 2012).

Brunette, P. and Wills, D. (1994) 'The Spatial Arts: An Interview with Jacques Derrida', in P. Brunette and D. Wills (eds) *Deconstruction and the Visual Arts: Art, Media, Architecture*, Cambridge: Cambridge University Press, 9–32.

Bucholtz, B.K. (2003) 'On Canonical Transformations and the Coherence of Dichotomies: Jazz, Jurisprudence, and the University Mission', *University of Richmond Law Review*, 37: 425–69.

Butler, J. (2004) *Undoing Gender*, Abingdon: Routledge.

——(2005) 'Affirm the Survival', *Radical Philosophy*, 129: 22–25.

Callahan, J.P. (1967) 'Doom of Cabaret Identification Law is Foreseen', *New York Times*, 8 September: 31.

Calmore, J.O. (1992) 'Critical Race Theory, Archie Shepp, and Fire Music: Securing an Authentic Intellectual Life in a Multicultural World', *Southern California Law Review*, 65: 2129–2230.

Caputo, J. (1997) *The Prayers and Tears of Jacques Derrida: Religion Without Religion*, Bloomington, IN: Indiana University Press.

Carr, W.H.A. (1960) 'Agent Called on Police "Fix" Story', *New York Post*, 16 November: 1.

Carson, L. (2011) 'Bail Schedules', *Criminal Justice*, 26, Spring: 12–17.

Cerulli, D. (1984) 'Crow Jim: No Gigs for Ofays', *Rogue*, January: 54–55, 77.

Chang, J. (n.d.) 'Brushed with Hip-hop Oil: The Terrific Return of Scritti Politti', *San Francisco Bay Guardian*. Online. Available HTTP: www.sfbg.com/noise/18/scritti.html (accessed June 2006 [URL no longer active]). [Copy on file with author.]

Charters, A. (1995) 'Editor's Introduction: "Essentials of Spontaneous Prose"', in A. Charters (ed.) *The Portable Jack Kerouac*, New York: Penguin, 481–82.

Charters, S.B. and Kunstadt, L. (1962) *Jazz: The History of the New York Scene*, New York: Doubleday.

Chemillier, M. (2009) 'La transcription musicale à l'ère de l'image animée: À propos des recherches sur l'improvisation et l'ordinateur avec le logiciel OMax (Ircam/Compagnie Lubat)'. Online. Available HTTP: ehess.modelisationsavoirs.fr/marc/publi/terrain/Transcription%20animee4revu.pdf (accessed 8 June 2012).

Chevigny, P. (1991) *Gigs: Jazz and the Cabaret Laws in New York City*, New York: Routledge.

Chilton, J. (1975) *Billie's Blues: A Survey of Billie Holiday's Career 1933–1959*, London: Quartet Books.

Citizens Union (1960) 'Citizens Union Calls Cabaret Licensing Justified'. Press Release, 12 December.

Cixous, H. (1991) 'Writing and the Law: Blanchot, Joyce, Kafka, and Lispector', in H. Cixous, *Readings: The Poetics of Blanchot, Joyce, Kafka, Kleist, Lispector, and Tsvetayeva*, trans. V.A. Conley, Minneapolis, MN: University of Minnesota Press, 1–27.

Cixous, H. and Derrida, J. (2004) 'The Language of Others'. Online. Available HTTP: http://jewishbookweek.com/archive/010304e/transcripts2.php (accessed 8 June 2012).

Clarke, D. (1994) *Wishing on the Moon: The Life and Times of Billie Holiday*, London: Penguin.

Cobussen, M. (2008a) 'Introduction', *New Sound*, 32: 5–7 (Special Issue: Improvisation).

——(2008b) 'Improvisation. An Annotated Inventory', *New Sound*, 32: 9–22 (Special Issue: Improvisation).

——(2002a) 'Deconstruction: Between Method and Singularity', in M. Cobussen, *Deconstruction in Music*. Interactive Online Dissertation. Available HTTP: www.deconstruction-in-music.com/navbar/index.html (accessed 8 June 2012).

——(2002b) 'Deconstruction in Music', in M. Cobussen, *Deconstruction in Music*. Interactive Online Dissertation. Available HTTP: www.deconstruction-in-music.com/navbar/index.html (accessed 8 June 2012).

——(2002c) 'Derrida's Ear', in M. Cobussen, *Deconstruction in Music*. Interactive Online Dissertation. Available HTTP: www.deconstruction-in-music.com/navbar/index.html (accessed 8 June 2012).

——(2002d) 'Justification', in M. Cobussen, *Deconstruction in Music*. Interactive Online Dissertation. Available HTTP: www.deconstruction-in-music.com/navbar/index.html (accessed 8 June 2012).

——(2002e) 'Music, Deconstruction, and Ethics', in M. Cobussen, *Deconstruction in Music*. Interactive Online Dissertation. Available HTTP: www.deconstruction-in-music.com/navbar/index.html (accessed 8 June 2012).

——(2002f) 'Scritti Politti', in M. Cobussen, *Deconstruction in Music*. Interactive Online Dissertation. Available HTTP: www.deconstruction-in-music.com/navbar/index.html (accessed 8 June 2012).

——(2002g) 'Silence, Noise and Ethics', in M. Cobussen, *Deconstruction in Music*. Interactive Online Dissertation. Available HTTP: www.deconstruction-in-music.com/navbar/index.html (accessed 8 June 2012).

Cobussen, M. and Finn, G. (2002) 'InterMezzo: Creativity and Ethics, in Deconstruction, in Music', *ECHO: a music-centered journal*, 4(2). Online. Available HTTP: www.echo.ucla.edu/Volume4-Issue2/intermezzo/index.html (accessed 8 June 2012).

Cohen, M.T. (1961) 'Affidavit for *Simone v Kennedy*', *Cabaret Law Clipping File*, Institute of Jazz Studies, Rutgers University.

——(1993) *The Police Card Discord*, London and Metuchen, NJ: Scarecrow Press and the Institute of Jazz Studies, Rutgers University.

Coleman, N. (1987) 'High Notes', *Observer*, 15 February: 31–34.

Coleman, O. and Derrida, J. (1997) 'Le musicien, le philosophe et las fanatiques', *Jazz Magazine* 473: 26–28.

——(2004) 'The Other's Language: Jacques Derrida Interviews Ornette Coleman, 23 June 1997', *Genre*, Summer: 319–28.

Collier, J.L. (1993) *Jazz: The American Theme Song*, New York: Oxford University Press.

Comte, A. (2001) 'Hyperfiction: A New Literary Poetics?', *Text*, 5(2). Online. Available HTTP: www.textjournal.com.au/oct01/comte.htm (accessed 8 June 2012).

Conley, V.A. (1990) 'Introduction', in H. Cixous, *Reading with Clarice Lispector*, trans. V.A. Conley, V.A. Conley (ed.), London: Harvester Wheatsheaf, vii–xviii.

Corbett, J. (1995) 'Ephemera Underscored: Writing Around Free Improvisation', in K. Gabbard (ed.) *Jazz Among the Discourses*, Durham, NC: Duke University Press, 217–40.

Cormack, B. (2007) *A Power to do Justice: Jurisdiction, English Literature, and the Rise of the Common Law, 1509–1625*, Chicago: University of Chicago Press.

Cornell, D. (1999) *Beyond Accommodation: Ethical Feminism, Deconstruction, and the Law*, New edn, New York: Rowman & Littlefield.

——(1992) *The Philosophy of the Limit*, New York: Routledge.

Cornell, D., Rosenfeld, M. and Carlson, D.G. (1992) *Deconstruction and the Possibility of Justice*, New York: Routledge.

Cotterrell, R. (1976) *Jazz Now: The Jazz Centre Society Guide*, London: Quartet Books.

Critchley, S. (2005) 'An Ethos of Reading', *Radical Philosophy*, 129: 26–28.

——(2003) 'The Other's Decision in Me (What Are the Politics of Friendship?)', in C. Norris and D. Roden (eds) *Jacques Derrida*, Volume IV, London: SAGE, 86–116.

Cross, J. (2012) '"Done In Convention": The Attestation Clause and The Declaration Of Independence', *Yale Law Review*, 121: 1236–70.

Crossan, M. (1998) 'Improvisation in Action', *Organization Science*, 9(5): 593–99 (Special Issue: Jazz Improvisation and Organizing).

Crouch, S. (1996) 'Bird Land', in R. Gottlieb (ed.) *Reading Jazz: A Gathering of Autobiography, Reportage and Criticism from 1919 to Now*, London: Bloomsbury, 1023–33.

——(1998) 'Blues to Be Constitutional: A Long Look at the Wild Wherefores of Our Democratic Lives as Symbolized in the Making of Rhythm and Tune', in R.G. O'Meally (ed.) *Jazz: The Jazz Cadence of American Culture*, New York: Columbia University Press.

Cruickshank, D. (2002) 'Lord Buckley Rides Again!', *Salon*. Online. Available HTTP: www.salon.com/people/feature/2002/06/26/buckley/print.html (accessed 8 June 2012).

CUAP (1949) 'Metropolitan Youth Commission (1949–50)', 1 January. Online. Available HTTP: www.mu.edu/cgi-bin/cuap/db.cgi?db=default&uid=default&view=1&db=default&uid=default&bool=and&ww=on&Content=beboppers&nh=7&mh=1 (accessed 8 June 2012).

——(1950a) 'Catholic Pupils Spearhead War on Bebopism: Student Council of 14 Schools Join Fight', 18 November. Online. HTTP: www.mu.edu/cgi-bin/cuap/db.cgi?db=default&uid=default&view=1&db=default&uid=default&bool=and&ww=on&Content=beboppers&nh=1&mh=1 (accessed 8 June 2012).

——(1950b) 'Lawless "Bop" Cliques Exist, Mayor Told: Youth Commission Reports Findings', 26 November. Online. Available HTTP: www.mu.edu/cgi-bin/cuap/db.cgi?db=default&uid=default&view=1&db=default&uid=default&bool=and&ww=on&Content=beboppers&nh=5&mh=1 (accessed 8 June 2012).

——(1950c) 'Letter from the Assistant City Attorney, 1950', 15 November. Online. Available HTTP: www.mu.edu/cgi-bin/cuap/db.cgi?db=default&uid=default&view=1&db=default&uid=default&bool=and&ww=on&Content=beboppers&nh=6&mh=1 (accessed 8 June 2012).

——(1950d) 'Teen Girls' Panel Offers the Cure for Bebopism', 3 December. Online. Available HTTP: www.mu.edu/cgi-bin/cuap/db.cgi?db=default&uid=default&view=1&db=default&uid=default&bool=and&ww=on&Content=beboppers&nh=12&mh=1 (accessed 8 June 2012).

Daquila, P. (2009a) 'About this project'. Online. Available HTTP: www.theimprovisers.org/about/index.html (accessed 8 June 2012).

——(2009b) 'Alarmingly off-script'. Online. Available HTTP: www.theimprovisers.org/notebook/nb6.html (accessed 8 June 2012).

——(2009c) 'Preparing for the Unpredictable'. Online. Available HTTP: www.theimprovisers.org/docu/docu4.html (accessed 6 June 2012).

Dardess, G. (1975) 'The Logic of Spontaneity: A Reconsideration of Kerouac's "Spontaneous Prose Method"', *Boundary 2*, 3(2): 729–46.

Davies, M. (1996) *Delimiting the Law, 'Postmodernism' and the Politics of Law*, London: Pluto Press.

——(2001) 'Derrida and Law: Legitimate Fictions', in T. Cohen (ed.) *Jacques Derrida and the Humanities*, Cambridge: Cambridge University Press, 213–37.

Davies, R. (1987) 'Player Kings and all that Jazz', *Observer Magazine*, 15 February: 24–29.

Davis, A. (1998) *Blues Legacies and Black Women: Gertrude "Ma" Rainey, Bessie Smith, and Billie Holiday*, New York: Pantheon Books.

Davis, F. (1996) 'Everycat and Birdland, Mon Amor', in R. Gottlieb (ed.) *Reading Jazz: A Gathering of Autobiography, Reportage and Criticism from 1919 to Now*, London: Bloomsbury, 1013–22.

Davis, M. (1996) 'Bird', in R. Gottlieb (ed.) *Reading Jazz: A Gathering of Autobiography, Reportage and Criticism from 1919 to Now*, London: Bloomsbury, 577–81.

Demsey, D. (2000) 'Jazz Improvisation and Concepts of Virtuosity', in B. Kirchner (ed.) *The Oxford Companion to Jazz*, Oxford: Oxford University Press, 788–98.

Dennis, J.L. (1993) 'Interpretation and Application of the Civil Code and the Evaluation of Judicial Precedent', *Louisiana Law Review*, 54: 1–17.

Derrida, J. (1976) *Of Grammatology*, trans. G.C. Spivak, Baltimore, MD: Johns Hopkins University Press.

——(1982a) 'Signature Event Context', *Margins of Philosophy*, trans. Alan Bass, Chicago: University of Chicago Press, 307–30. [Also published Derrida, J. (1988) *Limited Inc.*, G. Graff (ed.), Evanston, IL: Northwestern University Press, 1–23.]

——(1982b) 'White Mythology: Metaphor in the Text of Philosophy', *Margins of Philosophy*, trans. Alan Bass, Chicago: University of Chicago Press, 207–71.

——(1986) 'Declarations of Independence', *New Political Science*, 15: 7–15.

——(1987) 'The Laws of Reflection: Nelson Mandela, in Admiration', trans. M.A. Caws and I. Lorenz, in *For Nelson Mandela*, J. Derrida and M. Tlili (eds), New York: Seaver Books, 13–42.

——(1989) 'Psyche: Inventions of the Other', trans. Catherine Porter, in L. Waters and W. Godzich (eds) *Reading de Man Reading*, Minneapolis, MN: University of Minnesota Press, 25–65.

——(1992a) 'Before the Law', in J. Derrida, *Acts of Literature*, D. Attridge (ed.), New York and London: Routledge, 183–220.

——(1992b) 'The Law of Genre', in J. Derrida, *Acts of Literature*, D. Attridge (ed.), New York: Routledge, 221–52.

——(1992c) 'Ulysses Gramophone: Hear Say Yes in Joyce' in J. Derrida, *Acts of Literature*, D. Attridge (ed.), New York: Routledge, 256–309.

——(1992d) *The Other Heading: Reflections on Today's Europe*, trans. P.-A Brault and M. Naas, Bloomington, IN: Indiana University Press.

——(1994) *Specters of Marx: The State of the Debt, the Work of Mourning, and the New International*, trans. P. Kamuf, New York: Routledge.

——(1995a) 'Passages – from Traumatism to Promise', in J. Derrida, *Points … Interviews, 1974–1994*, E. Weber (ed.), Stanford, CA: Stanford University Press, 372–95.

——(1995b) 'There is No *One* Narcissism (Autobiophotographies)', in J. Derrida, *Points … Interviews, 1974–1994*, trans. Peggy Kamuf, E. Weber (ed.), Stanford, CA: Stanford University Press, 196–215.

——(1995c) *The Gift of Death*, trans. D. Wills, Chicago: University of Chicago Press.

——(1997a) 'For the First Time in the History of Humanity', in J. Derrida, *Politics of Friendship*, trans. G. Collins, London: Verso, 271–308.

——(1997b) 'Oligarchies: Naming, Enumerating, Counting', in J. Derrida, *Politics of Friendship*, trans. G. Collins, London: Verso, 1–25.

——(1997c) 'Politics and Friendship: A Discussion with Jacques Derrida', University of Sussex, 1 December. Online. Available HTTP: www.livingphilosophy.org/Derrida-politics-friendship.htm (accessed 8 June 2012).

——(1997d) *Politics of Friendship*, trans. G. Collins, London: Verso.

——(1998) *Monolingualism of the Other; or, The Prosthesis of Origin*, trans. P. Mensah, Stanford, CA: Stanford University Press.

——(1999) 'Hospitality, Justice and Responsibility: A Dialogue with Jacques Derrida', in M. Dooley and R. Kearney (eds) *Questioning Ethics: Contemporary Debates in Philosophy*, London: Routledge, 65–83.

——(2001a) 'Structure, Sign, and Play in the Discourse of the Human Science', in J. Derrida, *Writing and Difference*, trans A. Bass, London: Routledge, 351–70.

——(2001b) 'The Theater of Cruelty and the Closure of Representation' in J. Derrida, *Writing and Difference*, trans A. Bass, London: Routledge, 292–316.

——(2001c) 'Violence and Metaphysics: An Essay on the Thought of Emmanuel Levinas', in J. Derrida, *Writing and Difference*, trans. A. Bass, London: Routledge, 97–192.

——(2001d) *Deconstruction Engaged: The Sydney Lectures*, P. Patton and T. Smith (eds), Sydney: Power Publications.

——(2002a) 'Faith and Knowledge: The Two Sources of "Religion" at the Limits of Reason Alone', trans. S. Weber, in J. Derrida, *Acts of Religion*, G. Anidjar (ed.), New York: Routledge, 42–101.

——(2002b) 'Force of Law: The "Mystical Foundation of Authority"', trans. M. Quaintance, in J. Derrida, *Acts of Religion*, G. Anidjar (ed.), New York: Routledge, 230–98.

——(2002c) 'Nietzsche and the Machine', in J. Derrida, *Negotiations: Interventions and Interviews, 1971–2001*, trans. E. Rottenberg, E. Rottenberg (ed.), Stanford, CA: Stanford University Press, 215–56.

——(2002d) 'The Future of the Profession or the University Without Condition (Thanks to the "Humanities," What Could Take Place Tomorrow)', in T. Cohen (ed.) *Jacques Derrida and the Humanities: A Critical Reader*, West Nyack, NY: Cambridge University Press, 24–57.

——(2002e) *Positions*, Rev. edn, trans. A. Bass, London: Continuum.

——(2004a) 'Play – The First Name', trans. T.S. Murphy, *Genre: Forms of Discourse and Culture*, 37(2): 331–40.

——(2004b) 'The Last Interview', trans. R. Knafo, *SV*, November 2004. Online. Available HTTP: www.studiovisit.net/SV.Derrida.pdf (accessed 8 June 2012).

——(2004c) 'Unpublished Interview'. Online. Available HTTP: www.derridathemovie.com/readings.html (accessed 8 June 2012).

——(2005a) 'As If It Were Possible, "Within Such Limits" … ', in J. Derrida, *Paper Machine*, trans. R. Bowlby, Stanford, California: Stanford University Press, 73–99.

——(2005b) 'Liberty, Equality, Fraternity, or, How Not to Speak in Mottos', in J. Derrida, *Rogues: Two Essays on Reason*, trans. P.-A. Brault and M. Naas, Stanford, CA: Stanford University Press, 56–62.

——(2005c) 'Not Utopia, the Im-possible', in J. Derrida, *Paper Machine*, trans. R. Bowlby, Stanford, CA: Stanford University Press, 121–35.

——(2005d) 'Others Are Secret Because They Are Other', in J. Derrida, *Paper Machine*, trans. R. Bowlby, Stanford, CA: Stanford University Press, 136–63.

——(2005e) 'Shibboleth: For Paul Celan', in J. Derrida, *Sovereignties in Question: The Poetics of Paul Celan*, T. Dutoit and O. Pasanen (eds), New York: Fordham University Press, 1–64.

——(2005f) *Rogues: Two Essays on Reason*, trans. P.-A. Brault and M. Naas, Stanford, CA: Stanford University Press.

——(2006) *Geneses, Genealogies, Genres, and Genius: The Secrets of the Archive*, trans. B.B. Brahic, New York, Columbia University Press.

——(2007) 'A Certain Impossible Possibility of Saying the Event', trans. G. Walker, *Critical Inquiry*, 33: 441–61.

Derrida, J. and Dufourmantelle, A. (2000) *Of Hospitality*, trans. R. Bowlby, Stanford, CA: Stanford University Press.

Deutscher, P. (2005) *How to Read Derrida*, London: Granta Books.

DeVeaux, S. (1997) *The Birth of Bebop: A Social and Musical History*, London: Picador.

Dick, K. and Kofman, A.Z. (dirs) (2005) *Screenplay and Essays on the Film Derrida*, Manchester: Manchester University Press.

Donat, G.S. (1997) 'Fixing Fixation: A Copyright with Teeth for Improvisational Performers', *Columbia Law Review*, 97(5): 1363–1405.

Donoghue, D. (1982) 'The Arts Without Mystery', 1982 BBC Reith Lectures. Online. Available HTTP: www.bbc.co.uk/programmes/p00gq1s3 (accessed 8 June 2012).

Douzinas, C. (2005) 'Violence, Justice, Deconstruction', *German Law Review*, 6(1): 171–78 (Special Issue: A Dedication to Jacques Derrida – Justice).

Douzinas, C. and Warrington, R. with McVeigh, S. (1991) *Postmodern Jurisprudence: The Law of Text in the Texts of Law*, London: Routledge.

Down Beat (1961) 'Cabaret Card Situation Simmers', *Down Beat*, 28(1): 11.

Dugan, J. and Hammond, J. (1938) 'The Music Nobody Knows', in Programme for *'From Spirituals to Swing' (Dedicated to Bessie Smith)*, Carnegie Hall, New York City, 23 December: 3–4.

Dworkin, R. (1963) 'Judicial Discretion', *Journal of Philosophy*, 60(21): 624–38.

——(1986) *Law's Empire*, Oxford: Hart Publishing.

Eberle, E.J. and Grossfeld, B. (2006) 'Law and Poetry', *Roger Williams University Law Review*, 11: 353–401.

Edkins, J. (2005) 'Exposed Singularity', *Journal for Cultural Research*, 8(4): 359–86.

Ellison, R. (1953). *Shadow and Act*, London: Secker &Warburg.

——(1996) 'Minton's', in R. Gottlieb (ed.) *Reading Jazz: A Gathering of Autobiography, Reportage and Criticism from 1919 to Now*, London: Bloomsbury, 545–54.

Epstein, R.A. (2006) 'Intuition, Custom, and Protocol: How to Make Sound Decisions with Limited Knowledge', *NYU Journal of Law and Liberty*, 2: 1–27.

Erenberg, L. (1981) *Steppin' Out: New York Nightlife and the Transformation of American Culture, 1890–1930*, Westport, CN: Greenwood Press.

——(1998) *Swingin' the Dream: Big Band Jazz and the Rebirth of American Culture*, Chicago: University of Chicago Press.

Eschen, P.M. von (2004) *Satchmo Blows Up the World: Jazz Ambassadors Play the Cold War*, Cambridge, MA: Harvard University Press.

Esterhammer, A. (2004) *Spontaneous Overflows and Reviving Rays: Romanticism and the Discourse of Improvisation*, Vancouver: Ronsdale Press.

Fernandez, A.L. (2002) 'Let It Be: A Comparative Study of the Context Regulation of Recorded Music in the United States and the United Kingdom', *Penn State International Law Review*, 21: 227–57.

Finkelman, P. (1981) 'The First American Constitutions: State and Federal', *Texas Law Review*, 59: 1141–74.

Finkelstein, S. (1948) *Jazz: A People's Music*, New York: International Publishers.

Finn, G. (2008) 'One Time Alone: Improvisation Takes Place', *New Sound*, 32: 203–29 (Special Issue: Improvisation).

Fischlin, D. (2003) 'Take One/Rebel Musics: Human Rights, Resistant Sounds, and the Politics of Music Making', in D. Fischlin and A. Heble (eds) *Rebel Musics: Human Rights, Resistant Sounds, and the Politics of Music Making*, Montréal: Black Rose Books, 10–43.

——(2010) '"Wild notes" ... Improvisioning', *Critical Studies in Improvisation*, 6(2). Online. Available HTTP: www.criticalimprov.com/article/view/1358/1937 (accessed 2 September 2012).

Fischlin, D. and Ajay Heble (2004) 'The Other Side of Nowhere: Jazz, Improvisation, and Communities in Dialogue', in D. Fischlin and A. Heble (eds) *The Other Side of Nowhere: Jazz, Improvisation, and Communities in Dialogue*, Middletown, CT: Wesleyan University Press, 1–42.

——(2003) *Rebel Musics: Human Rights, Resistant Sounds, and the Politics of Music Making*, Montréal: Black Rose Books.

Fischlin, D. and Nandorfy, M. (2012) *The Community of Rights, The Rights of Community*, Montreal: Black Rose Books.

Fischlin, D., Heble, A. and Lipsitz, G. (forthcoming) *The Fierce Urgency of Now: Improvisation, Rights, and the Ethics of Co-creation*, Durham, NC: Duke University Press.

Fitzpatrick, P. (1992) *The Mythology of Modern Law*, London: Routledge.

——(2001a) 'Law Like Poetry – Burnt Norton', *Liverpool Law Review*, 23(3): 285–88.

——(2001b) *Modernism and the Grounds of Law*, Cambridge: Cambridge University Press.

——(2002) '"No Higher Duty": *Mabo* and the Failure of Legal Foundation', *Law and Critique*, 13: 233–52.

——(2003) 'Breaking the Unity of the World: Savage Sources and Feminine Law', *Australian Feminist Law Journal*, 19: 47–60 (Special Issue: Divining the Source: Law's Foundation and the Question of Authority).

——(2004) 'Dominions: Law, Literature, and the Right to Death', *Journal of Law and Society*, 31(1): 142–48.

——(2005a) 'Access as Justice', *Windsor Yearbook of Access to Justice*, 23(1): 3–16.

——(2005b) '"In God We Trust" Can Relieve Us of Trusting Each Other', *The Believer*, 3(8): 63–72.

——(2005c) 'In the End, or the Cause of Law', in A. Sarat and S. Scheingold (eds) *The Worlds Cause Lawyers Make: Structure and Agency in Legal Practice*, Stanford, CA: Stanford University Press, 463–68.

——(2011) 'Is Law Cosmopolitan?', in U. de Vries and L. Francot (eds) *Law's Environment: Critical Legal Perspectives*, Haag: Eleven International Publishing.

Fitzpatrick, P. and Joyce, R. (2007) 'Copying Right: Cultural Property and the Limits of (Occidental) Law', in F. Macmillan (ed.) *New Directions in Copyright Law: Volume 4: Protection of Traditional Knowledge and Culture*, Cheltenham: Edward Elgar, 171–92.

Fleming, M. (1998) 'Review of *Derrida and the Political*; *Feminist Interpretations of Jacques Derrida*', *Canadian Journal of Political Science*, 31(2): 420–21.

Fowler, G. (1949) *Beau James: The Life and Times of Jimmy Walker*, New York: The Viking Press.

Foy, H.M. (2010) 'On Judicial Discretion in Statutory Interpretation', *Administrative Law Review*, 62: 291–327.

Frank, J. (1949) *Courts on Trial: Myth and Reality in American Justice*, Princeton, NJ: Princeton University Press.

Freeman, I.H. (1960a) 'Mayor May Ease Nightclub Rules', *New York Times*, 25 November: 1, 30.

——(1960b) 'Cafe Drive Turns to Homosexuals', *New York Times*, 1 December: 30.

Freud, S. (1918) *Totem and Taboo: Resemblances between the Psychic Lives of Savages and Neurotics*, trans. A.A. Brill, New York: Vintage Books.

Fukuyama, F. (2004) 'Why There is No Science of Public Administration', *Journal of International Affairs*, 58(1): 189–201.

Gabbard, K. (1995a) 'Introduction: The Jazz Canon and Its Consequences', in K. Gabbard (ed.) *Jazz Among the Discourses*, Durham, NC: Duke University Press, 1–28.

——(2004) 'Improvisation and Imitation: Marlon Brando as Jazz Actor', in D. Fischlin and A. Heble (eds) *The Other Side of Nowhere: Jazz, Improvisation, and Communities in Dialogue*, Middletown, CT: Wesleyan University Press, 298–318.

Gallope, M. (2011) 'Is Improvisation Present?' Online. Available HTTP: cas.uchicago.edu/workshops/musichistorytheory/files/2011/10/GallopeImprovChapter10_19dblspc1.pdf (accessed 8 June 2012). [Also published in G. Lewis and B. Piekut (eds) *The Oxford Handbook of Critical Improvisation Studies*, Oxford: Oxford University Press.]

Gasché, R. (1986) *The Tain of the Mirror*, Cambridge, MA: Harvard University Press.

Gates, H.L. Jr. (1988) *The Signifying Monkey: A Theory of African-American Literary Criticism*, Oxford: Oxford University Press.

Gehring, P. (2008) 'The Jurisprudence of the "Force of Law"', in P. Goodrich, F. Hoffmann, M. Rosenfeld and C. Vismann (eds) *Derrida and Legal Philosophy*, Basingstoke: Palgrave Macmillan, 55–70.

Gelb, A. (1960a) 'Charges of Police Corruption', *New York Times*, 14 November: 1, 23.

——(1960b) 'City Will Study Cabaret Charges', *New York Times*, 15 November: 1, 33.

——(1960c) 'Inquiry on Police Weighed by State', *New York Times*, 16 November: 1, 44.

Gerard, C. (1995) 'Spirit, Soul and New Religions'. Online. Available HTTP: web.archive.org/web/20040716084631/http://www.utexas.edu/cola/depts/ams/Jazz/1–1/Spirit.html (accessed 8 June 2012).

Gillespie, J. (1979) *To Be or Not to Bop: Memoirs of Dizzy Gillespie with Al Fraser*, New York: Doubleday.

——(1996) 'Minton's Playhouse', in R. Gottlieb (ed.) *Reading Jazz: A Gathering of Autobiography, Reportage and Criticism from 1919 to Now*, London: Bloomsbury, 555–72.

Gilroy, P. (1995) '"... To Be Real": The Dissident Forms of Black Expressive Culture', in C. Ugwu (ed.) *Let's Get It On: The Politics of Black Performance*, London: ICA.

——(2000a) 'The Dialectics of Diaspora Identification', in L. Back and J. Solomos (eds) *Theories of Race and Racism: A Reader*, London: Routledge, 490–502.

——(2000b) *Between Camps: Nations, Cultures and the Allure of Race*, London: Penguin.

Gioia, T. (1997) *The History of Jazz*, New York: Oxford University Press.

Gitler, I. (1985) *Swing to Bop*, Oxford: Oxford University Press.

——(2001) *The Masters of Bebop: A Listener's Guide*, Updated and Expanded, Cambridge, MA: Da Capo Press.

Glassner, B. (2003) 'Rap Music and the Culture of Fear', *Entertainment and Sports Lawyer*, 21: 1.

Goldman, V. (n.d.) 'Ornette Coleman: Biography'. Online. Available HTTP: www.harmolodic.com/ornette/then_text.html (accessed 17 March 2007 [URL no longer active]). [Copy on file with author.]

Gomez, J. (1993) 'Do We Have a Chance Against the Far Right?', *New York Law School Law Review*, 38: 195–99.

Goodman, K. (2008) *Improvisation for the Spirit*, Naperville, IL: Sourcebooks.

Goodrich, P. (1999) 'Operatic Hermeneutics: Harmony, Euphantasy, and Law in Rossini's *Semiramis*', *Cardozo Law Review*, 20: 1649–71.

——(2005) 'J.D.', *German Law Review*, 15: 15–24.

——(2008) 'Un Cygne Noir', in P. Goodrich, F. Hoffmann, M. Rosenfeld and C. Vismann (eds) *Derrida and Legal Philosophy*, Basingstoke: Palgrave Macmillan, 227–37.

Goodrich, P., Hoffmann, F., Rosenfeld, M. and Vismann, C. (eds) (2008) *Derrida and Legal Philosophy*, Basingstoke: Palgrave Macmillan.

——(2008) 'Introduction: A Philosophy of Legal Enigmas', in P. Goodrich, F. Hoffmann, M. Rosenfeld and C. Vismann (eds) *Derrida and Legal Philosophy*, Basingstoke: Palgrave Macmillan, 1–18.

Gourse, L. (1995) *Madame Jazz: Contemporary Women Instrumentalists*: New York: Oxford University Press.

——(1997) *Straight, No Chaser: The Life and Genius of Thelonious Monk*, New York: Schirmer Books.

Gray, J.C. (1895) Judicial Precedents – A Short Study in Comparative Jurisprudence', *Harvard Law Review*, 9: 27–41.

Green, B. (1966) 'Jazz', *Observer*, 20 November: 32–36, 38–40, 42.

Griffin, F.J. (2001) *If You Can't Be Free, Be a Mystery: In Search of Billie Holiday*, New York: Free Press.

Grimston, J. (2012) 'Oh Well Done Class, You are All Total Flops', *Sunday Times*, 5 February: 15.

Grosz, E. (2003) 'Ontology and Equivocation: Derrida's Politics of Sexual Difference', in C. Norris and D. Roden (eds) *Jacques Derrida*, Volume IV, London: SAGE, 237–62.

Hadler, M. (1995) 'Jazz and the New York School', in K. Gabbard (ed.) *Representing Jazz*, Durham, NC: Duke University Press, 247–59.

Hägglund, M. (2008) *Radical Atheism: Derrida and the Time of Life*, Stanford, CA: Stanford University Press.

Haldar, P. (2004) '*L'Amour Fou*: The Subject *is* Forsaken in Love', paper presented at Association for the Study of Law, Culture and the Humanities (ASLCH) Annual Conference, Hartford, CT, 12–13 March.

Hall, T.S. (1999) 'The Score as Contract: Private Law and the Historically Informed Performance Movement', *Cardozo Law Review*, 20: 1589–1614.

Hallam, E. and Ingold, T. (eds) (2007) *Creativity and Cultural Improvisation*, Oxford: Berg.

Hart, H.L.A. (1994) *The Concept of Law*, 2nd edn, Oxford: Oxford University Press.

Haskins, J. (1977) *The Cotton Club*, London: Robson Books.

Hatch, M. (1998) 'Jazz as a Metaphor for Organizing in the 21st Century', *Organization Science*, 9(5): 556–57 (Special Issue: Jazz Improvisation and Organizing).

Hatch, M. and Weick, K.E. (1998) 'Critical Resistance to the Jazz Metaphor', *Organization Science*, 9(5): 600–604 (Special Issue: Jazz Improvisation and Organizing).

Hebdige, D. (1999 [1979]) *Subculture: The Meaning of Style*, London: Routledge.

Heble, A. (2000) *Landing on the Wrong Note: Jazz, Dissonance, and Critical Practice*, London: Routledge.

——(2003) 'Take Two/Rebel Musics: Human Rights, Resistant Sounds, and the Politics of Music Making', in D. Fischlin and A. Heble (eds) *Rebel Musics: Human Rights, Resistant Sounds, and the Politics of Music Making*, Montréal: Black Rose Books, 232–48.

——(2005) 'Editorial – Improvising Matters: Rights, Risks, and Responsibilities', *Critical Studies in Improvisation*, 1(2): 1–3.

Heble, A. and Siddall, G. (2000) 'Nice Work If You Can Get It: Women in Jazz', in A. Heble, *Landing on the Wrong Note: Jazz, Dissonance, and Critical Practice*, London: Routledge, 141–65.

Heble, A. and Siemerling, W. (2010) 'Voicing the Unforeseeable: Improvisation, Social Practise, Collaborative Research'. Online. Available HTTP: www.improvcommunity.ca/research/voicing-unforseeable-improvisation-social-practice-collaborative-research (accessed 8 June 2012). [Also published in Brydon, D. and Dvořák, M. (eds) (forthcoming) *Cross-Talk: Canadian and Global Imaginaries in Dialogue*, Waterloo, ON: Wilfred Laurier University Press.]

Heble, A. and Wallace, R. (forthcoming) *People Get Ready: The Future is Now!*, Durham, NC: Duke University Press.

Hentoff, N. (1959) 'Race Prejudice in Jazz: It Works Both Ways', *Harper's Magazine*, June: 72–77.

——(1961) *The Jazz Life*, New York: Dial.

——(1972) 'The Real Lady Day', *New York Times Magazine*, 24 December: 8–9, 18–19.

——(2001) 'Jazz: Music Beyond Time and Nations', in N. Hentoff, *The Nat Hentoff Reader*, New York: Da Capo Press, 94–100.

Hesse, H. (1929) *Steppenwolf*, New York: Henry Holt & Co.

Hill, L. (1997) *Blanchot: Extreme Contemporary*, London: Routledge.

Hoefer, G. (1961) 'Special Report: New York's Cabaret "Rhubarb"', *Cabaret Law Clipping File*, Institute of Jazz Studies at Rutgers University.

Holiday, B. (with Dufty, W.) (1992 [1956]) *Lady Sings the Blues*, New York: Penguin.

Holmes, S. (2009) 'In Case of Emergency: Misunderstanding Tradeoffs in the War on Terror', *California Law Review*, 97: 301–54.

Holt, J. (1990) 'Protecting America's Youth: Can Rock Music Lyrics Be Constitutionally Regulated?', *Journal of Contemporary Law*, 16: 53–75.

Hore, C. (1993) 'Jazz – A People's Music?', *International Socialism Journal*, Winter: 61. Online Available HTTP: pubs.socialistreviewindex.org.uk/isj61/hore.htm (accessed 8 June 2012).

Hoskyns, B. (1981) 'Where radical meets chic', *New Musical Express Magazine*, October. Online. Available HTTP: http://aggressiveart.org/sp_uk/interviews/spuk_1980_1.htm (accessed 8 June 2012).

House, H.W. (2008) 'Influence of the Natural Law Theology of the Declaration of Independence on the Establishment of Personhood in the United States Constitution', *Liberty University Law Review*, 2: 725–79.

Howe, M.A. (1999) *Genius Explained*, Cambridge: Cambridge University Press.

Hughes, L. (1961) 'Bop', in L. Hughes, *The Best of Simple*, New York: Hill & Wang, 117–19.

——(1958) 'Jam Session', in L. Hughes, *The Langston Hughes Reader*, New York: George Braziller, 107–8.

Hyman, P. (2004) *The Reluctant Metrosexual: Dispatches from an Almost Hip Life*, New York: Villard Books.

Ilma, V. (1934) 'The Nation's Youth: What Does It Want?', *New York Times*, 18 March.

Iyer, V. (2004) 'Exploding the Narrative in Jazz Improvisation', in R. O'Meally, B. Edwards and F. Griffin (eds) *Uptown Conversation: The New Jazz Studies*, New York: Columbia University Press, 393–403.

Jarrett, M. (1998) *Drifting on a Read: Jazz as a Model for Writing*, Albany, NY: SUNY Press.

——(2004) 'Cutting Sides: Jazz Record Producers and Improvisation', in D. Fischlin and A. Heble (eds) *The Other Side of Nowhere: Jazz, Improvisation, and Communities in Dialogue*, Middletown, CT: Wesleyan University Press, 319–49.

Jones, G. (1991) *Liberating Voices: Oral Tradition in African American Literature*, Cambridge, MA: Harvard University Press.

Jones, J. (2004) 'Wild Ones', *Guardian Weekend*, 11 December: 61–65.

Jost, E. (1994) *Free Jazz (The Roots of Jazz)*, New York: Da Capo Press.

Kahan, J.B. (1993) 'Bach, Beethoven, and the (Home) Boys: Censoring Violent Rap Music in America', *Southern California Law Review*, 66: 2583–2610.

Kant, I. (1951) *Critique of Judgment*, trans. J.H. Bernard, New York: Hafner Press.

Kaufman, C. (1980) 'The Scientific Method in Legal Thought: Legal Realism and the Fourteen Principles of Justice', *Saint Mary's Law Journal*, 12: 77–112.

Kaufman, F. and Guckin, J.P. (1979) *The African Roots of Jazz*, Sherman Oaks, CA: Alfred Publishing.

Kernfeld, B. (1995) *What to Listen for in Jazz*, New Haven, CT: Yale University Press.

Kerouac, J. (1995a) 'Essentials of Spontaneous Prose', in A. Charters (ed.) *The Portable Jack Kerouac*, New York: Penguin, 484–85.

——(1995b) 'Jazz of the Beat Generation – 1949', in A. Charters (ed.) *The Portable Jack Kerouac*, New York: Penguin, 222–32.

——(1995c) 'The Beginning of Bop – 1959', in A. Charters (ed.) *The Portable Jack Kerouac*, New York: Penguin, 555–59.

King, B. (2004) 'Review of Colin Nettelbeck, *Dancing with DeBeauvoir* (2004)', *API Review of Books*, 43 (2004). Online. Available HTTP: www.api-network.com/main/index.php?apply=reviews&webpage=api_reviews&flexedit=&flex_password=&menu_label=&menuID=homely&menubox=&Review=4650 (accessed 8 June 2012).

Kodat, C.G. (2003) 'Conversing with Ourselves: Canon, Freedom, Jazz', *American Quarterly*, 55(1): 1–28.

Kofsky, F. (1998a) *Black Music, White Business: Illuminating the History and Political Economy of Jazz*, New York: Pathfinder Press.

——(1998b [1970]) *John Coltrane and the Jazz Revolution of the 1960s*, 2nd edn, New York: Pathfinder Press.

Kronick, J.G. (1999) *Derrida and the Future of Literature*, Albany, NY: State University of New York Press.

Lake, S. (1985) 'Prime Time and Motion: Ornette Coleman', *Wire Magazine*, 19. Online. Available HTTP: www.thewire.co.uk/archive/interviews/ornette_coleman.html (accessed 17 March 2007 [URL no longer active]). [Copy on file with the author]

Laking, A. (2005) 'Jazz/law', email, 20 June.

Landgraf, E. (2011) *Improvisation as Art: Conceptual Challenges, Historical Perspectives*, New York: Continuum.

Lassonde, J. (2010) 'Thoughts on an Improvisation', *Critical Studies in Improvisation*, 6(1) 3 (Special Issue: *Lex Non Scripta*, *Ars Non Scripta*: Law, Justice and Improvisation). Online. Available HTTP: www.criticalimprov.com/article/view/1180/1710 (accessed 2 September 2012).

Laver, M. (2009) '"The Greatest Jazz Concert Ever": Critical Discourse, European Aesthetics, and the Legitimization of Jazz', *Critical Studies in Improvisation*, 5(1). Online. Available HTTP: www.criticalimprov.com/article/view/972/1620 (accessed 2 September 2012).

Leiboff, M. and Nield, S. (2010) *Law's Theatrical Presence, Special Issue of Law Text Culture*, 14: 1–399.

Leonard, N. (1962) *Jazz and the White Americans*, Chicago: University of Chicago Press.

Levinson, S. and Balkin, J.M. (1991) 'Law, Music, and Other Performing Arts', *University of Pennsylvania Law Review*, 139: 1597–1658.

Lewin, A.Y. (1998) 'Jazz Improvisation as a Metaphor for Organization Theory', *Organization Science*, 9(5): 539 (Special Issue: Jazz Improvisation and Organizing).

Lewis, G. (2004a) 'Afterword to "Improvised Music after 1950": The Changing Same', in D. Fischlin and A. Heble (eds) *The Other Side of Nowhere: Jazz, Improvisation, and Communities in Dialogue*, Middletown, CT: Wesleyan University Press, 163–72.

——(2004b) 'Improvised Music after 1950: Afrological and Eurological Perspectives', in D. Fischlin and A. Heble (eds) *The Other Side of Nowhere: Jazz, Improvisation, and Communities in Dialogue*, Middletown, CT: Wesleyan University Press, 131–62.

Lewis, G. and Piekut, B. (forthcoming) *The Oxford Handbook of Critical Improvisation Studies*, Oxford: Oxford University Press.

Lissner, W. (1966) 'Fingerprinting Rule In Cabarets to End', *New York Times*, 29 August: 1, 24.

Lussier, M. (2011) 'Book Review of *The Philosophy of Improvisation* by Gary Peters', *Critical Studies in Improvisation*, 7(2). Online. Available HTTP: www.criticalimprov.com/article/view/1778/2390 (accessed 2 September 2012).

Lyons, D. (1985) 'Formal Justice and Judicial Precedent', *Vanderbilt Law Review*, 38: 495–512.

Madson, P.R. (2005) *Improv Wisdom: Don't Prepare, Just Show Up*, New York: Bell Tower.

Maiorana, R. (1961) 'Police Rule Upheld on Cabaret Cards', *New York Times*, 1 March: 1, 28.

Malabou, C. and Derrida, J. (2004) *Counterpath: Traveling with Jacques Derrida*, trans. D. Wills, Stanford, CA: Stanford University Press.

Mandell, J.R. (2001) 'Trees that Fall in the Forest: The Precedential Effect of Unpublished Opinions', *Loyola of Los Angeles Law Review*, 34: 1255–95.

Manderson, D. (2000) *Songs Without Music: Aesthetic Dimensions of Law and Justice*, Berkeley, CA: University of California Press.

——(2003) 'From Hunger to Love: Myths of the Source, Interpretation, and Constitution of Law in Children's Literature', *Law and Literature*, 15: 87–135.

——(2010) 'Fission and Fusion: From Improvisation to Formalism in Law and Music', *Critical Studies in Improvisation*, 6(1) (Special Issue: *Lex Non Scripta*, *Ars Non Scripta*: Law, Justice and Improvisation). Online. Available HTTP: www.criticalimprov.com/article/view/1167/1717 (accessed 2 September 2012).

Manderson, D. and Caudill, D. (1999) 'Modes of Law: Music and Legal Theory – An Interdisciplinary Workshop Introduction', *Cardozo Law Review*, 20: 1325–29.

Maras, S. (1999) 'Audio-visualising Derrida', *Australian Humanities Review*, July 1999. Online. Available HTTP: www.australianhumanitiesreview.org/archive/Issue-July-1999/maras.html (accessed 8 June 2012).

Margulies, P. (1997) 'Doubting Doubleness, and All That Jazz: Establishment Critiques of Outsider Innovations in Music and Legal Thought', *University of Miami Law Review*, 51: 1155–94.

Martin, P.J. (2002) 'Spontaneity and Organisation', in M. Cook and D. Horn (eds) *The Cambridge Companion to Jazz*, Cambridge: Cambridge University Press.

Martinez, T.A. (2004) 'Perceptions of Racial Profiling: Rap Music, Utah, and Police in American Culture', *Utah Law Review*, 4: 945–60.

McCormick, J.P. (2001) 'Derrida on Law; or Poststructuralism Gets Serious', *Political Theory*, 29(3): 395–423.

McMullen, T. (2008) 'Book Review of *Sounding Out: Pauline Oliveros and Lesbian Musicality* by Martha Mockus', *Critical Studies in Improvisation*, 4(2). Online. Available HTTP: www.criticalimprov.com/article/view/903/1385 (accessed 2 September 2012).

——(2010) 'Subject, Object, Improv: John Cage, Pauline Oliveros, and Eastern (Western) Philosophy in Music', *Critical Studies in Improvisation*, 6(2). Online. Available HTTP: www.criticalimprov.com/article/view/851/1912 (accessed 2 September 2012).

Mc Namee, E. (2004) 'Once More Unto the Breach: Branagh's Henry V, Blair's war and the UK Constitution', in L.J. Moran, E. Sandon, E. Loizidou and I. Christie (eds) *Law's Moving Image*, London: The GlassHouse Press.

——(2009a) 'Eye-Witness: Memorializing Humanity in Steve McQueen's *Hunger*', *International Journal of Law in Context*, 5: 281–94.

——(2009b) 'The Theatre of Memory in Northern Ireland', *Masks: The Online Journal of Law and Theatre*, 1(1): 59–80.

McNeill, W. and Feldman, K.S. (eds) (1998) *Continental Philosophy: An Anthology*, Malden, MA: Blackwell.

Merriam, A.P. and Mack, R.W. (1960) 'The Jazz Community', *Social Forces*, 38(3): 211–22.

Metzer, D. (ed.) (1999) *Writing Jazz*, San Francisco, CA: Mercury House.

Meyer, L.B. (2000) *The Spheres of Music: A Gathering of Essays*, Chicago: University of Chicago Press.

Meyer, L.B., Frost, P.J. and Weick, K.E. (1998) 'Overture', *Organization Science*, 9(5): 540–42 (Special Issue: Jazz Improvisation and Organizing).

Miller, H.J. (2007) 'Derrida Enisled', *Critical Inquiry*, 33: 248–76.

Miller, J. (2000) 'Fight Prohibition – Get Up and Boogie', *New York Post*, 20 August. Online. Available HTTP: http://nycpost.com/08202000/postopinion/opedcolumnists/10293.htm (accessed February 2011 [URL no longer active]).

Mirvis, P.H. (1998) 'Practice Improvisation', *Organization Science*, 9(5): 586–92 (Special Issue: Jazz Improvisation and Organizing).

Mitgang, H. (2003) *Once Upon a Time in New York: Jimmy Walker, Franklin Roosevelt, and the Last Great Battle of the Jazz* Age, New York: Cooper Square Press.

Monson, I. (1995) 'The Problem with White Hipness: Race, Gender, and Cultural Conceptions in Jazz Historical Discourse', *Journal of American Musical Society*, 48(3): 396–422.

——(1996) *Saying Something: Jazz Improvisation and Interaction*, Chicago: University of Chicago Press.

Morgan, P. (2000) 'Something about Women and Monsters and a Bit of a Dance', *Postgraduate English*, 2. Online. Available HTTP: www.dur.ac.uk/postgraduate.english/morgan.htm (accessed 8 June 2102).

Morin, M.-E. (2006) 'Putting Community Under Erasure: Derrida and Nancy on the Plurality of Singularities', *Culture Machine*, 8. Online. Available HTTP: www.culturemachine.net/index.php/cm/article/viewArticle/37/45 (accessed 8 June 2012).

Morrison, T. (1992) *Jazz*, New York: PLUME.

Municipal Assembly of the City of New York, Aldermanic Branch (1926) 'Report of the Committee on Local Laws in Favor of Adopting a Local Law to Regulate Dance Halls and Cabarets and Providing for Licencing the Same', City of New York, 7 December, 572–74.

Muyumba, W.M. (2009) *The Shadow and the Act: Black Intellectual Practice, Jazz Improvisation, and Philosophical Pragmatism*, Chicago: University of Chicago Press.

Nachmanovitch, S. (1990) *Free Play: Improvisation in Life and Art*, New York: Jeremy P. Tarcher/Putnam.

Nancy, J.-L. (1991) *The Inoperative Community*, P. Connor (ed.), trans. P. Connor, L. Garbus, M. Holland and S. Sawhney, Minneapolis, MN: University of Minnesota Press.

Nancy, J.-L. and Fabbri, L. (2007) 'Philosophy as Chance: An Interview with Jean-Luc Nancy', *Critical Inquiry*, 33: 427–40.

Neal, M.A. (2004) '" … A Way Out of No Way": Jazz, Hip-Hop, and Black Social Improvisation', in D. Fischlin and A. Heble (eds) *The Other Side of Nowhere: Jazz, Improvisation, and Communities in Dialogue*, Middletown, CT: Wesleyan University Press, 195–223.

Nelson, C. (2001) 'Stare Decisis and Demonstrably Erroneous Precedents', *Virginia Law Review*, 87: 1–84.

Nettelbeck, C. (2004) *Dancing With DeBeauvoir: Jazz and the French*, Melbourne, Victoria: Melbourne University Publishing.

Newton, F. (1959) *The Jazz Scene*, Harmondsworth, Middlesex: Penguin.

New York Times (30 January 1922) 'Rector Calls Jazz National Anthem', *New York Times*: 16.

——(27 January 1925) 'Condemns Age of Jazz', *New York Times*: 12.

——(20 November 1926) 'Night Club Curfew is Hotly Assailed', *New York Times*: no page. [Copy on file with the author.]

——(18 June 1926) '3 A.M. Curfew Bill Offered By Walker', *New York Times*: no page. [Copy on file with the author.]

——(30 June 1926) '3 A.M. Curfew Foes Heckled By Walker', *New York Times*: 1, 10.

——(30 November 1926) 'Curfew Held Up Again', *New York Times*: no page. [Copy on file with the author.]

——(3 December 1926) 'Curfew Bill Change Sought by Aldermen', *New York Times*: no page. [Copy on file with the author.]

——(4 December 1926) 'Churches Plea Aids 3 A.M. Cafe Curfew', *New York Times*: no page. [Copy on file with the author.]

——(8 December 1926) 'Night Club Curfew Passes Aldermen', *New York Times*: 1, 9.

——(17 December 1926) '3 A.M. Curfew Bill Signed by Walker', *New York Times*: no page. [Copy on file with the author.]

——(18 December 1926) 'Mayor Would Lift Cabaret Curfew for Jan. 1; Dislikes Being "Spoilsport" New Year's Eve', *New York Times*: 36.

——(23 December 1926) 'Curfew Won't Halt New Year Parties', *New York Times*: 3.

——(19 May 1927) 'His Place is a Speak-Easy, Not Cabaret, He Tells Court', *New York Times*: no page. [Copy on file with the author.]

——(25 November 1930) 'Got $20,000 to Free 900 in Vice Cases, Prosecutor Confesses, Exposing Ring', *New York Times*: 1, 23.

——(27 November 1930) 'Innocent Girls Arrested', *New York Times*: 1.

——(29 November 1930) 'Mulrooney Starts Vice Squad Shake-Up by Demoting Seven', *New York Times*: 1, 4.

——(30 November 1930) 'Crain Acts to Jail Vice Ring Grafters', *New York Times*: 1, 26.

——(18 December 1930) 'Girls Accuse Police at Ouster Hearing', *New York Times*: 1, 16.

——(19 December 1930) 'Women Confused on Police Framers', *New York Times*: no page. [Copy on file with the author.]

——(23 December 1930) 'Roosevelt Pardons Six Women "Framed" by Police Vice Ring', *New York Times*: 1, 15.

——(27 December 1930) 'Hearing on Goodman Ordered by Seabury; Vice Verdict Upset, *New York Times*: 1, 3.

——(28 December 1930), 'Corrigan to Shift Many Court Aides; Delay for Goodman', *New York Times*: 1, 2.

——(16 January 1931) 'Woman of Standing Framed in Vice Case, Jailed for Ten Days', *New York Times*: 1, 2.

——(20 January 1931) 'Corrigan Says Girls Got Justice in Court', *New York Times*: 1, 4.

——(26 January 1931) 'Miller Under Fire as "Fixer" Today', *New York Times*: 1, 4.

——(4 February 1931) 'Vice Spy Says Police Forced Him to Flee', *New York Times*: 4.

——(6 February 1931) 'Mulrooney to Back New Curfew Bill', *New York Times*: no page. [Copy on file with the author.]

——(10 February 1931), 'Police End Delay on Frame-Up Cases', *New York Times*: no page. [Copy on file with the author.]

——(16 February 1931) 'Seabury Will Scan Police Bank Records in Wide Graft Hunt', *New York Times*: 1, 12.

——(17 February 1931) '$400,000 Speakeasy Graft from 125 Resorts is Laid to 2 Police "Collectors"', *New York Times*: 1, 14.

——(18 February 1931) '51 Police Bank Accounts Subpoenaed in Wide Hunt for "Higher-Ups" in Graft', *New York Times*: 1, 11.

——(20 February 1931) 'Policemen Defiant on $83,057 Deposits', *New York Times*: 1, 12.

——(23 February 1931) 'Police Move to Halt Bank Book Inquiry', *New York Times*: 1, 13.

——(24 February 1931) 'Police in "Vice Ring" Said to Sell Liquor', *New York Times*: no page. [Copy on file with the author.]

——(25 February 1931) 'Move to Prosecute Judge Norris Fails', *New York Times*: 1, 18.

——(2 March 1931) 'Investigates Acts of Another Judge', *New York Times*: no page. [Copy on file with the author.]

——(3 March 1931) 'Two Vicesquad Men to Face Jury Today', *New York Times*: no page. [Copy on file with the author.]

——(6 March 1931) 'Girl Swears Police Broke Arm in Raid', *New York Times*: 1, 4.

——(7 March 1931) 'Two Bail Bondsmen Indicted in Theft', *New York Times*: no page. [Copy on file with the author.]

——(8 March 1931) 'Seabury Examines Magistrate Dreyer', *New York Times*: 1, 2.

——(15 March 1931a) 'Police Must Tell of Bank Accounts', *New York Times*: no page. [Copy on file with the author.]

——(15 March 1931b) 'Huge Graft is Laid to Harlem Police', *New York Times*: no page. [Copy on file with the author.]
——(19 March 1931) 'Beaten and Framed by Vice Squad Men, Two Women Charge', *New York Times*: 1, 19.
——(22 March 1931) 'M'Laughlin Ousted From Police Force', *New York Times*: no page. [Copy on file with the author.]
——(23 March 1931) 'Vice Graft Traced in Harlem Inquiry', *New York Times*: no page. [Copy on file with the author.]
——(16 May 1931) 'Mayor's Crime Bill Advanced by Board', *New York Times*: no page. [Copy on file with the author.]
——(13 June 1931) 'Pass Walker Bill on Cabaret Curfew', *New York Times*: no page. [Copy on file with the author.]
——(4 February 1932) 'Police Satarized on Stage', *New York Times*: 25.
——(12 February 1933) 'Seabury Gives Up a $75,000 City Fee', *New York Times*: 1, 27.
——(15 August 1940) 'City to Fingerprint Night Club Staffs', *New York Times*: 1, 22.
——(25 September 1940) 'Union Loses Protest on Fingerprinting', *New York Times*: no page. [Copy on file with the author.]
——(1 December 1940) '13,348 Club Aides Fingerprinted', *New York Times*: no page. [Copy on file with the author.]
——(5 December 1940) 'Night Club Workers Fight Fingerprinting', *New York Times*: no page. [Copy on file with the author.]
——(21 December 1940) 'Night Club Rules are Held Too Broad', *New York Times*: no page. [Copy on file with the author.]
——(29 December 1940) 'Only One Fingerprinted in Day', *New York Times*: no page. [Copy on file with the author.]
——(7 May 1958) 'Samuel Seabury Dies on L.I. at 85', *New York Times*: 1, 35.
——(24 April 1959) 'Governor Signs School Loan Bill', *New York Times*: no page. [Copy on file with the author.]
——(15 May 1959) 'Trombonist Wins, Gets Cabaret Card', *New York Times*: 1.
——(30 August 1966) 'Two Small Victories', *New York Times*: no page. [Copy on file with the author.]
Nicholls, T. (2010) 'Speaking Justice, Performing Reconciliation: Twin Challenges for a Postcolonial Ethics', *Critical Studies in Improvisation*, 6(1) (Special Issue: *Lex Non Scripta*, *Ars Non Scripta*: Law, Justice and Improvisation). Online. Available HTTP: www.criticalimprov.com/article/view/1082/1705 (accessed 2 September 2012).
——(2012) *An Ethics of Improvisation: Aesthetic Possibilities for a Political Future*, Lanham, MD: Lexington Books.
Nichols, M.P. (1960) '"Hip Messiah" Loses Cabaret Card to Fuzz He Loves', *The Village Voice*, 3 November: 3, 6.
Nicholson, S. (1995) *Billie Holiday*, London: Victor Gollancz.
——(2005) 'Flashback: Stuart Nicholson on the 50th Anniversary of the Death of Charlie Parker', *Observer Music Monthly*, 18: 29.
Nitta, S.L.K. (2001) 'The Price of Precedent: *Anastasoff* v. *United States*', *University of Hawaii Law Review*, 23: 795–824.
Northrop, W.B. and Northrop, J.B. (1932) *The Insolence of Office: The Story of the Seabury Investigations*, New York: G.P. Putnam's Sons.
O'Brien, L. (1996) 'Sisters of Swing: Stardom, Segregation and 1940s/50s Pop', in S. Cooper (ed.) *Girls! Girls! Girls! Essays on Women and Music*, New York: New York University Press, 70–83.

O'Reilly, J. (1999) 'My Dinner with Derrida', *Independent*, 16 July. Online. Available HTTP: www.aggressiveart.org/sp_uk/interviews/spuk_1999_6.htm (accessed 8 June 2012).

O'Rourke, K.S. (2006) 'If You Can't Dance, You're in NY', *Washington Square News*, 27 January. Online. Available HTTP: www.nyunews.com/vnews/display.v/ART/2006/01/27/43d9f07ba4d07?in_archive=1 (accessed June 2006 [URL no longer active]). [Copy on file with author.]

OERD (1996) *The Oxford English Reference Dictionary*, Oxford: Oxford University Press.

Ogren, K.J. (1989) *The Jazz Revolution: Twenties America and the Meaning of Jazz*, New York: Oxford University Press.

Oliveros, P. (2005) *Deep Listening: A Composer's Sound Practice*, Lincoln, VT: iUniverse.

Osofsky, G. (1963) *Harlem: The Making of a Ghetto. Negro New York, 1890–1930*, New York: Harper & Row.

Ostransky, L. (1978) *Jazz City: The Impact of Our Cities on the Development of Jazz*, Englewood Cliffs, NJ: Prentice-Hall.

Panish, J. (1997) *The Color of Jazz: Race and Representation in Postwar American Culture*, Jackson, MS: University Press of Mississippi.

Pardo, D. (2009) 'Judicial Discretion in Talmudic Times and the Modern Era', *Cardozo Public Law, Policy and Ethics Journal*, 7: 429–54.

Peluso, D. and Lee, H. (1960) 'Big Night Spot Fights Suspension of Permit', *New York Daily News*, 23 November: 3, 6.

Peplowski, K. (1998) 'The Process of Improvisation', *Organization Science*, 9(5): 560–61 (Special Issue: Jazz Improvisation and Organizing).

Peretti, B.W. (1997) *Jazz in American Culture*, Chicago: Ivan R. Dee.

——(2007) *Nightclub City: Politics and Amusement in Manhattan*, Philadelphia, PN: University of Pennsylvania Press.

Perlman, A.M. and Greenblatt, D. (1981) 'Miles Davis Meets Noam Chomsky: Some Observations on Jazz Improvisation and Language Structure', in W. Steiner (ed.) *The Sign in Music and Literature*, Austin, TX: University of Texas Press, 169–83.

Perlmutter, E. (1960a) 'City Lifts Permits of 20 Night Spots', *New York Times*, 23 November: 1, 21.

——(1960b) 'Mayor to Relax Cabaret Rules', *New York Times*, 29 November: 1, 44.

——(1967) 'Identity Cards for Performers Exit to Applause', *New York Times*, 26 September: 53.

Perpich, D. (2005) 'Universality, Singularity, and Sexual Difference: Reflections on Political Community', *Philosophy and Social Criticism*, 31(4): 445–60.

Peters, G. (2005) 'Can Improvisation be Taught?', *International Journal of Art and Design Education*, 24(3): 299–306.

——(2009) *The Philosophy of Improvisation*, Chicago: University of Chicago Press.

Peters, J.S. (2008) 'Legal Performance Good and Bad', *Law, Culture and the Humanities*, 4: 179–200.

Petersen, H. (1998) 'On Law and Music: From Song Duels to Rhythmic Legal Orders?', *Journal of Legal Pluralism and Unofficial Law*, 44: 75–87.

Peterson, L. (1999) 'JazzStuff: Biographies – Charlie Parker', *The Jazzine*. Online. Available HTTP: www.jazzine.com/jazzstuff/biographies/charlie_parker.phtml (accessed 8 June 2012).

Petersson, J. (2005) 'Dance Activists File Lawsuit to Reform Cabaret Laws', *The Villager*, 75(7). Online. Available HTTP: www.thevillager.com/villager_114/danceactivists.html (accessed 8 June 2012).

Pilgrim, D. (2000) 'The Tom Caricature', Ferris State University Jim Crow Museum of Racist Memorabilia. Online. Available HTTP: www.ferris.edu/news/jimcrow/tom/ (accessed 8 June 2012).

Piper, T. (2010) 'The Improvisational Flavour of Law, the Legal Taste of Improvisation', *Critical Studies in Improvisation*, 6(1) (Special Issue: *Lex Non Scripta*, *Ars Non Scripta*: Law, Justice and Improvisation). Online. Available HTTP: www.criticalimprov.com/article/view/1191/1716 (accessed 2 September 2012).

Plato (1999) 'The Symposium', in *The Essential Plato*, trans. B. Jowett with M.J. Knight, New York: Quality Paperback Book Club, 679–762.

Pope, R. (2005) *Creativity: Theory, History, Practice*, London: Routledge.

Posner, E.A. (2012) 'Deference to the Executive in the United States After September 11: Congress, the Courts, and the Office of Legal Counsel', *Harvard Journal of Law and Public Policy*, 35: 213–44.

Postema, G.J. (1987) '"Protestant" Interpretation and Social Practices', *Legal Philosophy*, 6: 283–319.

——(2004) 'Melody and Law's Mindfulness of Time', *Ratio Juris*, 17(2): 203–26.

Pratt, G. and Johnston, C. (2007) 'Turning Theatre into Law, and Other Spaces of Politics', *Cultural Geographies*, 14: 92–113.

Prévost, E. (2004) 'The Discourse of a Dysfunctional Drummer: Collaborative Dissonances, Improvisation, and Cultural Theory', in D. Fischlin and A. Heble (eds) *The Other Side of Nowhere: Jazz, Improvisation, and Communities in Dialogue*, Middletown, CT: Wesleyan University Press, 353–66.

Pue, W. (2000) 'Policing, the Rule of Law, and Accountability in Canada: Lessons from the APEC Summit', in W. Pue (ed.) *Pepper in Our Eyes: The APEC Affair*, Vancouver: UBC Press, 3–26.

Rahmatian, A. (2005) 'Music and Copyright as Perceived by Copyright Law', *Intellectual Property Quarterly*, 3: 267–93.

Ramirez, M.K. (2009) 'Assessing the Values of Punishment: The State of Sentencing in the United States Criminal Justice System', *Drake Law Review*, 57: 591–642.

Ramshaw, S. (2003) 'Nearing the Wild Heart: The Cixousian "Feminine" and the Quest for Law's Origins', *Australian Feminist Law Journal*, 19: 11–27 (Special Issue: Divining the Source: Law's Foundation and the Question of Authority).

——(2004) '"He's My Man!": Lyrics of Innocence and Betrayal in *The People v. Billie Holiday*', *Canadian Journal of Women and the Law*, 16(1): 86–105 (Special Issue: Speaking Truth to Power: Remembering Marlee Kline).

——(2006) 'Deconstructin(g) Jazz Improvisation: Derrida and the Law of the Singular Event', *Critical Studies in Improvisation*, 2(1). Online. Available HTTP: www.criticalimprov.com/article/view/81/188 (accessed 2 September 2012).

——(2010a) 'The Creative Life of Law: Improvisation, Between Tradition and Suspicion', *Critical Studies in Improvisation*, 6(1) (Special Issue: *Lex Non Scripta, Ars Non Scripta*: Law, Justice, and Improvisation). www.criticalimprov.com/article/view/1084/1700 (accessed 2 September 2012).

——(2010b) 'Jamming the Law: Improvised Theatre and the "Spontaneity" of Judgment', *Law Text Culture*, 14: 133–59 (Special Issue: Law's Theatrical Presence).

——(forthcoming) 'Improvising (Il)legality: Justice and the Irish Diaspora, NYC, 1930–32', *Irish Journal of Legal Studies* (Special Issue: Irish Approaches to Justice).

Rehnquist, J.C. (1986) 'The Power that Shall Be Vested in a Precedent: Stare Decisis, the Constitution and the Supreme Court', *Boston University Law Review*, 66: 345–77.

Reynolds, S. (1988) 'Enigma Variation', *Melody Maker*, 5 March. Online. Available HTTP: www.aggressiveart.org/aof_files/interviews/aof_interview_p3b-3.htm (accessed 8 June 2012).

Roberts, C. (1991) 'Scritti Politti: Intellectual Hooliganism', *Melody Maker*, 2 March. Online. Available HTTP: www.aggressiveart.org/aof_files/interviews/aof_interview_p4–1.htm (accessed 8 June 2012).

Robinson, L. (1960) 'City to Bid Sinatra Testify on Cabarets', *New York Times*, 17 November: 1, 32.

Rogers, N. (2008) 'The Play of Law: Comparing Performances in Law and Theatre', *Queensland University of Technology Law Journal*, 8(2): 429–43.

Romano, T. (2002) 'The Safety Dance: You Can't Dance If You Want To', *The Village Voice*, 27 November. Online. Available HTTP: www.villagevoice.com/news/0248,romano,40202,1.html (accessed 8 June 2012).

——(2005) 'Short Memory: The Cabaret Law Still Exists. Why You Should Care', *The Village Voice*, 1 November. Online. Available HTTP: www.villagevoice.com/nyclife/0544,flylife,69576,15.html (accessed 8 June 2012).

——(2006) 'Annie Get Your Cell Phone Gun', *The Village Voice*, 25 July. Online. Available HTTP: www.villagevoice.com/nyclife/0630,romano,73960,15.html (accessed 8 June 2012).

——(2007) 'Cabaret Law Dances into Court', *The Village Voice*, 2 February. Online. Available HTTP: www.villagevoice.com/blogs/music/archives/2007/02/cabaret_law_dan.php (accessed 8 June 2012).

Ross, A. (2008) *The Rest is Noise: Listening to the Twentieth Century*, London: Fourth Estate.

Ross, R. (1972) *Bird Lives!: The High Life and Hard Times of Charlie "Yardbird" Parker*, London: Quartet Books.

Rottenberg, E. (2002) 'Inheriting the Future', in J. Derrida, *Negotiations: Interventions and Interviews, 1971–2001*, trans. E. Rottenberg, E. Rottenberg (ed.), Stanford, CA: Stanford University Press, 1–7.

Rzewski, F. (2002) 'Little Bangs: A Nihilist Theory of Improvisation', *Current Musicology*, 67–68: 377–86.

Sancton, T. (1990) 'Horns of Plenty', *Time Magazine*, 22 October. Online. Available: HTTP: www.time.com/time/magazine/article/0,9171,971423–1,00.html (accessed 8 June 2012).

Santoro, G. (2000) *Myself When I am Real: The Life and Music of Charles Mingus*, Oxford: Oxford University Press.

Sawyer, R.K. (2006) *Explaining Creativity: The Science of Human Innovation*, Cary, NC: Oxford University Press.

Sellers, S. (1991) *Language and Sexual Difference: Feminist Writing in France*, London: Macmillan Education.

Shapiro, S.J. (2007) 'The "Hart–Dworkin" Debate: A Short Guide for the Perplexed', *Public Law and Legal Theory Working Paper Series*, Working Paper No. 77, March: 54 pp.

Shaw, A. (1957) 'Ballad of the Bird: The Legend of Charles Christopher Parker', *Esquire*, December: 246–page unknown.

Shildrick, M. (2002) *Embodying the Monster: Encounters with the Vulnerable Self*, London: SAGE.

Sibley, J. (1961) 'Police Licensing of Clubs to End', *New York Times*, 17 January: 1, 42.

Siddall, G. (2005) '"I wanted to live in that music": Blues, Bessie Smith and Improvised Identities in Ann-Marie MacDonald's *Fall on Your Knees*', *Critical Studies in Improvisation*, 1(2): 10–19.

Siddall, G. and Waterman, E. (forthcoming) *Sounding the Body: Improvisation, Representation and Subjectivity*, Middletown, CT: Wesleyan University Press.

Silbey, S. and Ewick, P. (2003) 'The Double Life of Reason and Law', *University of Miami Law Review*, 57(3): 497–512.

Small, C. (1985) *Music of the Common Tongue. Survival and Celebration in Afro-American Music*, Hanover: Wesleyan University Press.

——(1998) *Musicking: The Meanings of Performing and Listening*, Middletown, CT: Wesleyan University Press.

Smith, J.D. (2004) 'Playing Like a Girl: The Queer Laughter of the Feminist Improvising Group', in D. Fischlin and A. Heble (eds) *The Other Side of Nowhere: Jazz, Improvisation, and Communities in Dialogue*, Middletown, CT: Wesleyan University Press, 224–43.

Smith, J.K.A. (2005) *Jacques Derrida: Live Theory*, New York: Continuum.

Snow, M. (2004) 'A Composition on Improvisation', in D. Fischlin and A. Heble (eds) *The Other Side of Nowhere: Jazz, Improvisation, and Communities in Dialogue*, Middletown, CT: Wesleyan University Press, 45–49.

Soocher, S. (1998) *They Fought the Law: Rock Music Goes to Court*, New York: Schirmer Books.

Stanton, D.C. (1986) 'Difference on Trial: A Critique of the Maternal Metaphor in Cixous, Irigaray, and Kristeva', in N. Miller (ed.) *The Poetics of Gender*, New York: Columbia University Press, 157–82.

Stone, J. (1964) *Legal System and Lawyers' Reasonings*, Stanford, CA: Stanford University Press.

Soules, M. (2004) 'Improvising Character: Jazz, the Actor, and Protocols of Improvisation', in D. Fischlin and A. Heble (eds) *The Other Side of Nowhere: Jazz, Improvisation, and Communities in Dialogue*, Middletown, CT: Wesleyan University Press, 268–97.

Spellman, A.B. (1985) *Four Lives in the Bebop Business*, New York: Limelight Editions.

Stanyek, J. (2004) 'Transmissions of an Interculture: Pan-African Jazz and Intercultural Improvisation', in D. Fischlin and A. Heble (eds) *The Other Side of Nowhere: Jazz, Improvisation, and Communities in Dialogue*, Middletown, CT: Wesleyan University Press, 87–130.

Stein, J. (2002) 'Life with the Father of Deconstruction', *Time Magazine*, 18 November. Online. Available HTTP: www.time.com/time/nation/article/0,8599,391685,00.html (accessed 8 June 2012).

Stewart, J. (2003) 'Freedom Music: Jazz and Human Rights', in D. Fischlin and A. Heble (eds) *Rebel Musics: Human Rights, Resistant Sounds, and the Politics of Music Making*, Montréal: Black Rose Books, 88–107.

Strain, V.L. (2011) 'Perfecting the Law: Legal Reform and Literary Forms in the 1590s and 1600s', unpublished thesis, University of Toronto.

Subotnik, R.R. (1996) *Deconstructive Variations: Music and Reason in Western Society*, Minneapolis, MN: University of Minnesota Press.

Székely, M.D. (2008) 'Thresholds: Jazz, Improvisation, Heterogeneity, and Politics in Postmodernity', *Jazz Perspectives*, 2(1): 29–50.

Szwed, J. (2002) *So What: The Life of Miles Davis*, London: Arrow Books.

Taylor, J. (2000) 'The Early Origins of Jazz', in B. Kirchner (ed.) *The Oxford Companion to Jazz*, Oxford: Oxford University Press, 39–52.

Thurschwell, A. (2008) 'Specters and Scholars: Derrida and the Tragedy of Political Thought', in P. Goodrich, F. Hoffmann, M. Rosenfeld and C. Vismann (eds) *Derrida and Legal Philosophy*, Basingstoke: Palgrave Macmillan, 152–64.

Todorov, T. (1999) *The Conquest of America: The Question of the Other*, Norman, OK: University of Oklahoma Press.

Toop, D. (2008) 'Search and Reflect: The Changing Practice of Improvisation', *New Sound*, 32: 139–51 (Special Issue: Improvisation).

——(1988) 'The Green Manifesto', *The Face*. Online. Available HTTP: www.aggressiveart.org/aof_files/interviews/aof_interview_p3b-2.htm (accessed 8 June 2012).

Townsend, P. (2000) *Jazz in American Culture*, Edinburgh: Edinburgh University Press.

Tucker, S. (2004) 'Bordering on Community: Improvising Women Improvising Women-in-Jazz', in D. Fischlin and A. Heble (eds) *The Other Side of Nowhere: Jazz, Improvisation, and Communities in Dialogue*, Middletown, CT: Wesleyan University Press, 244–67.

Tyler, A. (2012) 'The Forgotten Core Meaning of the Suspension Clause', *Harvard Law Review*, 125: 901–1117.

Tyler, T.R., Callahan, P.E. and Frost, J. (2007) 'Armed, and Dangerous (?): Motivating Rule Adherence Among Agents of Social Control', *Law and Society Review*, 41: 457–91.

Ullman, M. (1980) *Jazz Lives: Portraits in Words and Pictures*, Washington: New Republic Books.

University of Guelph (4 September 2007) 'Musical Improvisation, Social Change Focus of Major Research Grant'. Online. Available HTTP: www.uoguelph.ca/news/2007/09/musical_improvi.html (accessed 8 June 2012).

Ville, J., de (2011) *Jacques Derrida: Law as Absolute Hospitality*, London: Routledge.

——(2008) 'Sovereignty Without Sovereignty: Derrida's *Declarations of Independence*', *Law & Critique*, 19: 87–114.

Vitullo-Martin, J. (2003) 'Blackface Parodists Win in Court; Cops vs. Firefighters; Still No Dancing Allowed', *Gotham Gazette*. Online. Available HTTP: www.gothamgazette.com/article/crime/20030707/4/446 (accessed 8 June 2012).

Walsh, G. (1974) *Gentleman Jimmy Walker, Mayor of the Jazz Age*, New York: Praeger Publishers.

Ward, G.C. and Burns, K. (2001) *Jazz: A History of America's Music*, London: Pimlico.

Weick, K.E. (1998) 'Improvisation as a Mindset for Organizational Analysis', *Organization Science*, 9(5): 543–55 (Special Issue: Jazz Improvisation and Organizing).

Weinberg, T. (1999) 'Without Licence to Dance, No Cure for Ants in Pants', *Columbia News Service*, 9 April. Online. Available HTTP: http://cns.jrn.columbia.edu/apr09/nodance.html (accessed January 2001 [URL no longer active]). [Copy on file with the author.]

Weisbrod, C. (1999) 'Fusion Folk: A Comment on Law and Music', *Cardozo Law Review*, 20: 1439–58.

Whitney, J. (2005) 'Do You Wanna Dance?', *New York Magazine*, 21 November. Online. Available HTTP: http://newyorkmetro.com/nymetro/news/people/columns/intelligencer/15073 (accessed 8 June 2012).

Williams, M. (1961) 'Liner Notes', in O. Coleman, *Free Jazz: A Collective Improvisation by the Ornette Coleman Double Quartet*, New York: Atlantic Recording Corporation.

——(1970) *The Jazz Tradition*, Oxford: Oxford University Press.

Wills, D. (2006) 'Notes Towards a Requiem: Or the Music of Memory', *Mosaic*, 39(3): 27–46.

Woideck, C. (1998) *Charlie Parker: His Music and Life*, Ann Arbor, MI: University of Michigan Press.

Wolfe, J.C. (1993) 'Sex, Violence, and Profanity: Rap Music and the First Amendment', *Mercer Law Review*, 44: 667–86.

Young, E. (1930) 'Conjectures on Original Composition', in E.D. Jones (ed.) *English Critical Essays (Sixteenth, Seventeenth, and Eighteenth Centuries)*, London, Humphrey Milford; New York, Oxford University Press.

Zacharias, R. (2007) '"And yet": Derrida on Benjamin's Divine Violence', *Mosaic*, 40(2): 103–16.

Zartaloudis, T. (2005) 'The Case of the Hypocritical', *Law and Critique*, 16: 387–418.

Ziarek, E.P. (1997) 'From Euthanasia to the Other of Reason: Performativity and the Deconstruction of Sexual Difference', in E.K. Feder, M.C. Rawlinson and E. Zakin (eds) *Derrida and Feminism: Recasting the Question of Woman*, New York: Routledge, 115–40.

Zion, S.E. (1966) 'Mayor Backs End to Cabaret Law', *New York Times*, 20 January, 24.

Zlomislic, M. (2007) *Jacques Derrida's Aporetic Ethics*, Plymouth, MA: Lexington Books.

Sound recordings

Charlie Barnet and His Orchestra (1939) 'Cherokee', on *Charlie Barnet and his Orchestra 1939–1940*, Promo Sound AG.

Charlie Parker and Be Bop Boys/Ree Boppers/Ri Bop Boys (1945) 'Ko-Ko', on *Charlie Parker 1945–1947*, Classics Records.

Douglas, D. (2001) *Witness*, BMG Entertainment.

Scritti Politti (1982) 'Jacques Derrida', on *Songs to Remember*. Rough Trade Records.

Film

Dick, K. and Kofman, A.Z. (directors) (2002) *Derrida*, Jane Doe Films.

Cases

Chiasson v. NYC City Dept. (1986) 505 N.Y.S.2d 449, 132 Misc.2d 640 (Sup. Ct. NY Co., App. Panel).

Chiasson v. NYC City Dept. (1988) 524 N.Y.S.2d 649, 138 Misc. 2d 394 (Sup. Ct. NY Co., App. Panel).

Cummings v. Bond [1927] 1 Ch. 167.

Donoghue v. Stevenson (1932) A.C. 562 (HL).

Festa et al. v. NYC Dept. of Consumer Affairs et al. (2006) 12 Misc.3d 466, 820 N.Y.S.2d 452 (Sup. Ct. NY Co.), affirmed (2007) N.Y. Slip Op. 01476 (Sup. Ct. NY, App. Div.).

Friedman v. Valentine (1941) 177 Misc. 437, 30 N.Y.S.2d 891, affirmed (1943) 42 N.Y.S.2d 593, 266 A.D. 561 (Sup. Ct. NY, App. Div.).

New Honeymoon Danceland v. Valentine (1945) 59 N.Y.S.2d 637 (Sup. Ct. NY. Co.).

The People v. Greenberg and Slevin (1958) 12 Misc. 2d 396, 174 N.Y.S.2d 803 (NYC Mag. Ct.).

Simone v. Kennedy (1961) 212 N.Y.S.2d 838 (Sup. Ct. NY Co.).

Index